# FROM THE
# BODIES
# OF THE GODS

"These were ideas intensely debated by seminarians after the disclosures of the Dead Sea Scrolls. . . . As this book demonstrates, many passages in the Holy Scriptures are incomprehensible as anything but blatant descriptions of the Christian cult of the dead traceable back to the earliest religious rites of prehistory and prevalent throughout antiquity and medieval Catholicism."

CARL A. P. RUCK, PROFESSOR OF CLASSICAL STUDIES,
BOSTON UNIVERSITY, AND AUTHOR OF
*MUSHROOMS, MYTHS, AND MITHRAS*

"After this learned exploration of how necrophilia, hallucinogens, body fluids, human sacrifice, and ancestor worship powerfully influenced the major religions like Judaism and Christianity, it will be hard to view those venerable faiths and institutions in the standard, conventional way.

"During his stunning intellectual romp, Lee also provides fascinating, even 'heretical,' insights into such personages, places, and practices as the Roman catacombs, Last Supper, and Eucharist; Neolithic, Hebrew, Greek, and Egyptian burial rites; Horus, Prometheus, the Virgin Mary, Moses, Jesus, the Dominicans, and the Knights Templar; veneration of saintly relics and the Holy Grail, Minoan mead-making, corpse-painting, psychedelic mushroom-growing, anointing, witch-hunting, and goddess worship."

SANFORD BERMAN, AWARD-WINNING LIBRARIAN
AND AUTHOR OF *PREJUDICES AND ANTIPATHIES*

# FROM THE BODIES OF THE GODS

## Psychoactive Plants and the Cults of the Dead

EARL LEE

Park Street Press

Rochester, Vermont • Toronto, Canada

Park Street Press
One Park Street
Rochester, Vermont 05767
www.ParkStPress.com

Text stock is SFI certified

Park Street Press is a division of Inner Traditions International

**Library of Congress Cataloging-in-Publication Data**

Lee, Earl, 1954–
  From the bodies of the gods : psychoactive plants and the cults of the dead / Earl
Lee.
    p. cm.
  Includes bibliographical references (p.      ) and index.
  ISBN 978-1-59477-458-4 (pbk.) — ISBN 978-1-59477-701-1 (e-book)
  1. Cannibalism—Religious aspects. 2. Human sacrifice. 3. Funeral rites and
ceremonies. I. Title.
  GN409.L43 2012
  203—dc23

                                                                    2012001773

Printed and bound in the United States by Lake Book Manufacturing, Inc.
The text stock is SFI certified. The Sustainable Forestry Initiative® program
promotes sustainable forest management.

10 9 8 7 6 5 4 3 2 1

Text design and layout by Priscilla Baker
This book was typeset in Garamond Premier Pro with Blackfriar used as a display
typeface

Unless otherwise indicated all scriptural quotations are from the New American
Standard Bible (*The Holy Bible: Updated New American Standard Bible
Containing the Old Testament and the New Testament.* Grand Rapids, Mich.:
Zondervan, 1995).

To send correspondence to the author of this book, mail a first-class letter to the
author c/o Inner Traditions • Bear & Company, One Park Street, Rochester, VT
05767, and we will forward the communication, or contact the author through his
website at **www.goodreads.com/author/show/277396.Earl_Lee**.

*The great enemy of the truth is very often not the lie—*
*the deliberate, contrived and dishonest—*
*but the myth, persistent, persuasive, and unrealistic.*
*Belief in myths allows the comfort of opinion*
*without the discomfort of thought.*

JOHN F. KENNEDY

# Contents

## PART THREE
# Sweeney Todd among the Nightingales

# Acknowledgments

I thank Dr. Kathleen De Grave, Professor Randy Roberts, Professor Morgan McCune, Dr. Analisa DeGrave, and Dr. Nathan DeLee for their assistance in reading the manuscripts and suggesting improvements. I also thank Charles Bufe for his helpful suggestions during the process of completing the manuscript. And special thanks to Mindy Branstetter and the team at Park Street Press for their hard work and encouragement during this process.

*Perhaps the most paradoxical in this respect was Pedro Algorta. He did not come from a ranching family like the others—he was a sensitive socialist intellectual—and it was he who had justified eating those first slivers of human flesh by comparing what they were doing to eating the body and blood of Christ in the Holy Eucharist.*

PIERS PAUL READ,
*ALIVE: THE STORY OF THE ANDES SURVIVORS*

# A Eucharist of Flesh

For the past thirty years I have been researching material that many people would consider gruesome: the preparation of corpses, the use of bodily fluids from the dead, the torture of gods, and the mystical experiences of saints. It isn't just that I like horror stories, which I do; my research has led me to some startling conclusions about our contemporary religious practices. As I became more and more familiar with ancient religious rites, I saw the parallels to our own practices more clearly. Certainly cannibalism in any form is not part of the typical Western Sunday worship, but cannibalism lies at the root of much of our religious language and many of our stylized religious gestures. Even more important, it has everything to do with what Christian religions believe about death and divine revelation. This book will take you on the journey I took, slowly bringing the parallels to light.

I believe that, long before the beginnings of civilization, humans have been sacrificed and their skins and flesh used in religious rites. This is part of our history. The use of human fat in making sacred oils is well documented and generally accepted by archaeologists and historians.* Even more disturbing, however, is the fact that human flesh has

---

*W. Robertson Smith's *The Religion of the Semites* has long been a standard work for biblical scholars. In this book he states that the fat of human sacrifices was used to make sacred oils (Smith 1956, p. 384) and the use of human flesh in sacrificial meals was widespread (p. 366, n5).

been made into sacred foods. The process of harvesting the flesh from human bodies to create sacred foods is not as well understood, but it was a common practice throughout the Near East and also in many parts of Europe. I will document these practices, beginning in ancient Crete, and I will show how these religious rites spread to southern Europe and influenced the development of Western religion into the medieval era. Even as the ritual use of sacred food and oils was being suppressed within the Christian Church, from the fourth century on, the collection and display of human cadavers was becoming increasingly popular, especially during the Dark Ages, with a religious movement that historians call "the cult of the saints."

Sacred food and oils were once quite commonly used in religious rituals. It was not until the thirteenth century that such rites finally came to an end with the destruction of the Cathar Christians in southern France. Yet even after this, the use of human flesh continued for hundreds of years as part of necromantic rites among witches and some so-called heretical Christian groups, such as the Knights Templar.

In this book we will see that the practice of ritual cannibalism has been an essential part of Western religion for thousands of years. When I speak of ritual cannibalism, however, I mean not the eating of human flesh, raw or cooked. Rather, I am referring to specific religious rites using corpses, which include the ancient Minoan practice of rending human cadavers in order to harvest their flesh and the Egyptian practice of draining bodily fluids from decayed corpses so that they may be added to sacred foods, oils, salves, and unguents. I call these various religious practices necromantic, because they use human cadavers:

- to maintain an intimate (and often gastronomic) connection to the dead
- to communicate with the spirits of the dead
- to gain visions of the Spirit world, usually called heaven

A great deal has already been written about ordinary cannibalism, and eating human flesh is an interesting topic for college students enrolled in abnormal psychology or criminal justice studies or, perhaps, for students at the (I hope, imaginary) Hannibal Lecter School for the Culinary Arts. It's really only ritual cannibalism, however—cannibalism as part of religious rites—that concerns us here. Further, I am not interested in debating the modern theology of the Eucharist or examining the Christian concept of Transubstantiation—meaning the supernatural transformation of bread and wine so that they become the body and blood of Christ.* Even though this theological idea had its origins, historically, in the ancient practice of ritual cannibalism, the religious concept of Transubstantiation is a fairly recent innovation. My main interest in writing this book is to explore how human bodies were used to create sacred food and sacred oils and to explore the role these rites played in the origins of the Christian Church.

The evidence I have uncovered shows that Christianity began not as an offshoot of Judaism but through an attempt by a group of hardcore traditionalists to restore the old religious rites established by Moses. As a religious leader Jesus never intended to create a completely new religion. What he really wanted to do was restore the sacred rites of Moses but in the context of a more populist religion that was freed from the oppressive control of the Jerusalem Temple. Restoring these ancient rites included bringing back the use of sacred oils and sacred food, which were necessary for the Marzeah, the all-important feast for the dead.

According to Catholic scholars, the Marzeah was the source and model for both the Last Supper and the Agape Feast (described by the apostle Paul in 1 Corinthians 11:18–34).

---

*As in the Latin: *Corporis et Sanguinis Christi.* For those interested, Paul F. Bradshaw's *Eucharistic Origins* presents a good introduction to the history and theology of the Eucharist. The mystical rite for turning bread and wine into Christ's body and blood, however, would have been redundant in the early church. This is certainly the point made again and again by the Gnostics: they did not need a mystical substitute because they already possessed the true body of Christ.

The *Catholic Encyclopedia* is clear about the nature of the Agape Feast.

> This, at its origin, is clearly marked as funerary in its intention, a fact attested by the most ancient testimonies that have come down to us. Our Lord, in instituting the Eucharist, used these words: "As often as you shall eat this Bread and drink this chalice, you shall show forth the Lord's Death." Nothing could be clearer. Our Lord chose the means generally used in His time, namely: the funeral banquet, to bind together those who remained faithful to the memory of Him who had gone. (Leclercq 1907)

As described in the gospels, the original Last Supper was held at the time of Passover. The Agape Feast, however—which included the eating of Christ's flesh and the drinking of his blood—was essentially a funeral rite that was not limited to Easter but could be held at any time. At the Agape Feast the Eucharist was consumed as a way of memorializing Jesus Christ and all those who had died in Christ, or, as the *Catholic Encyclopedia* states of the Agape Feast, "the Eucharistic supper was fundamentally a funerary memorial." There is no escaping the fact that early Christians organized their most sacred ceremony of fellowship, the popular Agape Feast, along lines drawn primarily from the ancient Feast for the Dead, the Hebrew Marzeah.*

As Christianity slowly emerged from the shadows to become the dominant religion of the Roman Empire, the funerary nature of the Christian religion grew and then came into full flower in the fourth century with what is often called "the cult of the saints." Those not familiar with the cult of the saints will be surprised by the Catholic Church's preoccupation or, dare I say, their obsession with the bodies

---

*Amos 6:7 and Jeremiah 16:5. Philip King defines the Marzeah as "a pagan ritual that took the form of a social and religious association. . . . Some scholars regard the funerary marzeah as [a] feast for—and with—deceased ancestors (or Rephaim, a proper name in the Bible for the inhabitants of Sheol)" (King 1988, p. 35). See also Armstrong 1998, p. 109.

of the dead. Christian churches preserved and displayed the bones of saints (which they believed held the power to cure diseases and perform miracles), and they held ceremonies and festivals in cemeteries—often at the tombs of martyrs, saints, and bishops. Christian saints played much the same role in the fourth century as that played earlier by "the blessed dead" in rites of the first Christians (Davies 1999, p. 81). The blessed dead were, essentially, all those who had already died in Christ.

The purpose of this book is to lay the foundation for understanding how the ancient cult of the dead—in its Semitic, Egyptian, and Greek forms—contributed to the beginnings of the Christian religion. Even more important, we will explore why the prehistoric cult of the dead has held such power over Western civilization—so much so that its echoes are still heard today in our literature, film, and other arts.

This book encompasses much more than the secrets of the Christian Church. It also examines evidence from several other religious traditions in Europe and the Americas. We will briefly examine the sacred (or cursed) corpses of these cultures and their many icons and religious symbols. In ancient Crete, for example, the Minoans venerated the skin of Prometheus as it was stretched out and pierced with nails on a mountaintop. In Egypt priests worshipped before the image of Osiris, with the goddess Isis in the form of a falcon standing on his corpse. The goddess/falcon was portrayed as procreating with the corpse of Osiris in order to conceive from his dead body his only begotten son, Horus. This was a powerful symbol for the Egyptians in their elaborate cult of the dead. Remarkably, many of these ancient symbols have persisted, and some have been carried over into modern literature and art and, especially, into horror films. Today we have the living dead corpses of Dracula, Frankenstein, the Mummy, and many other undead ghouls and zombies. And perhaps we can see in the distance, beyond these strange horrors, the seabirds whirling in a cloud over the form of the deathless white whale, Moby Dick, impaled and scarred with iron harpoons and bound with hemp ropes like the biblical Leviathan.

This book is, in some ways, a new approach to old problems. For example, scholars have had great difficulty understanding the origins and purpose of the Egyptian burial rites set forth in the Egyptian Book of the Dead. I believe that I have found an explanation for why the ancient Egyptians performed such complex burial rites. A century ago the great British Egyptologist Sir E. A. Wallis Budge expressed some astonishment at the bizarre funeral rites of the Egyptians, especially their use of bodily fluids—taken from corpses—in their most holy rituals. At the same time Budge was certain that the Egyptians must have had a good reason for using the putrefying fluids, even if he could not logically make out what it was. He had faith in the basic rationality of the Egyptians, and we should approach this topic with the same kind of faith in our distant ancestors.

Ultimately I hope that this book provides a clear explanation, albeit an unusual one, for the complex burial rites of the Egyptians, Greeks, earliest Hebrews, and early Christians, and also for the heretical Christian sects of the medieval era.

The title of this book may seem cryptic, but it reflects the complexity of the subject. I propose to cover a body of material that can't be covered easily in a single book. I doubt that it can be covered well in a dozen books. My hope here is to lay a trail of crumbs for others to follow. This work is essentially a prologue to many other lines of inquiry. It's only the first examination of this topic, and I believe it will serve as a guide for future scholars.

At the beginning of his book *Greek Myths and Christian Mystery,* the great Jesuit scholar Hugo Rahner quotes from the early church leader Clement of Alexandria: "Come, I will show you the Word and the mysteries of the Word, and I will give you understanding of them by means of images familiar to you" (*Protrepticus XII*).

I can think of no better words to introduce this work, because I intend to display the lost mysteries of Christianity that were once quite familiar to Clement and his followers at the beginning of the Christian era.

## PART ONE

# Unveiling the Corpse of Jesus

*Artists of the early and mid-Victorian period were not great respecters of persons. In their quest for knowledge of anatomy, a group of artists including Gibson robbed graves. They came across, recorded Gibson, a very beautiful girl, about sixteen; her face was full and round. How sweet and innocent she looked in death! She was shrouded in white linen and sprinkled over with bits of red wool, like flowers.*

RONALD PEARSALL,
*THE WORM IN THE BUD*

# 1

✠

# Surviving Remnants of the Cult of the Dead

Four thousand years ago ritual cannibalism and other necromantic rites were quite common in many parts of the ancient world. Although most of these rites have vanished from the scene, distinct echoes continue to reverberate to the present day. To discover any remaining traces of cannibalistic rites is a challenging task. Often, it means keeping an eye open for the unusual event or the unexplained detail.

For example, we can refer to the strange funeral of a Catholic priest, Father François Bérenger Saunière: On January 17, 1917, in Rennes-le-Château, a small village in southern France, the local priest suffered a serious stroke. As his condition slowly worsened, his approaching death became a painful ordeal. Father Saunière was in terrible agony as he lay on his deathbed. From a neighboring parish another priest rushed to his bedside to perform last rites—but, after listening to Saunière's confession, this priest arose and walked out of the bedroom. Apparently disturbed by the confession, the neighboring priest refused to give Extreme

Unction to the dying man, and he abruptly left Father Saunière's death-bed to return to his own parish.* A few days later, on January 22, 1917, Father Saunèire finally died (Baigent et al. 1982, p. 9).

For a Catholic priest to refuse last rites to a brother of the cloth is exceptional, but what followed the next morning after Father Saunière's death was even more unusual. The local villagers, following Father Saunière's written instructions, held a strange funeral service for the dead priest—a very revealing service, indeed. According to *Holy Blood, Holy Grail,* "his body was placed upright in an armchair. . . . [Saunière was] clad in an ornate robe adorned with scarlet tassels. One by one certain unidentified mourners filed past, many of them plucking tassels of remembrance from the dead man's garment" (Baigent et al. 1982, p. 10).

According to the authors of *Holy Blood, Holy Grail,* the unusual rite performed at Father Saunière's funeral was similar to the burial rites that had been used several centuries earlier by a Christian sect called the Cathars. Although the Cathars were once the most influential Christian sect in this part of France, they had been branded as heretics and eventually were wiped out as part of a crusade organized by the Catholic Church in 1208. So why, at the beginning of the twentieth century, would a Roman Catholic priest want to be buried according to what was apparently an old Cathar rite, taken from a creed that had died out more than five hundred years before? Further, why would the mourners agree to participate in this rite?

As stated, in the twelfth century, the Cathars were the dominant Christian sect in the south of France. Unlike the Catholic priests who had a reputation for sexual abuses and corruption, the Cathar "good men" and "good women" were known for their piety and charity (Rahn 2006, p. 91). They defied the authority of Rome and enjoyed the full support of both the nobility and the peasants in the region. The rulers

---

*The Catholic rite of Extreme Unction involves anointing the dying person by rubbing a holy oil on his sensory organs. This rite is meant to assist the dying person by confirming him in his faith and preparing him for death.

of this part of southern France, called Languedoc, were sympathetic to Catharism, and they strongly opposed efforts by the Catholic Church to punish the Cathars. Because of this blatant resistance to the Church of Rome, in the year 1208 Pope Innocent III ordered a crusade against the Cathars, and he denounced them and all their supporters as heretics. Some historians call this invasion of southern France the Albigensian Crusade after the city of Albi, which had strong Cathar connections.

The pope had no trouble finding plenty of volunteers for the war, mainly because the Catholic knights, by going on this French crusade, received all the political and financial advantages of crusaders, without having to travel very far from home. Compared to the poorer lands in the north of France, the lands of southern France were quite wealthy; and the promise of gold, jewels, and rich estates inspired many French nobles to join the crusade. These Catholic invaders plundered the treasures of southern France with the blessing of both the pope and the French king.

During the war, however, an odd event took place. Several leaders of the Cathar church approached the enemy camp and asked to speak with Simon de Montfort, the leader of the Catholic army. These heretic Cathars offered to show de Montfort the body of Christ in the flesh so that he could see with his own eyes that the Cathars were the true Christians and that the Catholic Church was false. Historians are not sure what, exactly, the evidence was that the Cathars wanted to show him, but de Montfort apparently believed that they wanted him to witness their version of the Eucharist.*

Simon de Montfort was, no doubt, aware that the Cathars had often criticized the Catholic Eucharist as false and being no better than plain bread, compared to the Cathar's own true Eucharist.

---

*The Cathar Christians were perhaps hoping that their enemy de Montfort, like the Pharisee Saul, could be persuaded to change sides in the conflict. Saul had actively persecuted the Christians on behalf of the Jerusalem Temple. When he accepted Christianity after his vision on the road to Damascus, he changed his name to Paul and went on to evangelize for "the poor"—which is how James the Just, Peter, and the other apostles were known at that time.

The historian A. E. Waite was sufficiently puzzled by this event to write, "It would look as if there were strange claims about concerning the Eucharist as practiced by some or other of the sects in Southern France, where the Albigensian Crusade was raging" (1993, p. 406).

Unfortunately for the Cathars, Simon de Montfort flatly refused their offer and brusquely sent them away.

With most of Europe now turned against the Cathars, their heresy couldn't last much longer. In the twenty years from 1209 to 1229, an army of thirty thousand crusader knights easily occupied and conquered the former Cathar territories, and the pope made sure that new pro-Catholic rulers were installed there. The few Cathar priests who survived the war were later hunted down by the Inquisition and burned at the stake. A new religious order, the Dominicans, was established in 1220 specifically to root out what was left of the Cathar heresy. After the Cathar territories were conquered, former Cathars who survived the war—both nobles and peasants—were forced to wear white armbands or yellow stars on their clothes so that they could be watched by the authorities. Between 1290 and 1329, the remnants of the Cathar church were finally crushed, and the Cathars' heretical beliefs and rituals came to an end—at least that is the official story.

In *Holy Blood, Holy Grail*, Michael Baigent, Richard Leigh, and Henry Lincoln present evidence that Father Saunière had discovered several remarkable secret documents in the late 1880s while renovating an ancient church in the small town of Rennes-le-Château. Furthermore, they allege that these documents proved that the Cathars' religious beliefs and rituals developed directly from those of the earliest Christians. Their book also suggests that these beliefs represent a purer strain of Christianity than that of the Roman Catholic Church. They claim, too, that Father Saunière had become a closet Cathar, and this was why the Catholic priest who heard his deathbed confession refused to give him last rites.

Here is a peculiar aside to the story of Father Saunière: while he was renovating his small church in Rennes-le-Château, the priest added stained-glass windows representing the Stations of the Cross—the fourteen episodes of Christ's Passion, the time from his arrest to his burial. Many Catholic churches display the Stations of the Cross either in sculpture or in stained glass, but there are some odd details in the stained glass of Father Saunière's church. According to *Holy Blood, Holy Grail*, the glass for Station 14 depicts Christ's body being placed in the tomb under a dark sky. Because it's well known that Jesus was buried before sundown according to Jewish law, the suggestion that the authors make is that the stained-glass image shows Christ's body being taken *out* of the tomb (Baigent et al. 1982, p. 9). This idea is, of course, wholly inconsistent with orthodox Christianity, but this window—and several others—suggest that Father Saunière held some rather peculiar religious ideas.*

The authors of *Holy Blood, Holy Grail* suggest that it was through Father Saunière's research into the history of the Cathar church that he discovered the Cathars' ancient funeral rites. They have no explanation for why he did this, but Saunière, for some reason, chose to have his funeral service completed in accordance with these heretical Christian rituals.† According to a contemporary account, the priest's corpse was placed upright in a chair, and the mourners walked past, "plucking tassels of remembrance from the dead man's garment." To this day no one has been able to explain the symbolism of removing reddish-colored tassels from the corpse.

As mysterious as all of this may seem, it's certainly not the only or even the most peculiar part of this story. Father Saunière's funeral

---

*Although there is a good deal of controversy over what Saunière may have discovered in the church, there is no question about his interest in local Catharism.

†In *The Sion Revelation: The Truth about the Guardians of Christ's Sacred Bloodline*, Lynn Picknett and Clive Prince are often critical of *Holy Blood, Holy Grail*, but they state that this funeral "was not a later invention by the Priory of Sion mythmakers" and that this "curious ritual" could indeed have had a special significance for the local people of Rennes-le-Chateau (2006, p. 154). Recently, several archaeologists have found Egyptian religious relics in this area, which might also explain where this rite first originated, assuming there are religious ties between Egypt and France that extend to the distant past.

may very well have been performed according to the ancient Cathar ceremony, but if it's a Cathar rite, where did this ceremony originate? Is it truly an early Christian rite, or is it something far older?

This funeral rite may in fact be older than the Cathars and much older, even, than the Christian Church itself. Indeed, this funeral rite is probably far older than the pyramids of Egypt. I have found references to similar funeral rites dating back to early Neolithic times (see, for example, Vulliamy). Father Saunière's funeral rite imitated the ancient funeral rites of the prehistoric cults of the dead: religious rites that were based on ritual cannibalism.

The act of removing red tassels from Father Saunière's corpse in 1917 reflects a rite that is at least seven thousand and perhaps more than twenty thousand years old. There is, however, a significant difference in the rites. As part of Father Saunière's funeral the mourners walked past the body, and each one removed a red tassel or pom-pom from the corpse, but in the ancient ceremonies there were no red tassels. Instead, worshippers removed reddish-colored mushrooms from the corpse, and the corpse was not nearly as fresh as Father Saunière's.*

---

*Although Father Saunière was sitting upright in a chair, it was more common for the corpse to be in a prone position. Nevertheless, it's easy to find a historical precedent for placing the corpse in a chair. In paintings and illustrations made in ancient Egypt numerous images show the mummified corpse of Osiris sitting in a chair and presiding over funereal rites. In addition to being the god who ruled over the next world, Osiris was also a fertility god, and I have found a few images of him lying in a prone position, with plants growing out of his body (for example, Budge 1969b; 1973, 1:58). The worship of Osiris easily predates the building of the earliest pyramids in Egypt at the end of the Old Kingdom. The Minoans of Crete may also have placed some of their deceased in an upright position (Alexiou 1969, p. 119).

# 2

✠

# Sacred Oils, Sacred Foods

## SACRED OILS

I am constantly amazed by how little people know about Jesus Christ. There seems to be a complete disconnect between the average Christian and the information that has been unearthed over the past century by historians and archaeologists. It's not as if this information is hidden away in dusty journals in a darkly lit corner of a private archive. Most of it's easily available in public libraries and on the Internet. Yet it seems that many people would rather read the latest sentimental bio-novel about Jesus, such as Anne Rice's *Christ the Lord,* or watch a violent fantasy, such as *The Passion of the Christ,* rather than be bothered with information about who Jesus was and what he taught.

For example, the word *christ* is not Jesus's last name. It's not even a Hebrew word. The English word *christ* is based on the Greek word *khristós,* meaning "a christened one," or "an anointed one." The authors of the Christian scriptures used *Christus* as a translation for the Hebrew *Messiah (Māšîah),* which means, literally, "an anointed one [of Yah-weh]." Thus when the first Christians wrote about Jesus the Christ, they meant quite literally Jesus the Anointed [of the Lord] or Jesus the Messiah. This fact is widely accepted by Bible translators. For example, depending on which English translation you happen to use, when you read Matthew 16:16 the translators describe Jesus as either Christ or Messiah—depending on the translator's preference for one word or the other in the context. Similarly, the apostle Paul frequently wrote about Jesus Christ, meaning Jesus [the] Christ, but he never wrote "Christ the Messiah," because he understood enough Greek and Hebrew to know that this would be redundant (Barnstone 639). It would be similar to writing King the Lord or Dad the Father.

This is hardly new information, however. In his popular book *The Golden Bough,* which was first published in 1890, Sir James Frazer explains that the word *messiah* was originally used as a title for the one who was anointed. Frazer states that for a person who was anointed, "the application of the holy oil to his head was believed to impart to him directly a portion of the divine spirit. Hence he bore the title of Messiah, which with its Greek equivalent Christ, means no more than 'the Anointed One'" (1961, 1:21).

If modern historians and Bible translators are familiar with the origin and meaning of the word *christ*—and they've known it for more than a century—why do so few people today make the connection among anointing, christening, and Christ? Even more difficult to understand: Why has the rite of anointing been downplayed or abandoned by so many modern Christian churches—including almost all of the churches that claim to be "Bible-based"?

The act of anointing religious and political leaders was a common practice in many parts of the Near East, which includes ancient Palestine. In the Hebrew scriptures we read that Moses's brother Aaron was anointed, as were many priests and all of the kings, and, because they were anointed, they were also called messiahs (Butz 2010, p. 187). Hebrew priests are often described as being anointed in the books of Exodus, Leviticus, and Numbers. According to Hebrew tradition the priests and kings were called God's anointed, and because of this anointing they had a special religious status. For example, to do physical violence to one of God's anointed was considered to be an attack on God—and thus equal to blasphemy. Psalms 105:15 states: "Do not touch My anointed ones, And do My prophets no harm" (New American Standard Bible). The Darby Bible (1890) translation is even more emphatic: "Put not your hand on those who have been marked with my holy oil. . . ." Being anointed was a kind of first-century union card for anyone who wanted to be taken seriously as a religious leader. It was also important to be anointed by a highly respected religious figure so that no one could question the authority of the anointed to preach, as some of Jesus's enemies tried to do (John 8:13).

According to the gospels Jesus was anointed early on in his career by an unnamed woman, probably according to a Nazarene rite (Luke 7:36–38):

> Now one of the Pharisees was requesting Him to dine with him, and He entered the Pharisee's house and reclined *at the table*. And there was a woman in the city who was a sinner; and when she learned that He was reclining *at the table* in the Pharisee's house, she brought an alabaster vial of perfume, and standing behind *Him* at His feet, weeping, she began to wet His feet with her tears, and kept wiping them with the hair of her head, and kissing His feet and anointing them with the perfume.

Some scholars have wondered: How was she "a sinner"? Most people assume that her sin was sexual in nature.* More recently some scholars suggest that it was her religious beliefs that were not respectable, and thus sinful from the point of view of the Jewish majority. Why Jesus would accept her anointing is still a mystery, at least to most scholars.

---

*She was likely viewed as being similar to the Samaritan woman whom Jesus met at Jacob's Well (John 4:4–42). There are hints that the woman's sinful life could have been of a religious nature, which might include working as a priestess at a local shrine, which the Bible authors often associate, rightly or wrongly, with the pagan practice of ritual prostitution (as in Genesis 38:21–29).

Although the gospels do not record it, Jesus was probably also anointed by John the Baptist, because an anointing with sacred oils often followed the rite of baptism. In several religious traditions converts are spiritually cleansed by baptism and then sealed by being anointed with sacred oils. There is evidence for this in the *Didache* and in the writings of St. Ignatius (Logan 2006, p. 79). Later, shortly before his death, Jesus was anointed by Mary of Bethany, who applied "a pint of pure nard" to his feet and dried his feet with her hair (John 12). Some people suggest that Mary was the unnamed woman with the alabaster jar who anointed him earlier in Luke and in Matthew 26:6–13 and Mark 14:3–9. Each of the gospels includes an anointing story, and each time, Jesus is anointed by a woman.

Apparently the importance of the anointing rites was not limited to the living. After his death, Jesus was taken to the tomb, and a surprisingly large amount of ointment—perhaps as much as seventy-five to one hundred pounds of myrrh and aloe—was used to prepare his corpse.* After his corpse was entombed, the Gospel of Mark describes a group of women going to his tomb in order to anoint him with still more ointment, and this was how they came to discover "the mystery of the empty tomb" (Mark 16:1–8).

Jesus's followers believed in the importance of anointing, just as Jesus did. He is often identified as one of God's anointed—a messiah. Jesus himself explained the importance of being anointed. In Luke 4:18 he says, "The Spirit of the Lord is on me, because he has anointed me to preach the gospel to the poor. He has sent me to proclaim release to the captives and recovery of sight for the blind, to set free those who are oppressed." This passage in Luke is similar to Matthew 12:18 and John 3:34, and all three passages appear to point to Isaiah 61:1, in which the prophet says: "The Spirit of the Lord God is upon me, because the Lord has anointed me to bring good news to the afflicted; He has sent me to bind up the brokenhearted, to proclaim liberty to captives and freedom to prisoners."

---

*According to historian Byron McCane this amount sounds rather unusual, because "a few bottles of ointment might suffice for washing an ordinary corpse, but for Jesus no less than one hundred pounds will do" (2003, p. 101–2).

In both Luke and Isaiah heavy emphasis is placed on the act of anointing as the means by which God's spirit was bestowed on humans. Being anointed was what made a person a messiah. As one of the anointed, Jesus was now possessed by the divine spirit, "for the consecration of the anointing oil of his God is on him" (Leviticus 21:12).

Being anointed also held wide-ranging religious implications. Because he had been anointed, no one was permitted to lay hands on Jesus or harm him in any way, according to Hebrew tradition (1 Chronicles 16:22). His criticism of the Temple and his claim that he was the Son of Man and the Messiah were serious enough to provoke his enemies, yet the priests and their agents didn't risk attacking him physically. They might hurl verbal abuse and perhaps even quietly encourage the crowd to stone Jesus, but they didn't dare throw the first stone for fear of committing a crime against one of God's anointed (John 8:7).

Furthermore, that Jesus was baptized (and very likely anointed) by John the Baptist probably gave him extra credibility among the common people so that physically attacking him might also provoke a violent reaction from John's followers. Many people still remembered John the Baptist, and John's martyrdom at the hands of Herod was, no doubt, still fresh in their memory. During the time of Jesus's ministry many of John's followers likely felt a connection to Jesus as a righteous man who had been baptized (and perhaps anointed) by their teacher. The author of Acts implies that some of John's supporters became Christians after John was beheaded and Jesus was crucified (Acts 18:24–19:6).

Mainly because of all the biblical references, we know that Jesus was an anointed one, a messiah. Indeed, many of Jesus's followers believed that he was, in fact, the long-awaited Messiah described in Hebrew scripture. The Messiah was a religious leader who would unite the people, like Moses. However, most Jews believed that this promised Messiah would also be a military leader, much like Joshua, who would liberate Palestine from foreign control, as was promised in 2 Samuel 7:12–16 and Isaiah 9:6–7.

For a child will be born to us, a son will be given to us;

And the government will rest on His shoulders;

And His name will be called Wonderful Counselor, Mighty God,

Eternal Father, Prince of Peace.

There will be no end to the increase of *His* government or of peace,

On the throne of David and over his kingdom,

To establish it and to uphold it with justice and righteousness

From then on and forevermore.

The zeal of the LORD of hosts will accomplish this.

Some Jews thought that the Messiah would be the famous military leader Joshua himself, who would return from the dead and free the Jews from Roman oppression. Others thought that the Messiah would be someone filled with the spirit of Joshua, and he would defeat the Romans. Jesus's claim to be a messiah and perhaps even the Messiah seems to play into these ideas, in part because the names Joshua and Jesus are almost identical—Yehoshua and Yeshua in Hebrew are like William and Will in English. In first-century Palestine many families named their boys Yeshua (for the same reason that Jesus is a popular name in many Hispanic communities today). It's no wonder that people thought Jesus might somehow be the great Hebrew leader Joshua, son of Nun, whose military exploits are described in the Hebrew scriptures of Exodus, Numbers, and Joshua.

As Jesus began his ministry there was confusion, even among some of his followers, over whether he was really the powerful Messiah promised in the Hebrew scriptures. For many of his fellow Jews this question was settled when Jesus was arrested and crucified by the Romans. His death proved to them that Jesus was not the military leader who would defeat Rome; but at least for some of his followers, his arrest and execution did not end the speculation about who Jesus really was.

The disappearance of his corpse and the other events following his death caused his closest followers to begin to ask: If Jesus was the true

Messiah, could he really die? Some likely believed, based on the promise of Psalms 16:10, that Jesus could not remain dead. Yahweh would not permit the Messiah's corpse to rot in the earth, just as Yahweh would not permit the author of Psalms to remain dead. The author of Psalms states: "For You will not abandon my soul to Sheol; Nor will You allow Your Holy One to undergo decay." This idea is later affirmed in Acts 2:25–31, in which the exact words from Psalms are directly applied to the corpse of Jesus (Komarnitsky 2009, p. 115). This idea is repeated by the apostle Paul in his speech recorded in Acts 13:35–36. At least some of Christ's followers believed—perhaps even from the time of his death—that his body could not see corruption and that Jesus would soon return from Sheol, the land of the dead.

In the weeks after Christ was crucified there was among his followers the idea that this was not the end. Jesus would return from the dead—at least this is how the author of Acts puts it: "But God raised Him up again, putting an end to the agony of death, since it was impossible for Him to be held in its power" (Acts 2:24).

Fifty days after his crucifixion his apostles gathered to eat a meal for the Jewish festival of Shavuot. During this meal it's said that they experienced something remarkable. They had been anointed in accordance with the holiday season (as in 1 Samuel 10:1) before they sat down to eat. Then the Holy Spirit descended upon the apostles as each one was enveloped in a supernatural fire.

> When the day of Pentecost had come, they were all together in one place. And suddenly there came from heaven a noise like a violent rushing wind, and it filled the whole house where they were sitting. And there appeared to them tongues as of fire distributing themselves, and they rested on each one of them. And they were all filled with the Holy Spirit and began to speak with other tongues, as the Spirit was giving them utterance. (Acts 2:1–4)

This supernatural experience we call the Pentecost event (*pentecost* is the Greek word for *Shavuot,* meaning "fifty days"). As a result of this event, the apostles came to believe that Jesus had, in fact, been the true Messiah and that his violent death had ushered in the kingdom of God. This experience at the feast of Pentecost was the beginning of Christianity, and this meal became the model of the Agape Feast: Christians came together for a meal that memorialized the death and resurrection of Jesus Christ. At these meals they ate the flesh and drank the blood of Jesus, as he had commanded, and they also anointed each other with sacred oils, according to the Jewish tradition (Logan 2006, p. 78). During these feasts people often experienced a state called *theolepsy,* or "being possessed by God." From this experience many people received gifts of the Spirit, which included prophecy, discernment, tongues, healing, and other spiritual endowments. This much, at least, is clear from various historical studies of the early Christian Church, but it's unclear how they came to experience these spiritual gifts.

After the first Pentecost the title of Messiah no longer focused on Jesus's role as the one who was anointed. Now he was the anointing one. His followers believed that Jesus was much more than the expected and all-too-human military Messiah for whom the Jews had been waiting. Instead, the name Jesus the Anointed One came to define his role as the direct source of God's anointing. It was through the power of the anointing that the Holy Spirit entered the physical body, and the initiate could receive spiritual gifts and be in Christ. Many of his followers believed that with this powerful anointing all of humanity could one day be spiritually transformed (Romans 6).

The importance of anointing with holy oils cannot be overstated, for the oils are given high praise in both the Hebrew and in early Christian traditions.

Take also for yourself the finest of spices: of flowing myrrh five hundred *shekels,* and of fragrant cinnamon half as much, two hundred and fifty, and of fragrant cane two hundred and fifty, and of cassia five hundred, according to the shekel of the sanctuary, and of olive

oil a hin. You shall make of these a holy anointing oil, a perfume
mixture, the work of a perfumer; it shall be a holy anointing oil.
(Exodus 30:23–5)

The Chrism is superior to baptism, for it is from the word "Chrism"
that we have been called "Christians," certainly not because of the
word "baptism." And it is because of the Chrism that "the Christ" has
his name. For the Father anointed the Son, and the Son anointed the
apostles, and the apostles anointed us. He who has been anointed possesses everything. He possesses the resurrection, the light, the cross,
the Holy Spirit. (Gospel of Philip 74:12–21; Robinson 1988, p. 153)

The act of anointing was the central rite of the early Christian
Church. Why is it, then, that today so little emphasis is given to anointing and so much emphasis is placed on other rites, such as baptism?

During the years after his crucifixion, Jesus very quickly evolved
into the true and only source of the power of God's anointing, and it
was through the supernatural power of the anointing that Jesus's followers came to be in Christ. Once they were anointed, they saw themselves as part of the body of Christ, the Corpus Christi.* Based on this
new conception of who and what Jesus was, Jesus came to be called, by
both John and Paul, "the firstborn from the dead," or "the first-begotten
of the dead" (Revelation 1:5; Colossians 1:18). In their eyes Jesus was
the foundation stone of a new race of men and women who were both
living and dead (Romans 6:13). Paul examines this idea more fully in
1 Corinthians 15:20, in which he says, "But now Christ has been raised
from the dead, the first fruits of those who are asleep."

Just as the Anabaptists were named for their practice of rebaptism,

---

*Christening of new religious converts was common among the Egyptians but not
among the first-century Jews, who practiced circumcision (which, ironically, was also a
practice that originated with the Egyptians). In the Armenian church, Christians are still
thought of as the anointed ones, and in that faith they have a special anointing oil called
*muron,* which is used every seven years. The recipe for this oil includes more than forty
herbs and spices.

or second baptism (the baptism of adults who had already been baptized as infants), it's obvious that the followers of Jesus were named for their distinctive practice of christening their initiates. This, at least, is the claim that was made by Bishop Eusebius (263–339 CE) in his *Ecclesiastical History* (chapter 4) and by Theophilus of Antioch, who wrote in a letter to a pagan scholar:

> And about your laughing at me and calling me Christian, you know not what you are saying. First, because that which is anointed is sweet and serviceable, and far from contemptible. For what ship can be serviceable and seaworthy, unless it be first anointed? Or what castle or house is beautiful and serviceable when it has not been anointed? And what man, when he enters into this life or into the gymnasium, is not anointed with oil? And what work has either ornament or beauty unless it be anointed and burnished? Then the air and all that is under heaven is in a certain sort anointed by light and spirit; and are you unwilling to be anointed with the oil of God? Wherefore we are called Christians on this account, because we are anointed with the oil of God. (Theophilus, *To Autolycus,* 1:12)

In time, the name Christian was given to anyone who had been ritually anointed and had thus become one with Jesus Christ (Acts 11:26, 26:28; and 1 Peter 4:16). Yet this idea of becoming one with Jesus through a rite of christening was the same process that had already been going on for thousands of years in Egypt with the followers of Horus. They too were anointed and thus became one with their god, and with this anointing rite they gained the promise of eternal life in a supernatural realm governed by Osiris, Horus's heavenly father. Osiris was the primary god of Egypt. He ruled over the afterlife, and he perpetually provided his followers with food and drink in Tuat, the Egyptian heaven.*

---

*The Turin Canon, which provides some of our most important information on Egypt's early history, specifically describes the predynastic rulers of Egypt as followers of Horus. By the end of the Old Kingdom, Horus had become the son of Isis and Osiris.

The similarities between Jesus and Horus are quite striking. In fact several nineteenth-century scholars claimed that Jesus was really just another name for Horus, and that Christianity was nothing more than a newly rebranded mystery cult—a heavily Judaized version of the Horus cult. Recently several books have been written along this line, such as Timothy Freke and Pete Gandy's *The Jesus Mysteries: Was the "Original Jesus" a Pagan God?* Their book expands on the arguments made by several nineteenth-century scholars who discovered—once the French scholar Jean Champollion learned in 1822 how to decipher Egyptian hieroglyphs—that the Egyptian religion was remarkably similar to Christianity.

These were amazing discoveries, but the theory that Christianity came directly out of first-century Horus worship, like a knockoff Gucci handbag, is a bit off the mark. Even though the religious rites of Moses and, later on, the rites of the Christian Church were both influenced by Egyptian rites, the origins of the Hebrew religion are deeply rooted in the religious practices of ancient Bronze Age Palestine. And even though there are many parallels between the worship of Jesus and the worship of Horus, of all the similarities the most significant is the use of sacred oils made from the bodies of the dead.

The sacred oils used in the Hebrew christening rites were not ordinary. Typically several drugs were added to them, including hallucinogenic plants and a large amount of cannabis (Godbey 1930, p. 222). The book of Exodus describes one of the original recipes for the sacred oil of the Hebrews as containing "250 shekels worth of Kannabosm" (Exodus 30:22–23). Although there has been a good deal of debate on this topic recently, *Kaneh Bosm* almost certainly refers to cannabis.*

These holy oils, used in both the Egyptian and the Christian anointing, gave the new convert a powerful, life-changing vision of their god. The apostle John describes the effects of this vision: "As for you,

*Because of the work of Polish anthropologist Sula Benet, the Hebrew University of Jerusalem announced in 1980 that her interpretation of Kaneh Bosm (also *Kineboisin*) as hemp blossoms was essentially correct. Previously it was thought to be *calamus,* an herb that may have some hallucinogenic properties and was used in North American shamanism.

the anointing which you received from Him abides in you, and you have no need for anyone to teach you; but as His anointing teaches you about all things, and is true and is not a lie, and just as it has taught you, you abide in Him" (1 John 2:27).

Being anointed with this sacred oil was very important; but for the initiate to believe himself to be in Christ, and to have Christ in him, it seems the sacred oils had to include the flesh of other Christians who had died and become part of "the blessed dead." And the most valued oil was that taken from bodies of the Christian martyrs who had been tortured and suffered death for their faith.

These holy oils were made from the bodies of those who were already part of the Corpus Christi—those who had died in Christ. The theology of the first Christians reflects their belief that their new converts had absorbed the sacred flesh taken from the body of the god, and these converts now possessed and were possessed by the spirit of their god, whom they often called Lord Jesus. They were now "in Christ" just as the Christ was a Spiritus Sancti, a "holy ghost" dwelling within them.

Understanding the meaning of this ritual practice of anointing is the key to understanding early Christian theology. The earliest Christians understood they were to be followers of Christ's teachings, and, much more important, they had the undeniable and life-changing experience of being anointed with the Corpus Christi, an ointment made from the body of someone who had himself been anointed in Christ.

Thanks to this powerful anointing, the Christian initiates became part of a kind of blessing chain going all the way back to the first and original Corpus Christi, the spiritual body of Jesus, the Christened One himself.* For the new believer becoming part of and being in Christ meant that he shared in Christ's immortality and that he gained entrance to the Christian heaven. For many Christians this also meant sharing in miraculous visions and experiencing the gifts of the Spirit that came while using the sacred food and oils.

---

*J. M. Carroll's *Trail of Blood, or Following the Christians Down through the Centuries from the Days of Christ to the Present Time* (1931) demonstrates the psychological power of this idea. See also Logan 2006, p. 78*ff.*

A firm belief in the power of these anointing oils comes from the Egyptians, through Moses, and later through the continuing influence of Egyptian rites and practices on early Christianity. In her recent book *Golden Shrine, Goddess Queen: Egypt's Anointing Mysteries,* Alison Roberts makes the case for the anointing rite as the most important rite in Egyptian religion: "Far from disappearing once Egypt came under Roman rule, these New Year rites evolved into the Christian anointing mysteries, as recorded in the canonical gospels."

Roberts, a British Egyptologist, suggests a fairly late date for the adoption of the Egyptian anointing rite, but the scriptural evidence suggests that the Hebrews used an anointing rite much earlier, from the time of Moses and his brother Aaron, who was the first biblical figure (as far as we know) to be called the anointed one. The evidence for a strong Egyptian influence on the Hebrew religion is based on similarities in holy vestments and rites and even the design of the Hebrew altars. In terms of theology, the similarities are even more striking. For example, if you compare Pharaoh Akhenaten's *Hymn to the Aten* (fourteenth century BCE) to Psalms 104:24, written at least six centuries later, the influences vividly demonstrate how much the Hebrews borrowed from Egyptian ideas. We can also see the similarities in rites and liturgy in the ancient Hebrew prayer for cleansing referred to in Psalms 51, which was apparently based on the much older rites for cleansing the corpse that had been used by the Egyptians for thousands of years (Glazov 2001, p. 159).

According to Acts 7:22 the early Christians looked to Moses as the founder of their faith, and they took pride in the fact that Moses was "learned in all the wisdom of the Egyptians." Because Moses had been educated in the pharaoh's court, his knowledge of the Egyptian rites almost certainly included the complex burial rites for washing and anointing the dead, not to mention the Opening of the Mouth ceremony described in the Egyptian Book of the Dead.*

---

*See also Benjamin Urrutia's article on the Opening of the Mouth ceremony in *Scripta Hierosolymitana: Publications of the Hebrew University of Jerusalem* 28 (1982): 222–23.

According the great British Egyptologist Sir E. A. Wallis Budge:

As in the *Book of Opening the Mouth* the words spoken by the Kher-heb, or chief officiating priest, were believed to change the meat, and bread, and wine into divine substances, so in the Liturgy also the formula, which was said over each element, was supposed to change it into a divine and spiritual food, which was partaken of by the souls of the gods and of the dead. The material elements of the offerings were eaten by the priests and the relatives of the dead, and the act of eating brought them into communion with the blessed dead and with the gods. The age of the belief in the transmutation of offerings cannot be stated, but it is certain that it was well known to the Egyptians under the Fifth Dynasty, and there is reason to think that it was not unknown to their ancestors in the latter part of the Neolithic Period, and that it is coeval with the indigenous African belief in the immortality of the soul, and in a life beyond the grave. (1994, p. ix)

The resemblance of these Egyptian funeral rites to the Agape Feast is obvious. During Jesus's lifetime, Moses was still highly regarded as a prophet in both Palestine and Egypt. Many spiritual healers and magicians called on his name to cure diseases, but while the Christians embraced Moses's Egyptian connections, the priests of the Jerusalem Temple were leery of these old connections to pagan Egypt.

Among the rites used for preparing the bodies of the dead, the Egyptians had a special rite for collecting bodily fluids from cadavers. This was one of several necromantic rites that the ancient Egyptian priests developed with great care and exactitude. They mixed rancid bodily fluids from decaying corpses with narcotic powders and the juices pressed from hallucinogenic plants. The resulting paste was used in making sacred oils and ointments. As part of their religious rites, the Egyptian priests applied these fluid effluxes and sacred oils to the faces of the dead and the dying, after which the dying very likely saw a vision of their fate.* Citing the Coffin Texts from the tomb of Seti, Erik Hornug goes on to describe the remarkable effects of the liquid effluxes taken from the corpse: "Wondrous powers of renewal were ascribed to the discharges of the murdered Osiris already in early mortuary texts" (2001, p. 39). The divine corpse of Osiris, and the many corpses of his followers, had over the centuries provided the fluids for the Egyptian anointing.

The use of these sacred oils would tend to comfort the dying, relieve pain, and perhaps even give them pleasant visions of Tuat, the Egyptian heaven. For the unlucky ones, however, these oils might bring horrific visions of the pain and torture that they could expect to experience in the afterlife. Much depended on the convictions of the dying penitent, who believed that in the afterlife good deeds would be rewarded and evil deeds would be punished. After death each person's heart was weighed by the divine scales; those found wanting were fed to a crocodile-headed monster, and those blessed souls who were justified by the scales enjoyed eternal life in the Egyptian heaven.

More important, the Egyptian priests used sacred oils in public ceremonies to anoint new converts to the cult of the god Horus. The sacred oils often gave these new believers profound visions of their god, which in turn helped to confirm the initiates in their new faith. After the anointing ritual the initiates are actually described as having become a Horus (Temple and Temple 2009, fig. 8.37). The practice of ritually anointing new believers was quite common throughout the ancient world, and it was especially prevalent in Egypt.

In a sense the converts to Horus were undergoing an important

---

*This Egyptian rite is similar to the Catholic Extreme Unction. In the Catholic rite the sense organs must be anointed. If the rite must be performed quickly, then an abbreviated form can be used, "But, after applying the thumb to the forehead, we would instantly, and without making the sign of the cross, pass it over one eye, over the nose and lips, and then apply it to one ear. We should thus have the unction of all the organs, the forehead holding the place of the hand. We are convinced this could be done as quickly as the words of the form above given could be pronounced. In most cases, even the hand, after the ear, could be anointed within the time" (O'Kane 1883, p. 365).

transition into a new state of existence and were given rites similar to those used for the dead (Gershenson 1991, p. 115). The anointing rite used by the ancient Egyptians and by Moses was similar to that used later by the followers of Jesus. During the postexile period (after 538 BCE) the Jerusalem Temple rejected many of these Egyptian rites as part of their effort to eliminate foreign influences. By the first century the Jerusalem Temple had successfully purged all these pagan influences from Judaism. Yet the early Christians embraced these ancient Mosaic initiation rites as a kind of inheritance that came to them through Jesus Christ, thus bypassing the morally corrupt priesthood in Jerusalem who had rejected both Jesus and the rites of Moses.

## SACRED FOODS

The use of holy oils is clearly documented in the early writings of the Christians, but now we must turn to the more unusual methods used to ready the bodies of the dead: the rites used in the preparation of the sacred foods.

Ritual cannibalism was often linked to ancestor worship, which was widespread throughout the Mediterranean and the Near East going back to prehistoric times. Archaeologists call these ancient religions cults of the dead, because they required ritual interactions with the dead. As part of their burial rites these communities maintained contact with the spirits of the dead by being anointed with sacred oils and by eating sacred foods that were prepared for the burial feast. Among the Hebrew tribes, these feasts often included using a powerful drink called the "cup of consolation" (Jeremiah 16:7). The Hebrew cup of consolation was sometimes also called "the drink of the dead," or *Kispu,* and it was often spiked with a variety of drugs, including opium, wormwood, and various hallucinogens (Godbey 1930, p. 225). Based on Isaiah 57:9 and other sources, some scholars believe that these feasts for the dead not only included the use of sacred oils but also the inhaling of special kinds of incense that allowed mourners to believe that they had traveled to the land of the dead to visit their ancestors (Godbey 1930, p. 219).

In the religion of Osiris, one of the oldest of the cults of the dead, the Egyptian priests developed elaborate rites and liturgies for maintaining spiritual (and physical) contact with the dead. They reveled in complex burial rituals and in elaborately staged ceremonies for the gods. In *Death, Burial and Rebirth in the Religions of Antiquity*, Jon Davies suggests, "It is quite permissible to regard the extraordinary religion of Egypt as an ornate 'cult of the dead'" (1999, p. 62). Davies also examines the influence of Egypt during the Iron Age on the Hebrew attitudes toward the disposal of the dead.

Centuries earlier, however, during the Bronze Age (3300–1200), the ancient cults of the dead, such as those in Crete and in Palestine, were fairly straightforward—even pragmatic or utilitarian—in how they made use of human remains. This is especially true in the comparison of these cults and the more complex religion of Egypt. In both Crete and Palestine people in communities stored cadavers near at hand in simple stone and rock tombs so the bodies could be used to make sacred food and oils used in their religious rites. As the Hebrews came more and more under the influence of Egypt, the local cults of the dead in Palestine began to adopt more complex ideas and elaborate rites.

As I pointed out in the introduction, throughout the Near East and also among the Hebrews the funeral feasts were called Marzeah. During these feasts the celebrants performed burial rites, consumed specially prepared food and drink, and anointed themselves with holy oils (King 1988, p. 37). According to the *Catholic Encyclopedia,* the Agape Feast, used by the earliest Christians to celebrate the death (and resurrection) of Jesus the Christened One, was derived from these ancient Hebrew burial feasts. "This, at its origin, is clearly marked as funerary in its intention, a fact attested by the most ancient testimonies that have come down to us. Our Lord, in instituting the Eucharist, used these words: 'As often as you shall eat this Bread and drink this chalice, you shall show forth the Lord's Death'" (Leclercq 1907).

Yet the difficult problem for historians today is to explain how and why the ancient Hebrew burial feast—a rite that the Jerusalem Temple had suppressed for nearly two centuries—could suddenly resurface at the beginning of the first century CE to become one of the central rites of the new Christian Church.*

The four gospels and the Acts of the Apostles document major conflicts between the followers of Christ and the leaders of the Jerusalem Temple. Less clear is exactly why these two groups were in conflict. The Christian Church has long maintained that it was Jesus's claim to be the long-awaited Messiah that led to his conflict with the Temple hierarchy. Later Jewish writings also tend to support this explanation; in them Jesus is viewed as one of many failed claimants to the title Messiah. If this, however, had been the only point of contention between the two parties, then the execution of Jesus by the Romans should have ended the debate. Clearly the Temple priests believed that Jesus was not their Messiah. He was certainly not anything like the Messiah that the Jews were led to expect by descriptions in their prophetic books.

If Jesus had been the Jewish expected Messiah of prophecy, he would have formed an army, defeated the Romans, and then driven them into the sea. Instead (at least from the point of view of his Jewish brethren), the death of Jesus on the cross was proof that he was not the Messiah that the Jews had been awaiting for so long. Furthermore, his death on the tree marked Jesus as irredeemably cursed in the eyes of his fellow Jews (Deuteronomy 21:23). Because Jesus not only had failed to lead the revolt against Rome but also had been executed as a criminal, he could not be the Messiah. At least that was the opinion of most Jews. The notion put forward in later Christian theology of Jesus as some kind

---

*The Last Supper is a Christianized version of the Marzeah feast. The story of the Last Supper establishes the theological justification for eating the body and blood of Christ. The catacombs of Rome have numerous images of the Last Supper as a typical burial feast. According to J. Romilly Allen, "During the era of the persecution of the Christian Church by the Roman Emperors, between the years 64 BCE and 303 BCE, religious art is entirely confined to the underground cemeteries which were purposely made inaccessible by means of concealed entrances and other precautionary measures" (2004, p. 9).

of rejected Messiah who died as a criminal in order to redeem human-kind merely obscures the more significant historical conflict between the Jerusalem Temple and the first Christians.

During the twentieth century there was a great deal of debate over how the Jerusalem Temple reacted to the challenge posed by the apoca-lyptic preaching of Jesus. A serious effort has been made to portray the priests as victims of an impossible dilemma: How could they maintain good relations with Roman overlords without alienating the common Jews? How could they deal with this itinerate preacher who was stirring up trouble with his tales of a Kingdom of God?

These all sound like serious concerns. But were they reasons enough to plot against Jesus? Did the Pharisees really see him as a threat? Ulti-mately, we must discover the real reason for the strong hostility that existed between the earliest Christians and the priests of the Jerusalem Temple.

Perhaps the real argument between the Temple and Jesus was a conflict over the rites for the blessed dead. The problem was not so much over Jesus's claim to be the Messiah, although the claim worried the authorities because of Jesus's ties to dangerous reactionaries, such as John the Baptist. In reality the conflict involved Jesus's role as the leader of a religious faction that wanted to restore the rites for the blessed dead, including the Marzeah Feast, along with the use of sacred oils and sacred food and all that this implied about the sacred nature of the bodies of the blessed dead. The Yahwist priesthood in Jerusalem had suppressed the Marzeah Feast in the kingdom of Judah for five hun-dred years and tried to do so in nearby Samaria and Galilee for nearly two hundred years. Because these pagan necromantic rites were associ-ated with the old Hebrew cult of the dead, the priesthood had struggled against them in a religious conflict that dated back several centuries.

To be exact, this conflict between Jesus and the Temple was primar-ily over the rites for the 'elohe 'abiw, or the Elohim, which Asian reli-gions often call the divine ancestors (as in Genesis 28:22). In Palestine they were sometimes called "the blessed dead" in both the Hebrew and the Christian religions. (References to the blessed dead appear in Revelations 14:13 and the late-first-century Ascension of Isaiah IX, 8–9.) Ancestor worship was quite common throughout the ancient world, and the blessed spirits of the dead were also referred to as the righteous dead or even "the grateful dead" (when the spirits of the dead reward people for good conduct toward the dead). Stories about these spirits were common in Near Eastern folklore, and a popular story about the grateful dead found its way into the Jewish Book of Tobit, written sometime before 50 BCE.*

The religion of Egypt was a cult of the dead, though perhaps a lot more complex than the Hebrew cult. The influence of Egyptian rites on early Hebrew religion is quite clear. In his book on the religions of antiquity, Jon Davies explores the religious influences of Persia, Babylon, Egypt, and Canaan on the Hebrew religion, as it existed in the kingdom of Judah. Davies believes that in its earliest form, the Hebrew religion began as "an Iron Age (ca. 1200–580 BCE) 'Judahite' cult of the dead" (1999, p. 62). Other scholars have also come to this conclusion, including Elizabeth Bloch-Smith, who believes that over a long period of time, the Hebrew cult of the dead was "an integral aspect of Judahite and probably Israelite society" (1992, p. 222).

Hebrew funeral practices were quite firmly entrenched in Hebrew society, and these rites had survived centuries of interplay between the Hebrew and Egyptian religions. The funeral rites for the blessed dead were integrated into Hebrew social life early on, as is demonstrated by the archaeological evidence of gravesites in Israel, in Judah, and

---

*Some traces of the old religion persist to this day. For example, in the film *Half Baked* (1998), called a stoner comedy, the character Brian buys a pouch that supposedly contains the ashes of Grateful Dead guitarist Jerry Garcia (1942–1995). Toward the end of the film Brian and his friends get into a fight with some drug dealers, during which Brian drops the pouch of ashes. The ghost of Jerry Garcia leaps from the ashes and hits the villain over the head with a guitar, thus saving Brian and his friends. The ghost then vanishes. In contrast, in the film *Night of the Living Dead* (1968) a brother and sister are attacked in a graveyard by one of the hungry dead—or the zombies that perhaps should be called "the ungrateful dead." This film focuses on the dangers posed by the living dead, who have come back to life and hunger for the flesh of the living.

(amazingly enough) even in the vicinity of Jerusalem (Davies 1999, p. 78). The clannish nature of these family-based burial rites sometimes created divided loyalties, and, more important, they tended to dilute the power of the political and religious elites centered in Jerusalem. Yet over the centuries as the Hebrew religion became more and more focused on Yahweh, considerable political pressure was exerted to establish his centralized worship in Jerusalem. In Judah, the Jerusalem Temple worked to end both the Mazerah burial rites and the veneration of ancestors at local shrines.

How did this conflict first begin? The religion of Abraham was Semitic in origin, and it no doubt included Near Eastern funereal rites, including the Marzeah and probably Canaanite/Semitic rites for communicating with the spirits of the dead, which included using incense.* Later on, during the time the Hebrew people were in Egypt, the Hebrews probably adopted similar Egyptian practices. Archaeologists have recently found several caverns in Palestine where special kinds of sacred incense were inhaled in order to contact the dead, and these caverns held several examples of totemlike bronze serpents (Godbey 1930, p. 220). These sacred icons are probably similar to the Brazen Serpent worshipped by Moses in the desert (Numbers 21:4–9). The Hebrew scriptures describe Moses as crafting the image of a serpent out of bronze and hanging it on a pole. His followers could "look upon" the bronze icon in order to overcome the dangerous effects of snakebite.

Several prominent historians, including Budge and Frazer, have concluded that the rites established by Moses were based on Egyptian practices, and during their captivity in Egypt the Hebrews probably also developed a familiarity with the Egyptian funereal rituals for preparing the bodies of the dead (Glazov 2001, p. 159).

For example, the Jewish patriarch Jacob was mummified in Egypt using a process that took forty days to complete, with seventy days

---

*It's likely that the incense included myrrh, frankincense, and galbanum. These were burned on an incense altar. People had to pass this altar before approaching Yahweh (Hillman 2008, p. 104).

reserved for the mourning rites (Genesis 50:1–12). Additional Hebrew mourning rites were performed for Jacob when his body was taken to his homeland for burial. Evidently the Hebrews at the time of Jacob and Joseph saw no conflict between the Egyptian and the Hebrew burial practices. Joseph arranged for his father's body to be honored by both religions before it was finally interred in Palestine.

By the time of the Exodus of the Hebrew people from Egypt, sometime before 1200 BCE, the Hebrew religion was overlaid with Egyptian religious rites. After the Exodus the Hebrew religion continued as a Semitic/Egyptian hybrid for nearly a thousand years. But beginning perhaps as early as the eighth century BCE the Hebrew religious authorities tried to discourage the traditional Marzeah Feasts. The priests tried to restrict the Hebrew cult of the dead and to stop the practice of making offerings to the dead (Bloch-Smith 1992, p. 223). It also became the Jerusalem Temple's official policy to try to discredit the dead. The Temple priests attacked rural shrines and spirit oracles as unreliable and dangerous (Davies 1999, p. 78). The common people were often admonished to rely on Yahweh and his priests, instead of seeking guidance from the blessed dead. Isaiah 8:19 states, "When they say to you, 'Consult the mediums and the spiritists who whisper and mutter,' should not a people consult their God? Should they consult the dead on behalf of the living?"

It seems the priests in Jerusalem wanted be rid of their rivals, the local holy men who made sacrifices and accepted tithes on behalf of the blessed dead. Yet many Hebrews resisted the authorities in Jerusalem; family and traditional ties to local shrines and graves often took precedence over the demands of the priests far away in Jerusalem. The old Mosaic rites persisted in spite of intense criticism coming from Jerusalem—and then the religious persecutions began.

During this time King Hezekiah (716–687 BCE) began several religious reforms, destroying idols and removing cult objects—which included the famous Brazen Serpent, which was taken out of the Temple and destroyed (2 Kings 18:4). The Jerusalem priests were especially determined to suppress the old funeral rites that they claimed were corrupted with dangerous Egyptian and Canaanite ideas and should be eradicated. Later, in about 622 BCE, under King Josiah the attacks against the many rural shrines intensified throughout Judah. Described in 2 Chronicles 34, Josiah led a program of religious genocide against the local priests.

> For in the eighth year of his reign while he was still a youth, he began to seek the God of his father David; and in the twelfth year he began to purge Judah and Jerusalem of the high places, the Asherim, the carved images and the molten images. They tore down the altars of the Baals in his presence, and the incense altars that were high above them he chopped down; also the Asherim, the carved images and the molten images he broke in pieces and ground to powder and scattered *it* on the graves of those who had sacrificed to them. Then he burned the bones of the priests on their altars and purged Judah and Jerusalem. (2 Chronicles 34:3–5)

The book of Deuteronomy reflected these attitudes and formally established the Yahweh-only views embodied in King Josiah's religious reforms. Although the king was somewhat successful in destroying the high places and sacred groves in his kingdom, the funeral feasts continued to be performed. As far as the average Hebrew was concerned, rites for his dead ancestors took precedence over the demands coming from Jerusalem. That situation, however, changed dramatically a few decades later. The Babylonian armies defeated the Hebrew army in 597 BCE, ending several decades of relative independence for the kingdom of Judah. The Hebrew elite was taken into captivity in Babylon, and this disastrous event triggered a major reevaluation of the old Mosaic beliefs.* During this time the Hebrew leaders questioned why they had lost the favor of Yahweh and been forced into captivity. The Hebrew priesthood decided that it was the popular support for the Hebrew cult

---

*The northern kingdom of Israel had already fallen to the Assyrians in 732 and again in 720 BCE, and its population was dispersed. Its peoples became known as the Ten Lost Tribes of biblical tradition.

of the dead that had caused this disaster. The rites for the dead were too much like the pagan rites of the Canaanites and the Egyptians and were therefore unacceptable to Yahweh. In their eyes Yahweh had turned away from his people because of their stubborn loyalty to these old rites.

Then, after sixty years in exile, the Hebrews were finally delivered. The Persian army defeated the Babylonians, and the Persian king became their new master. The Hebrews soon developed close relations with their liberators, the Persians, and the Persian king Cyrus the Great allowed them to return to Jerusalem. He even financed the rebuilding of their Temple, which was eventually completed under the Persian king Darius the Great. During this time the Hebrews came into direct contact with the Zoroastrian religion of the Persians, and it was probably during this period that the Hebrews adopted some of the Persian attitudes toward the dead. Unlike the Egyptians, the Persians saw the bodies of the dead as a source of spiritual pollution—especially the bodies of holy men and women, for they believed that these corpses tended to attract evil spirits (Davies 1999, p. 43). Typically, the Persians placed their dead in high towers, where birds ate the corpses. Probably because of Persian influences, the Hebrew priesthood also came to view the bodies of the dead as being spiritually taboo and even dangerous.

After the return of the Hebrew elite from Babylon in 537 BCE, the priesthood was even more determined to reform Judaism as part of their monotheistic, Yahweh-only campaign. This included blaming the Hebrews who still performed the pagan rites for the blessed dead. The priests claimed that by failing to rely on Yahweh those Hebrews who had followed the Hebrew cult of the dead were responsible for their earlier defeat by the Babylonians (Isaiah 8:21). It was their unwillingness to rely on Yahweh that caused Yahweh to withdraw his spiritual protection from Judah. The cult of the dead was now to be blamed for their long captivity in Babylon.

After their return from the Babylonian captivity and now securely in power, the priests in Jerusalem set out to suppress some of the old rites established by Moses and remove all Egyptian influences. Of course the priests' determination to get rid of the rural holy men was both self-serving and theological. The Yahweh-only policy was partially based on the fact that they did not want to share power (or tithes) with the many local priests and holy men whose shrines were scattered all across Palestine. During the Second Temple period (520 BCE–70 CE) the authorities in Jerusalem extended their influence and further developed their Yahweh-only theology.

The funeral rites for the blessed dead were suppressed to some extent—at least in the areas controlled by the authorities in Jerusalem— but some of the priests at the sacred groves, caves, and high places (which were beyond the borders of Judah and thus beyond the political reach of Jerusalem) continued to practice the traditional rites. In most of the territories north of Judah—including Israel and Galilee—people continued to enjoy a certain amount of religious freedom for several centuries, at least until these territories were conquered by the Jewish Hasmonean kings (140–37 BCE). Then these territories were forced to accept the religious authority of the Jerusalem Temple.

After the conquest of the northern territories the priests of Yahweh were even more determined to concentrate religious sacrifices in Jerusalem. From this time on all sacrifices were to be made in Jerusalem and religious power was to be centered in the Jerusalem priesthood. This meant destroying all the remaining holy shrines, high places, and sacred groves in the northern territories of Israel and Galilee.

Completely ending the old funeral rites was, however, much more difficult, because long-standing family loyalties and local traditions favored the occasional burial rites and the Marzeah Feasts. According to Davies, "Inevitably, 'the authorities' sought, in Judah as throughout Jewish history, to moderate and hopefully to suppress this quintessentially ancient Near Eastern practice; the dialectic of the struggle continued in both Jewish and Jewish-Christian religion and history" (1999, p. 63).

The Jerusalem Temple did what it could to suppress the funeral feasts for the blessed dead. Ultimately the priests succeeded in ending the feasts within conventional Judaism, but for the more unconventional religious groups, such as the Nazarenes, the rites persisted. It is likely that the resistance to the Jerusalem priests' authority was centered in Galilee and, to some extent, in Jewish communities in Egypt (Baigent 2006, p. 144*ff.*).

Through the centuries several rival sects developed within Judaism, including the Nazarenes, who were still loyal to the old cult of the dead. The stubborn Nazarenes eventually formed the mustard seed of what became the new Christian cult (Butz 2010, p. 58). In recent years several scholars have come to the conclusion that Christianity developed out of the old Hebrew cult of the dead. These scholars include Lewis Bayles Paton, the author of *Spiritism and the Cult of the Dead in Antiquity,* and more recently the famous Jewish scholar Shalom Spiegel (1899–1984). As Davies notes, "In his quiet way, Spiegel at various points indicates a degree of agreement with the notion that, in Christianity, Judaism gave rise to a pagan cult of the dead, in particular a cult of sacrifice, a return [he implies] to an ancient legacy predating both Judaism and Christianity" (1999, p. 64).

Some Hebrews remained loyal to the old rites for the blessed dead, which still persisted in the face of intense religious persecution from Jerusalem. Eventually many of these people became the first Christians.

Some areas north of Jerusalem, and especially Galilee, resisted the so-called reforms coming from the Jerusalem Temple. This is why the Pharisees said, "No prophet arises out of Galilee" (John 7:52). They knew that many Galileans continued to practice the old rites of the blessed dead, and any religious leader coming from there was probably, at the very least, spiritually compromised. This included the new claimant to the title of Messiah, whom they called Jesus the Galilean. They were certainly skeptical of Jesus's religious views, and much of what he preached caused them concern. He was not a traditionalist— at least not in the way they were.* Jesus seems to have taken every opportunity to challenge the religious authorities, but from the

---

*Recently this view of Jesus as a religious outsider has gained some new adherents as, for example, Pieter F. Craffert in his *The Life of a Galilean Shaman: Jesus of Nazareth in Anthropological-Historical Perspective.*

perspective of a radical traditionalism. He speaks as someone who has centuries of anti-authoritarian tradition backing his religious views.

At first Jesus presented himself as a reformer rather than a radical. But the priestly establishment probably considered Jesus to be—much like John the Baptist—a dangerous reactionary.* Adopting Jesus's ideas would have meant a fundamental shift in power away from the priests in Jerusalem. Would they permit the rites for the blessed dead to be restored? This was very unlikely. Ultimately Jesus failed in his effort to reshape early-first-century Judaism to be more like the diffused and localized Hebrew religion that had existed a thousand years earlier. Instead, Jesus was arrested and executed, most likely at the instigation of the high priest and powerful members of the Sanhedrin.

Little of this was recorded in the Christian scriptures. The conflict over rites for the blessed dead was largely carried out behind the scenes, because neither group wanted a direct and open conflict over the way the Jerusalem Temple had suppressed the old Hebrew cult of the dead. Even though the Jerusalem Temple had rejected the Egyptian rites centuries earlier, the priests were still a bit leery about revisiting the old conflict. The Temple priests had already suppressed these rites (where they could), and the Jerusalem priests were not interested in reviving this old controversy, especially during a time when the priesthood was coming under intense criticism for their exploitation of the poor with their endless demands for tithes and sacrifices.

Unlike the Jerusalem priesthood, the early Christians took pride in their Egyptian connections, and they boasted that Moses was "learned in all the wisdom of the Egyptians" (Acts 7:22). Even more amazing, the Christians did not hesitate to compare the crucified Jesus to the "brazen serpent" of Moses, the same Egyptian icon that the Jerusalem priests had removed from the Temple and destroyed: "As Moses lifted up the serpent in the wilderness, even so must the Son of Man be lifted up;

---

*Recently archaeologists have explored a cave that they think belonged to John the Baptist. See Shimon Gibson's *The Cave of John the Baptist.*

so that whoever believes will in Him have eternal life" (John 3:14–15).

This statement is a rejection of the Jewish priesthood and its laws, which state, "He who is hanged is accursed of God" (Deuteronomy 21:23). It seems more than likely that Jesus's goal was not to create a new religion but simply to reform Judaism by restoring the traditional rites of Moses as they existed before the Babylonian captivity.* These rites would include the Marzeah Feast. It seems clear that the religious role of the blessed dead was the essential point of conflict between the Jerusalem Temple and the first Christians. This realization is, perhaps, the most remarkable (and completely unexpected) discovery that we could imagine. Recognizing the influence of the Hebrew cult of the dead on Christianity helps us to interpret some of Jesus's teachings that have, for many centuries, remained confusing or obscure. For example, in Matthew 15:11, Jesus makes a rather odd statement: "It is not what enters into the mouth that defiles the man, but what proceeds out of the mouth, this defiles the man."

This sounds like an attack on the Jewish dietary laws, but these words seem strange, because on other occasions Jesus strenuously defends Mosaic law. Further, his brother, James the Just, was famously devoted to the law of Moses. Why then would Jesus tell people to ignore the dietary laws of Moses? Perhaps this statement is not really about whether we should eat pork. Perhaps Jesus is talking not about the dietary laws at all, but about the sacred foods.

This statement from Matthew 15 probably did not originate with Jesus, but it was very likely a common argument used by Nazarenes to defend the ancient rites of the dead and, in particular, the eating of sacred foods. Because most of the Hebrews living in Judah at that time would have considered any contact with the dead to be a serious spiritual problem, a slogan or catchphrase defending sacred foods was necessary. In Matthew 15:11, Jesus defends the use of sacred foods, not the

*Lewis Paton's book is the definitive early work on this topic, but Rachel S. Hallote's *Death, Burial, and Afterlife in the Biblical World* is an excellent recent source that is both insightful and easy to read.

eating of unclean animals. He would have been, no doubt, horrified by the way these words were later used to justify abandoning the dietary laws of Moses. Jesus did not intend to discredit Mosaic law (Matthew 5:17–20). Instead his goal was to fulfill and restore the law, primarily by restoring the proper respect toward the blessed dead.

There have been many attempts to explain Jesus's words, though the scholars fail to understand that this statement is tied logically to the earlier verses of Matthew 15:4–7. Here Jesus compares Yahweh's commandment to honor our parents with the priests' claim that we can tithe to the Temple instead and ignore the requirement that we honor our parents. Jesus addresses the priests:

> Why do you break the commandment of God because of your traditions? For example, God said, "Honor your father and your mother" and "Whoever curses father or mother must be put to death." But you say that whoever tells his father or mother, "I have given to God whatever support you might have received from me," does not have to honor his father. Because of your traditions you have destroyed the authority of God's word. You hypocrites! Isaiah was right when he prophesied about you. (*GOD'S WORD Translation*, 1995)

In spite of what this passage seems to suggest, we can be fairly sure that the priests were not suggesting that good people should allow their parents to starve in the street. There is, however, a better interpretation of this passage. If we view Jesus as the leader of a sect that wishes to give the blessed dead the reverence that is due them, this passage makes sense. Essentially, Jesus accuses the priests of failing to honor the blessed dead, called here their fathers and mothers, by claiming the tithes and the prayers due these dead ancestors. Jesus's audience would have understood the command to honor their fathers and mothers to include, by extension, all of the family's ancestors. This command to "honor" includes maintaining the family tombs, a familial duty that usually fell to the eldest son (Davies 1999, p. 56); but instead of honoring the dead, the priests demanded that prayers, tithes, and sacrifices go to the Jerusalem Temple, the honors that rightly should have gone to local shrines, tombs, and cemeteries. Jesus attacks the priests for not honoring their ancestors with the old rites, and shortly after, in Matthew 15:11, he defends sacred food. As a whole, Matthew 15 is a coherent attack on the Jerusalem Temple based on Jesus's commitment to the old ways of Moses and the Hebrew cult of the dead.

These accusations against the priests were serious, but the most serious accusations are saved for Matthew 23:29–33. In these verses Jesus accuses the priests not only of greed and hypocrisy but also of benefiting from the murder of Yahweh's prophets.

> Woe to you, scribes and Pharisees, hypocrites! For you build the tombs of the prophets and adorn the monuments of the righteous, and say, "If we had been *living* in the days of our fathers, we would not have been partners with them in *shedding* the blood of the prophets." So you testify against yourselves, that you are sons of those who murdered the prophets. Fill up, then, the measure *of the guilt* of your fathers. You serpents, you brood of vipers, how will you escape the sentence of hell?

Some scholars suggest that Jesus speaks of fairly recent events (perhaps even hinting that the Temple priesthood was complicit in the arrest of John the Baptist). In this passage Jesus attacks the priests for failing to support those who, like John, spoke for righteous causes—not to mention other now long-forgotten prophets who were denigrated in their lifetimes and harassed by the religious authorities. According to Jesus, the priests are now busily erecting fabulous marble tombs for these dead prophets— which are only monuments to their own priestly wealth, power, and glory.

Matthew also contains several references that probably relate to sacred food: the holy cup, which the priests have befouled (Matthew 23:25–26); the experience of spiritual knowledge (*gnosis*), which they have prevented (Matthew 23:13–14); and the whitewashed tombs of their ancestors, which they have rendered unclean (Matthew 23:27).

This attack on the Temple priests plays on the common Jewish notion that the dead are unclean; but to Jesus it's the priests, not the bodies of the holy men and women, who are unclean.

> Woe to you, scribes and Pharisees, hypocrites! For you clean the outside of the cup and of the dish, but inside they are full of robbery and self-indulgence. You blind Pharisee, first clean the inside of the cup and of the dish, so that the outside of it may become clean also. Woe to you, scribes and Pharisees, hypocrites! For you are like whitewashed tombs which on the outside appear beautiful, but inside they are full of dead men's bones and all uncleanness. So you, too, outwardly appear righteous to men, but inwardly you are full of hypocrisy and lawlessness. (Matthew 23:25–28)

It is the spiritual corruption of the priests, not the act of coming into contact with the dead that makes them unclean.

The Gospel of Matthew presents sacred food as one of several disputes that Jesus has with the priestly hierarchy in Jerusalem, but the Gospel of John moves this conflict front and center. In John 6:48–66 we see direct confrontation between Jesus and the beliefs of his necrophobic contemporaries. The very idea of ritual cannibalism was repugnant to many Jews, and this passage shows their rejection of Jesus and his message. Many of those who wished to become his disciples were unable to accept this teaching and left him.

> "I am the bread of life. Your fathers ate the manna in the wilderness, and they died. This is the bread which comes down out of heaven, so that one may eat of it and not die. I am the living bread that came down out of heaven; if anyone eats of this bread, he will live forever; and the bread also which I will give for the life of the world is My flesh." Then the Jews *began* to argue with one another, saying, "How can this man give us *His* flesh to eat?" So Jesus said to them,

"Truly, truly, I say to you, unless you eat the flesh of the Son of Man and drink His blood, you have no life in yourselves. He who eats My flesh and drinks My blood has eternal life, and I will raise him up on the last day. For My flesh is true food, and My blood is true drink. He who eats My flesh and drinks My blood abides in Me, and I in him. As the living Father sent Me, and I live because of the Father, so he who eats Me, he also will live because of Me. This is the bread which came down out of heaven; not as the fathers ate and died; he who eats this bread will live forever." These things He said in the synagogue as He taught in Capernaum. Therefore many of His disciples, when they heard *this* said, "This is a difficult statement; who can listen to it?" But Jesus, conscious that His disciples grumbled at this, said to them, "Does this cause you to stumble? *What* then if you see the Son of Man ascending to where He was before? It is the Spirit who gives life; the flesh profits nothing; the words that I have spoken to you are spirit and are life. But there are some of you who do not believe." For Jesus knew from the beginning who they were who did not believe, and who it was that would betray Him. And He was saying, "For this reason I have said to you, that no one can come to Me unless it has been granted him from the Father." As a result of this many of His disciples withdrew and were not walking with Him anymore.

In this passage from the Gospel of John we see that by the end of the first century the sacred food had become the preeminent issue for Jews who wanted to become followers of Christ. It was clearly an obstacle for anyone who believed that they should avoid contact with the dead.

The reality, however, was that they feared much more than just taking "flesh" from the bodies of the dead and then adding it to sacred oils. That would be shocking enough to the Jews who listened to this teaching. What was left hidden was, perhaps, even more disturbing. Those who rejected this public teaching outlined in the Gospel of John almost certainly rejected the more bizarre implications of a theology focused on the bodies of the dead.

What they did not know was that the followers of Jesus were firmly committed to growing hallucinogenic mushrooms on the bodies of the dead, and these reddish-colored mushrooms were harvested from the flesh of the dead—just as they were symbolically harvested from the corpse of Father Saunière in 1917—so that the Christians could experience the divine through eating from the bodies of the dead.

After so many centuries, trying to identify the specific varieties used in Palestine, Egypt, or Greece would be an impossible task. It's like trying to figure out dog breeds from reading a history book.

By growing hallucinogens on the bodies of the dead, harvesting them, and then adding them to sacred oils and sacred foods, the followers of Christ put themselves well beyond what most of their Jewish contemporaries were willing to do. Those who followed Jesus—the Christians who respected the old Hebrew funeral rites in the form of the Agape Feast—already knew that the use of sacred plants taken from the bodies of the dead was a serious stumbling block to new recruits. Their fellow Hebrews, who had been taught for several generations to avoid all contact with the dead in order to not be spiritually polluted, would probably balk at eating these foods or using sacred oils made from the bodies of the dead.

The Christians were right to worry about the use of sacred foods, because the foods did become an obstacle to recruiting Jews to this new faith. As history has demonstrated, Paul was much more successful in recruiting the (much less fastidious) pagans to the new cult of Christ. The pagans were clearly more necrophile compared to the necrophobic Hebrews, and the pagans were also more open to the teachings of this newly resurrected Hebrew cult of the dead. After all, the Christian cult had a great deal in common with both the Greek and Egyptian mystery religions, which—like the Hebrew cult of Moses—had their origins in the prehistoric cult of the dead.

The use of sacred food, wines, and oils was an essential part of the new Christian Church. Early Christians described the sacred foods using several euphemisms, including the Body of Christ, the Lamb of God, the New Wine, the Water of Life, and the Precious Blood. Christians used the sacred foods to experience the indwelling of the Holy Ghost and to receive the spiritual teachings of Christ.* Once the novice Christian had partaken of sacred foods and been sealed with sacred oils, the initiate often had a direct experience or knowledge (gnosis) of the living Christ and, like Paul, could speak with authority on spiritual matters. According to Paul this new spiritual authority was manifested as special gifts of the Spirit—a blessing that should be desired by all Christians. Paul said, "Pursue love, yet desire earnestly spiritual gifts, but especially that you may prophesy."†

In the first few centuries after Christ's death, the rite of Confirmation involved both baptism and anointing with sacred oils that gave the initiate an intimate knowledge of the supernatural world. For example, "And then remember that you received the seal of the Spirit; the spirit of wisdom and understanding, the spirit of counsel and strength, the spirit of knowledge and godliness, and the spirit of holy fear, and preserved what you received. God the Father sealed you, Christ the Lord strengthened you, and gave the earnest of the Spirit in your heart, as you have learned in the lesson from the Apostle" (St. Ambrose "Concerning the Mysteries" 7:42). The use of sacred food persisted for several centuries as an essential part of the new Christian faith. The sacred foods provided new believers with an infallible vision of the kingdom of God, with Lord Jesus as its supernatural king, in much the same role held by Osiris in the Egyptian afterlife.

The Agape Feast—during which Christians anointed themselves with sacred oils and partook of sacred foods, sometimes to the point of folly (that is, inebriation)—was solidly established by St. Paul in his missionary work among the gentiles, and he insisted on the importance of sacred foods: "Is not the cup of blessing which we bless a sharing in the blood of Christ? Is not the bread which we break a sharing in the body of Christ?" (1 Corinthians 10:16).

---

*As described in 1 John 2:20, 27. See also New Wine at Hosea 4:10.

†1 Corinthians 14:1. See also Acts 8:14–17, 19:5–6; Ephesians 1:13, 4:30; and Hebrews 6:2. Many modern theologians have speculated on why Christians no longer receive these spiritual gifts. Obviously, once the use of sacred foods and oils came to an end, so did the spiritual gifts.

Paul was committed to the Agape Feast in spite of some problems with believers who actually became "drunk" with the Eucharist (1 Corinthians 11:20–32). Scholars seem to have overlooked the fact that if this public drunkenness were simply a problem with drinking too much wine the church leadership could easily have controlled the amount of wine at the table, but if the primary goal was to achieve a kind of spiritual drunkenness using sacred food, then this drunkenness could not be easily managed, much less completely eliminated from the Agape Feast.

A century later the church father Tertullian was still promoting the Agape Feast while making serious efforts to combat the rival feasts of the pagans. He was strongly committed to the Eucharist.

> The flesh, then, is washed, so that the soul may be made clean. The flesh is anointed, so that the soul may be dedicated to holiness. The flesh is signed, so that the soul too may be fortified. The flesh is shaded with the imposition of hands, so that the soul too may be illuminated by the Spirit. The flesh feeds on the Body and Blood of Christ, so that the soul too may fatten on God. They cannot, then, be separated in their reward, when they are united in their works. (Tertullian "The Resurrection of the Dead" 8:2)

It's likely that the Christians of Tertullian's time saw the Agape Feast as a strong selling point for the Christian churches compared to the more elitist pagan feasts of Mithraism and other cults, which often limited their membership to wealthy aristocrats.

One of Tertullian's contemporaries, Clement of Alexandria, was also strongly committed to the Agape Feast. At the same time he was—like Paul and Tertullian—very critical of those churches that abused the Eucharist and the Agape Feast and church members who started drunken arguments and even fighting.* Interestingly, Clement seems to have advo-

---

*The apostle Paul was concerned about these disruptions, as was Pope Clement I, who wrote several letters directed to churches in which the authority of the bishops had been challenged.

cated separating the charitable feasts for the poor from the religious Agape Feast. The feasts for the poor were considered charitable works, and the Agape Feast was clearly for the religious purpose of instruction and partaking of the Eucharist (Keating 2009, p. 78*ff*.). In recent years Clement has become something of a controversial figure in that it's alleged that he possessed a longer version of the Gospel of Mark called *The Secret Gospel of Mark,* which was reserved for those Christians who were spiritually advanced. Whether or not we accept this assertion, we must ask ourselves why Clement supported two separate meals. Why not combine a meal for the poor with the Agape Feast—unless there was a special Eucharist that could not be shared with those who were less spiritually advanced. It seems likely that during Clement's lifetime there was an effort to create a separate, ordinary Communion that consisted of plain wine and bread for the uninitiated, reserving for the spiritually mature Christians the true substance of the body of Christ: the sacred foods and sacred oils.

The Agape Feast was very important to the apostle Paul and also for many of the early Christians, but even more significant is that these feasts were often held in graveyards and catacombs. This fact helps to explain why Roman officials viewed the first Christians as being similar to the Hebrews but also different in significant ways. The Romans described the first Christians as some kind of burial cult or graveyard society, which was different from the Hebrews, who were fastidious, perhaps even phobic, in handling their dead (Wilken 1984, p. 31*ff*.). Unlike the Christians, for the first-century Hebrews any direct physical contact with the dead was to be avoided so that the faithful did not become ritually impure (Numbers 19:16–18). Yet physical contact with the dead was clearly not a problem for the Christians in Rome, who chose to hold their Agape Feasts in the underground catacombs and in graveyards for more than three hundred years. In fact, when the emperor Valerian (195–260 CE) wanted to punish the Christians, he did so by making it illegal for them to go to their cemeteries.

Although Catholic historians have tried to suggest that the Christians decided to meet in the catacombs because of intense religious persecution, recently several scholars have expressed serious doubt about the length and severity of these persecutions.* Did Christians meet in the catacombs mainly to avoid persecution? Hardly. And later on it was the church authorities themselves who began to block the entrances to the catacombs to control access to the tombs. This would have been unnecessary, unless many Christians actually wanted to visit the catacombs in order to celebrate their Agape Feast in the traditional way—that is, by associating with the blessed dead. Enjoying a physical proximity to the dead was highly valued by ordinary Christians. This was clearly part of their tradition, despite the later efforts of the church hierarchy to stop it.

More recently Ramsay MacMullen, Ph.D., suggests, based on the archaeological evidence, that there simply wasn't enough floor space in Christian homes and churches to accommodate the large number of Christians who existed at the time, from 200 to 400 CE. He argues that the majority of Christians were still regularly meeting in graveyards in order to worship, perhaps even preferring to worship in the old ways: among the dead (2009, p. 9ff.). Yet once the Christian Church had a firm hold on the levers of political power in Rome, this quickly changed. The church undertook the enormous task of building churches all over the Empire, largely to accommodate the large numbers of Christians who would have to be coaxed (or forced) away from the graveyards.

Over time the private feasts and rites for the dead were forcefully discouraged by the bishops, who wanted all Christian rites to become official ceremonies held in churches. This is clear to modern scholars, including Robin Jensen: "Church leaders were attempting to transfer these customary practices from the cemeteries to the church by encouraging mourners to observe the anniversary of a loved one's death with alms and

---

*See, for example, Marta Sordi's *The Christians and the Roman Empire*. The year 381 marks the date of the Council of Constantinople, which was called by the emperor Theodosius to confirm the Nicene Creed. This was the official end of all the other varieties of belief. The Christian churches that viewed Jesus Christ as human or a lesser being, including the Arians, were outlawed by the emperor's decree.

eucharistic offerings rather than food shared at a tomb" (2008, p. 120).

It appears that, like the priests of the Jerusalem Temple several centuries earlier, the Christian priests in Rome were trying to divert the alms and offerings away from the celebrations for the dead and directly into church coffers. Yet the Agape Feast was clearly a solid institution, and it would take several generations before these rites could be completely absorbed into the official church celebrations.

During the fourth century the church officials moved the Agape Feast into the churches, and new rules were written to govern the way the feasts were conducted. Primarily this meant stopping the corpse from being given the Eucharist. For example, in 393 CE the African churches passed regulations against placing the sacred host in the mouth of the dead person and also ruled against performing the Eucharist in the presence of a dead body. As Robin Jensen observes: "The need for such rules shows that by the late fourth century, the eucharist—taken in the church and at its altar rather than at the grave—must have become part of the ritual surrounding most Christian funerals, and that certain practices—like the feeding of the consecrated elements of the sacrament to a corpse (*viaticum*)—have a long tradition" (2008, p. 142–43).

The Christian rite of putting the Eucharist in the mouth of the corpse is clearly related to similar Greek and Egyptian rites, including the Greek rite for putting a sop of bread into the mouth of the corpse.

In recent years more scholars have looked at the burial rites of the Christians and in particular the continuation of rites from pagan cults of the dead. For example, Ramsay MacMullen has written extensively on this subject, and no less an authority than Helmut Koester says of MacMullen's writings on the early church:

He brings forward impressive evidence, mostly archaeological, for the third and especially the fourth century CE, showing the persistent predominance of pagan rituals among the vast majority of Christians, especially in burial practices and veneration of the dead. While only a small minority of them went to church, most could have been found celebrating the memory of the departed with food and wine at the cemeteries, often in a manner that their bishops hardly approved.*

The ritual use of sacred food and drink—the New Wine, the Water of Life, the Precious Blood—along with various sacred oils was continued by many groups of Christians into late antiquity (300–600 CE), but as the Roman church gained political power, the church authorities began to turn against the old rites. What was the problem for the authorities? Any believer who had a spiritual vision considered his or her spiritual authority to be equal to or even above that of the official priesthood. (This was certainly the attitude that the apostle Paul displayed toward some of the leaders of the Christian Church who lived in Jerusalem.) As Christianity spread across the Empire, many churches that used these necromantic foods and oils—now often called Gnostic churches—resisted the bureaucratic authority of the Catholic bishops. This was an impossible situation for the Roman church, because it was determined to establish the authority of Rome over all the other churches in the Empire. By the end of the fifth century the Roman church had decided that the use of sacred foods and oils must be completely suppressed. With the military support of the emperor, the Roman church now had the political power to do this.

Eventually the Roman army succeeded where mere debate and persuasion had failed. Sacred foods were declared heretical throughout Christendom, and the Christians who used these foods were largely exterminated all across the Empire. Except for some writings placed in jars and buried in the Egyptian desert, what the Catholic churches called "gnostic" Christianity ceased to exist within the Empire. Yet in spite of the Roman crackdown, the making of necromantic foods and

---

*Quote from Koester's review (on cover) of MacMullen's book: Ramsey MacMullen is professor emeritus of history and classics at Yale University and the recipient of a lifetime award for scholarly distinction from the American Historical Association. The award citation calls him "the greatest historian of the Roman Empire alive today." Helmut Koester is the John H. Morison Research Professor of Divinity and Winn Research Professor of Ecclesiastical History at Harvard University.

oils still continued in remote parts of Europe. Over time sacred foods became associated with the so-called occult practices of witches and with heretical churches, such as that of the Cathars. Even after the passing of several centuries, legends about the sacred foods persisted, becoming associated with stories of the Knights Templar and, more particularly, the Holy Grail (Lee 2000, p. 23*ff.*).

Yet the Catholic church, though suppressing the use of holy oils and holy foods, continued to support the theology of the blessed dead by channeling the raw emotions of these private funeral ceremonies into the more public—and church-sponsored—veneration of martyrs and saints. This religious movement is often called the cult of saints. The church-sanctioned veneration of saints' bodies and their various finger bones, leg bones, skulls, and other body parts persisted for centuries. The mania for finding and displaying holy relics sometimes reached absurd levels. For example, several churches claimed to have and often put on public display bits of dried skin that were supposed to be the foreskin of the baby Jesus!

As part of this grim new mania for relics, the church authorities opened the doors of the catacombs and set up a lively business in the tourist trade, which continues to this day. Even after the fall of the Roman Empire the cult of the saints continued to thrive in Christian Europe. The role of shrines, relics, tombs, and holy pilgrimages connected with the sacred bodies of the saints came to dominate the church for more than a thousand years. Even in Mark Twain's era the relics of saints were still a powerful draw for tourists visiting Europe. In his *Innocents Abroad,* Twain describes the relics of the cathedral in Milan.

The priests showed us two of St. Paul's fingers, and one of St. Peter's; a bone of Judas Iscariot (it was black,) and also bones of all the other disciples; a handkerchief in which the Saviour had left the impression of his face. Among the most precious of the relics were a stone from the Holy Sepulchre, part of the crown of thorns (they have a whole one at Notre Dame) a fragment of the purple robe worn by the Saviour, a nail from the Cross, and a picture of the Virgin and Child painted by the veritable hand of St. Luke. This is the second of St. Luke's Virgins we have seen. Once a year all these holy relics are carried in procession through the streets of Milan. (1869, p. 180)

As strange as all this may seem to us today, in the first centuries of the Christian era the display and veneration of relics was culturally and spiritually important in European countries, particularly as they slid slowly into the long night of the Dark Ages. The collapse of religious ideals was paralleled by the social collapse of the Roman Empire. Unfortunately, by focusing on collecting and piling up bones and dried flesh, the Catholic cult of the saints proved to be only a crude and degraded parody of the earlier Christian cult of the dead.

## CONCLUSION

Historians typically use the word *necromantic* to describe the secretive religious practices—identified as witchcraft—that were common throughout Europe during the Middle Ages and later, even into the modern era. These secret rites are necromantic because they often involve summoning the spirits of the dead. They were assumed to be heretical, because they were clearly in direct conflict with the official theology, rites, and powers of the Church of Rome, which now declared itself in the Nicene Creed to be "The One, Holy, Catholic, and Apostolic Church of Rome."

Over the centuries the Church of Rome has gone to great lengths to suppress these necromantic practices. During the twelfth and thirteenth centuries the church conducted several inquisitions in Europe, including a major military crusade in southern France. As we have seen, this part of the French Mediterranean was home to an important group of heretics, the Cathars, sometimes (and perhaps ironically) called "the Good Christians." The Cathars were known for their purity, poverty, and piety, and they often preached against the moral corruption of the Church of Rome.

The Cathar churches were destroyed in a twenty-year crusade (1209–1229), and an official papal Inquisition was then begun as part of what we today would call a cleanup operation. Newly formed in 1216, the Dominican order led this Inquisition to root out any left-over heretics and their necromantic practices that might still be hiding in remote parts of the Pyrenees, mountains that separate France and Spain. This effort was not entirely successful (Butz 2010, p. 274).

The fate of Christianity as a true cult of the dead was diverted by political forces and suppressed by force of arms, but this was not the end. The Christian cult of the dead survived just as the Hebrew cult of the dead had survived: through tradition and family loyalties. The desire to maintain family honor is a primal motive that cannot be easily suppressed—in spite of efforts by church and state to suppress these loyalties to kith and kin.

Jon Davies points out in *Death, Burial and Rebirth in the Religions of Antiquity:*

> As we shall see, it is this aspect of death which gives rise to repeated controversy in, for example, Judaism, where temptations to accord to the dead a capacity to help or advise the living, or even to intercede with God, are regarded by "the authorities" as a most dangerous heresy. It is difficult, however, to find any religious culture which is able to suppress such 'cults of the dead' completely . . . (1999, p. 18).

Before we can truly understand the Hebrew cult of the dead and how Christianity sprang from this ancient belief, we must first understand the cult and its origins.

# 3

✠

# The Red Corpse

The funeral of Pope John Paul II was televised worldwide on April 8, 2005. With the possible exception of the funerals of Princess Diana and Michael Jackson, it was the most watched funeral in history. People who saw the display of John Paul's body were probably surprised by the brilliant red cassock and white vestments.* The vestments were the traditional garments used at a papal funeral. The mourners were probably unaware that red was the traditional color used for burying the dead. Although mourners today wear black and the deceased is also often dressed in dark colors, the use of red as a funereal color goes back many thousands of years.

In *Immortal Man: A Study of Funeral Customs and Beliefs in Regard to the Nature and Fate of the Soul,* archaeologist and literary scholar C. E. Vulliamy includes a chapter titled "The Cult of the Dead" in which he describes a number of peculiar burial practices that were quite common

---

*In a popular, humorous photo President George W. Bush kneels near the pope's body and says (according to the caption), "What happened to Santa?" Of course, Santa's robes are also bright red and white, much like the red and white *Amanita muscaria* mushroom (Ott 1976, p. 97).

in the Neolithic era. Vulliamy lists several cultures in which the corpse is painted red or covered with red paste. Historians and archaeologists have puzzled over this odd burial practice for years but have not come up with a satisfactory explanation for it. Indeed, no one has explained why so many ancient people color their dead with red paste or red clay before they bury them. Vulliamy names dozens of societies in which the corpse is colored red. Vulliamy describes the practice in Africa.

> The funeral use of red is frequent in Africa. The Niam-Niam [a cannibal people] adorned the dead body with skins and feathers and dyed it with red wood. In the Congo the corpse is dried over a slow fire, and then plastered from head to foot with red clay, or reddened by being rubbed all over with oil and powdered camwood. The Ndolo covered the body with a paste made from red bark. Beecham relates how the Fanti people used to bedeck the dead man in all his finery and lay him out on a sofa, under a silk umbrella, in a room entirely hung with red cloth. Modern Africans continue the ancient custom, and still colour their dead with camwood powder and fat, with greasy preparations of iron oxide, or with oil and red earth. (1997, p. 45)

Vulliamy states that the practice of painting corpses red is at least twenty thousand years old and was common throughout the ancient world. This practice was especially popular from 7000 to 3000 BCE but slowly died out in Europe as people developed the use of iron. Archaeologists have not yet explained why the increased use of iron tools and weapons is related to the decline in the practice of painting corpses red.*

---

*In *Food of the Gods: The Search for the Original Tree of Knowledge,* Terence McKenna suggests that the shift of ancient cultures from bronze weapons to iron weapons coincided with a major shift in religious practices. These ancient cultures moved from using hallucinogenic plants and mushrooms to using beer and wine in sacred rites. This change occurred because Bronze Age mushroom-using cultures were conquered by technologically advanced invaders—nomadic peoples who used iron weapons and who also consumed alcohol in their religious rites.

Perhaps through painting their corpses red these earlier mushroom-using peoples were attempting to imitate or even stimulate the growth of red-capped mushrooms on the corpses of their dead. These mushrooms were probably one of several reddish-colored hallucinogenic varieties of psilocybin mushrooms that grew wild in North Africa and many parts of Europe. It would be reasonable to expect that by eating mushrooms grown on corpses the mourners at a funeral service likely expected to see visions of the afterlife, and they might have believed that they were communicating with the dead. The mourners might also have believed that some part of the dead's life force continued on within them as the result of eating the mushrooms.*

The idea of growing sacred plants on the bodies of the dead may seem bizarre, but there are many religious images in Egypt, Crete, Palestine, Norway—indeed, all across Europe—that represent this idea. Often peoples disguised this practice in their religious art. The mushrooms are usually replaced by birds or growing plants, but the images of plantlike shapes standing on corpses appear over and over again in ancient literature and art. The most popular of these images was probably that of the Egyptian goddess Isis in the form of a hawk standing on the corpse of her husband, Osiris.

The practice of growing mushrooms on the bodies of the dead began with an amazing discovery: a mushroom shaman was buried in a shallow grave, and some time later his corpse was unearthed. It was discovered that his body was covered with dozens of tiny mushrooms. In all likelihood the clothing of the mushroom shaman was heavily impregnated with mushroom spores. This growth is certainly suggested by the image of the Tassili mushroom shaman, found in a cave in southern Algeria, which may be more than ten thousand years old. In this

---

*See, for example, Hartland 1908–1927, p. 575. In the horror film *Shrooms* (2006) a group of American tourists travel to Ireland to gather hallucinogenic mushrooms in the forest and experience a mushroom "trip." One variety of hallucinogenic mushrooms, according to the story, has the power to let someone communicate with the dead and see visions of the future.

cave painting the body of a shaman, wearing a beelike mask, is covered in mushrooms. In all probability it was the discovery of just such a mushroom-laden corpse that led ancient people to venerate the dead as a source of divine wisdom.

Putting red clay on the corpse was a kind of sympathetic magic, and, more practically, the clay also tended to suppress the natural acids that the human body produces shortly after death. The acids had to break down naturally over time or somehow be suppressed before the body could become a host for the mushrooms.* The use of clay served this function perfectly. Furthermore, the red clay could be mixed with fat and bodily fluids taken from older corpses to promote the growth of new mushrooms. If the fluids were taken from an older corpse that had already germinated, these bodily fluids were already laden with mushroom spores. In fact, the ancient Egyptians used a word meaning *to germinate* in their funerary prayers and while praying over a corpse.

The transfer of bodily fluids from old corpses to a fresh corpse is documented in the writings of the ancient Egyptians, and scholars have long been puzzled by this practice. The British Egyptologist Sir E. A. Wallis Budge devotes part of *The Liturgy of Funerary Offerings* to trying to understand why the Egyptians transferred fluids from one corpse to another. Ultimately he is unable to suggest a clear reason for this rite (1994, p. 54).

The Egyptians appear to have continued the practice of coloring corpses with red pigments at least into the third century CE. The

---

*Baking the corpse would have the same effect. This was a common practice in the Congo (Vulliamy 1997, p. 45). We can note that in the ancient Greek celebrations of Dionysus, the celebrants covered themselves with clay. Andrew Lang suggests an African origin for this practice, but why the Greeks would adopt this practice has never been adequately explained (1996, 1:274–6). It is also worth noting that the twenty-thousand-year-old stone statue known as the Venus of Willendorf was covered with a coating of red clay as were many religious objects and statues in prehistory (Russell 1998, p. 17). For movie buffs we might also note the Billy Zane film *Memory* (2006), in which South American natives cover themselves with red-colored ocher made from the brain-tissue of corpses.

evidence for this practice, from earliest times, is extensive. According to Budge, "The wall paintings in Egyptian tombs, etc., often contain representations of men whose bodies are coloured red, and in papyri containing vignettes of the Book of the Dead the body of Osiris is frequently given this colour. From these it is clear that the Egyptians were in the habit of painting their bodies with red pigment" (1969b; 1973, 2:257).

Budge then gives a list of modern African tribes who ritually paint their own bodies, including a tribe in which the wealthy "mix the ashes of cow dung with their unguents, and when smeared with them their bodies have a dusky red tint." In addition to oils, many of these reddish-colored salves contain clay, ashes, and animal fats.*

These unguents containing bodily fats and fluids—sometimes mixed with red clay or oils—were applied to a fresh corpse, and after this application the body slowly decayed. It seems more than likely that once the flesh decayed sufficiently the corpse began to produce mushrooms from the spores contained in the fluids taken from older corpses.† Later on the mushrooms could be gathered in a religious ceremony.‡ This theory explains why many prehistoric societies dressed their corpses with red clay and oils as part of their burial rites.

Any explanation of this Neolithic burial practice must also account for why it died out. If Neolithic peoples believed that covering their dead with red paste or red clay was important, then why did they stop

---

*Even the Sphinx originally had a red face to indicate his holy and divine nature. Furthermore, religious jewelry shaped like the holy symbols of the Egyptian faith were often made from red stone, including the famous eye of Horus. A female icon, the *tjet,* said to represent the blood of Isis, was also made of red, semiprecious stone. These icons were often placed in Egyptian graves.

†The Egyptians took forty to seventy days to prepare a body for burial. This time period seems to be consistent with mushroom growth, based on Stamets's *The Mushroom Cultivator.*

‡It would be similar to the Cathar burial rite. It seems impossible to avoid the idea that Holy Communion is a direct descendant of an ancient ceremony in which people file past the corpse, and each removes a red mushroom in remembrance and in order to partake of the spirit of the deceased (Wilken 1984, p. 31*ff.*).

doing it? Further, why did this practice stop just as these peoples began using iron tools and weapons?

Terence McKenna, in *Food of the Gods,* suggests an answer. He believes that early mushroom-worshipping people were invaded and conquered by nomadic tribes (1992, p. 18). Throughout the Mediterranean area the gods of the old cults of the dead were replaced with newer wine- and beer-drinking gods. The older, pastoral religions were pushed aside, and new hierarchical (and typically patriarchal) religions followed in their stead. This process sometimes took several centuries to complete as the old religions were destroyed by military conquest and their leaders were exterminated. The suppression of the Cathars by the king of France and Pope Innocent III is only one of the more recent examples of this kind of crusade, but there have been many similar episodes in history.

The Hebrew scriptures, for example, tell how the cult of Yahweh did everything in its power to crush the older Palestinian Hebrew and Canaanite fertility cults—many of which used hallucinogenic plants. In the northern kingdom of Israel in the ninth century BCE, King Ahab acted with the help of the prophet Elijah to destroy the 450 priests of Baal. This event, described in 1 Kings 18, is portrayed as a rousing success for Yahweh and his followers. Their strict monotheism triumphed over the laxness of the competing priests. In truth, it was both a political victory for King Ahab and a decisive victory of the Yahwehist priests over the rural shrines and their holy men. Despite the religious propaganda written by the priests (and later included in the Hebrew scriptures) most of these rural priests of Baal were merely guardians of small temples and regional shrines, many of which were associated with local stories about Moses, Joshua, and other famous religious figures. The holy men at these shrines typically performed sacrificial rites for a variety of Hebrew and Canaanite gods, including Yahweh.

Elijah's crusade against the rural shrines provided King Ahab with an excuse to round up and kill the rural priests and holy men.

Elijah wanted to establish the dominance of Yahweh over the other gods, which in turn supported King Ahab's political ambitions. This is a matter not of one religion being spiritually better than another. As Patrick Tierney explains in *The Highest Altar,* the prophet Elijah and King Ahab proceeded to execute these rural holy men by making them human sacrifices to Yahweh* to bring rain and thereby break a persistent drought. Of course, though, the real purpose was political: to consolidate religious and political authority with the elite of Israel.[†]

Throughout history church and state have combined forces to purge the old pagan religions. The sacrifice of the priests of Baal (like the extermination of the Cathar "heretics") represents only one of the many holy crusades against the cults of the dead that have taken place over the centuries all across Europe and the Middle East.

---

*Elijah thus proved that he was not morally superior to the priests of Baal—at least not in his attitude toward human sacrifice. For a comprehensive work on the influence of human sacrifice on Christianity, we can refer to J. M. Robertson's *Pagan Christs: Studies in Comparative Hierology.* For the full argument, read the unabridged text.

†Similarly, in eleventh-century Norway, King Olaf made an alliance with the Christian Church in order to wipe out the worship of Thor and the other Norse gods, because he wanted one all-powerful church to help him unify the country under his own rule (Du Chaillu 1889, 1:464*ff.*). It was in the political interest of King Olaf to promote Christianity over the rural cults and local shrines. In return for his efforts on behalf of the church, King Olaf was sanctified as St. Olaf. Many Norsemen left Norway rather than submit to the king. They migrated to Britain, northern France, and other parts of Europe.

# 4

✠

# Ritual Cannibalism and Magic Foods

According to Dan Russell's *Shamanism and the Drug Propaganda,* the use of hallucinogenic plants was virtually universal in the ancient world. In addition to psilocybin and other hallucinogenic mushrooms, like the *Amanita muscaria,* dozens of plants have psychoactive properties. Ancient peoples were well acquainted with their cultivation, collection, and use. According to Russell these plants (and potions made from them) include such familiar religious symbols as "the Burning Bush, the Tree of Life, the Cross, the Golden Bough, the Forbidden Fruit, the Blood of Christ, the Blood of Dionysus, the Holy Grail (or rather its contents), the Chalice (*Kalyx:* flower cup), the Golden Flower (*Chrysanthemon*), Ambrosia (*Ambrotos:* immortal), Nectar (*Nektar:* overcomes death), the Sacred Lotus, the Golden Apples, the Mystic Mandrake, the Mystic Rose, the Divine Mushroom (teonanacatl), the Divine Water Lily, Soma, Ayahuasca (Vine of the Soul), Kava, Iboga, Mama Coca and Peyote Woman" (Russell 1998, p. 1).

The desire to experience the divine by using hallucinogens was common among ancient peoples. At least in their beginnings, almost all modern religions used hallucinogens in their religious rites. Originally people found and gathered hallucinogenic plants in the wild for their own use. Over time they organized the gathering and preparation of the plants into sacred rituals. The social use of many of these hallucinogenic and narcotic plants was fairly benign or even beneficial: they helped develop tribal cohesion.

Using these plants in a religious context meant that these ancient peoples looked to a common set of tribal ancestors for spiritual guidance during these rites. In most cases being able to identify with tribal and family ancestors carried a survival advantage: shared religious visions often served to link individuals into a strong social group. Yet sometimes using hallucinogens to see into the afterlife can be a double-edged sword: this kind of power can easily be abused by the unscrupulous priest or shaman or by a political leader who wants to claim divine sanction for self-serving actions. The use of religiously motivated violence extends into modern times. For example, Timothy Knab's *A War of the Witches* is a contemporary account of how some Mexican shamans used their knowledge to gain revenge, power, and money. In a local conflict between groups of *pistoleros* (gunmen) and *brujos* (witches) that took place in the 1930s, a local brujo was crucified by a mob in the village plaza, an act that led the Mexican authorities to intervene to end the war. This sort of conflict between social groups continues even today in societies where religion sparks social division.*

In the chapters that follow we will see how the modern Eucharist of Christianity grew out of the ancient cults of the dead by way of Egyptian, Greek, and Middle Eastern rites. Historically, a Semitic cult of the dead was overlaid with Egyptian rites, allegedly by a religious figure called Moses, who migrated to Palestine with a small tribe of followers, most likely people of mixed Hebrew and Egyptian ethnic-

---

*Similarly, in recent years the almost limitless power of religious clerics in Iran was quickly abused by the more unscrupulous clerics, especially in the absence of any organized opposition to their political demands (Dalrymple 2008, p. 217).

ity. This new religion became the Hebrew cult of the dead, and it dominated the area around Jerusalem from about 1200 BCE until the defeat of the Hebrew armies by the Babylonians in 587. Over the next ten years the Hebrew elite was carried away into a Babylonian captivity that lasted about sixty years. When the elite eventually returned to Jerusalem they were determined to reform their religion under one god, Yahweh, and destroy all the "corrupt" pagan and Egyptian influences. This process required more than three hundred years and was never completely successful, because the funeral rites of the old Hebrew cult of the dead continued to be performed, even near Jerusalem, up to the second century BCE (Armstrong 1998, pp. 75–76).

In about 30 CE a charismatic leader called Jesus the Galilean (a.k.a. Jeshua ben Joseph) tried to reassert these old funeral rites in a public campaign against the Jerusalem Temple. He failed to restore the old Hebrew rites, but his followers later broke away from mainstream Judaism. These followers of Jesus the Nazarene—especially the apostle Paul—successfully promoted the religious idea of Jesus as "the christened one" among many secularized Jews and pagans. The pagans already had extensive experience with Greek cults (based on the old Minoan cult of the dead), and they were quite open to this new amalgamation of Hebrew, Greek, and Egyptian ideas.

The earliest followers of Jesus Christ were familiar with the practices of these cults, and some church leaders—like the apostles Paul and John—did not hesitate to use the power of hallucinogenic and sacred plants to create their own visions and bind their followers into a tightly knit community of believers. They created sacred food and holy oils that had the power to give people visions and a full knowledge and possession of supernatural truths. The ultimate triumph of Christianity over its pagan rivals is, in part, a tribute to the almost magical power of the blood of Christ.*

---

*In southern Mexico the mushroom cult seems to have survived by merging with the Catholic religion of the Spanish overlords. Today the local psilocybin mushrooms are still called "the blood of Christ" by people in this area (Ravicz 2007, p. 48).

After the first few centuries of the early Christian Church, the true nature of the sacred blood became a closely held secret, and the sacred oils were restricted to smaller and smaller groups as we can see in this statement made in 416 CE by Pope Innocent: "That this power of a bishop, however, is due to the bishops alone, so that they either sign or give the Paraclete the Spirit. . . . For to presbyters it is permitted to anoint the baptized with Chrism whenever they baptize . . . but with Chrism that has been consecrated by a bishop; nevertheless it is not allowed to sign the forehead with the same oil; that is due to the bishops alone when they bestow the Spirit, the Paraclete" (Denzinger 2002, p. 3).

Here the bishops extend their power over who can be anointed and how. Later, sacred food and oils were completely suppressed by the church leaders. Over time the church slowly transformed itself from a primitive mushroom cult into a highly organized (and politically astute) alcohol-based religion. Eventually the use of all the hallucinogenic foods and ointments was denounced as heretical. In the medieval era, after the heretic churches were wiped out, the few people who still used hallucinogens were labeled witches.

There is a good deal of evidence for the use of hallucinogens among the earliest Christians, including the writings of both the early church fathers and their pagan critics. The earliest Christians were frequently accused of committing antisocial crimes, including cannibalism (Keating 2009, p. 67). Yet this was a crime they were guilty of committing only to the extent that they used the bodies of their dead to create necromantic foods. The accusation of cannibalism was put forward by Roman authorities who apparently believed the stories to be literally true, at least based on what they could learn about the Christian Agape Feast. Modern Christian authors suggest that this accusation came from a simple misunderstanding of the Eucharist. They argue that because during the Mass, worshippers partook of the body and the blood of Christ, perhaps pagans misunderstood this as an act of cannibalism.* On the other hand, we know that many pagan religions had rituals that were very similar to those in the Mass. Certainly this was the case with the worship of Isis and Osiris (which was popular in Rome), and it was also true of the religion of Dionysus in Greece. Why, then, would the pagans, who were quite familiar with Osiris worship and understood its (mostly) symbolic nature, claim that the Christians were involved in some kind of cannibalism unless there was some truth to the charge?

Likely some of the early Christians did practice a form of ritual cannibalism by growing hallucinogenic mushrooms on the bodies of the dead. It was not a literal or simple cannibalism as we understand it—but it was close enough to attract the attention of several Roman authorities. In most respects, the Romans were open to a wide variety of religious practices. Indeed, some of the popular pagan rituals were bizarre in their own right. The Romans were also familiar with some of the more peculiar practices that were current in northern Europe (such as the practice of British warriors to go into battle naked and painted blue). That accusations of cannibalism came up at all suggests that the Christians did something that was significantly different from practices of most of the other religious cults in Rome.

It's likely that the followers of the apostle John, in particular, practiced ritual cannibalism, including the use of mushrooms grown on cadavers to make sacred food and oils. As Clark Heinrich suggests, the religious imagery of the Gospel of John and the book of Revelation clearly point to the use of hallucinogens in early Christian rites. Furthermore John explicitly mentions the use of a sacred ointment that gave an initiate an immediate knowledge (gnosis) of a powerful and compelling spiritual reality. In 1 John 2:27, the apostle John states, "As for you, the anointing which you received from Him abides in you, and

---

*Among some of the earliest Christians in Rome, the Mass included slaughtering a lamb whose blood was gathered in a cup so that it might be drunk by the communicants (Robertson 1911, p. 320).

you have no need for anyone to teach you; but as His anointing teaches you about all things, and is true and is not a lie, and just as it has taught you, you abide in Him."

John clearly believed that a Christian initiate had an immediate and direct experience of the divine by using this holy ointment. The initiate was now in Christ just as the body of Christ was in him. A profound understanding of Christ's teachings could be absorbed with the ointment made from the bodies of those who had already died in Christ and had become part of the Corpus Christi. This is perhaps why both Paul and John call Jesus "the first begotten of the dead" (Revelation 1:5; Colossians 1:18), for it's from his body that all the others who come after him received the Holy Spirit.

In addition to his defense of the Holy Spirit in his epistles, John's gospel subtly reinforces the idea of the transmission and germination of the Holy Spirit from one generation to the next: "Truly, truly, I say to you, unless a grain of wheat falls into the earth and dies, it remains alone; but if it dies, it bears much fruit" (John 12:24).

Although there was some opposition to John's writings, at least from the Church of Rome, the books written by John (or his followers)—including John's epistles, the Gospel of John, and Revelation—were quite popular in some churches, and these books were officially added to the Christian scriptures.

A leader whose theology was quite similar to that of John was the prominent church father Ignatius of Antioch, who attacked those Christians who rejected the true Eucharist: "They abstain from the Eucharist and from prayer, because they confess not the Eucharist to be the flesh of our Savior Jesus Christ, which suffered for our sins, and which the Father, of His goodness, raised up again" (Ignatius of Antioch "to the Smyrnaeans" 7.1).

Several modern scholars have noted the conflict within the early church among several groups that used sacred food and oils. There was an argument over which food and oils were truly "of Christ." Some groups—such as the church in Antioch—claimed to have a direct connection to the physical body of Christ, while others emphasized the purely spiritual aspect of the body of Christ. St. Ignatius seems to have sided with those who emphasized the physical body as the true source of the spiritual. In *The Gnostics,* A. H. B. Logan sees Ignatius of Antioch as one who emphasized the physical Christ as the source of the sacraments: "Thus he appeals to Christ's genuine human experiences as the basis for the Christian sacraments, mentioning Christ receiving ointment on his head to breathe immortality on the church, Christ's baptism 'to purify the water', then the Eucharist, the 'drug of immortality'" (2006, p. 78). For Ignatius the sacraments of Anointing, Baptism, and the Eucharist were all physical acts that were vital to salvation.

During the next two centuries the Christian Church prospered all across the Roman Empire. But at this point in church history something amazing happened: after centuries of secrecy, hidden in the shadows, the Christian Church—now becoming politically powerful and financially secure—proclaimed truths that its faithful only whispered about before. The Christian cult of the dead was now ready publicly to embrace the dead—and it did so with two vital documents written in the third and fourth centuries, the *Didascalia Apostolorum* and the *Apostolic Constitutions.* For the first time these two documents publicly repudiate the idea that the human corpse was somehow unclean (McCane 2003, p. 115). The reasoning behind this idea: from the Christian perspective, the dead are not really dead but simply asleep in Christ. In particular, the *Didascalia Apostolorum* states, "therefore do you approach without restraint to those who are at rest, and hold them not unclean" (*Didascalia Apostolorum* 6.22, cited in McCane 2003, p. 115). Similarly and perhaps more revealingly, the *Apostolic Constitutions,* or the *Teaching of the Apostles,* attacks some Christians for refusing the Eucharist:

Others, again, of them do refuse certain meats, and say that marriage with the procreation of children is evil, and the contrivance of the devil; being ungodly themselves, they are not willing to rise again from the dead on account of their wickedness. Wherefore also they ridicule the resurrection, and say, "We are holy people, unwilling to eat and to drink"; and they fancy that they shall rise again from the dead [which they will, but as] demons without flesh, who shall be condemned forever in eternal fire. Fly therefore from them, lest ye perish with them in their impieties. (*Apostolic Constitutions* 1:26)

This defense of sacred food seems to suggest that the resurrection from the dead largely depended on partaking of the Eucharist. Written some time between 375 and 380 CE, this statement continues with further teachings about why we should revere the bones and relics of the dead, along with a reference to the first Pentecost in which Jesus ate and drank with the apostles.

At about this same time, St. Jerome (347–420 CE) advocated for Christians to separate themselves further from the Jews and their belief in the impurity of corpses. As we might expect, St. Jerome was also a strong advocate for full participation by everyone in the funeral aspects of the Christian cult of the dead. According to Professor Byron McCane in *Roll Back the Stone: Death and Burial in the World of Jesus,* "The cult of the dead had come out into the open, and Christians were leading the way. Jerome not only participated in the cult of the dead, he gave it his written approval and argued that it was a Christian duty to take part" (2003, p. 117).

This and other energetic appeals were directed to all Christians, who were now openly directed to accept the dead as if they were still members of the community, and many churches openly enjoyed this practice. Even the churches in Palestine, at the heart of Judaism, were now embracing the dead, so that "by the fifth and sixth centuries, Christians in Palestine had brought the remains of corpses right into their church buildings" (McCane 2003, p. 121). They did this in a way that distinguished them from their Jewish brethren, who were still quite leery of being in the presence of a corpse, much less including a cadaver in a religious service.

There was now a Christian cult of the dead that was separate and distinct from its Jewish origins. The dead were now the living dead in Christ.

> Drawing therefore upon energies that had long persisted below the surface of social life in Palestine, Christians transformed a secret Jewish cult of the Dead into an open Christian one. Explicitly denying the impurity of corpses, they began to do in public what had previously been done only in private, and to do on a large scale what had earlier been done only on a small scale. (McCane 2003, pp. 122–23)

During this time the Christian Church had grown so rapidly that it may be an open question how many churches were still using the same recipe for making the blood and flesh of Christ. The use of psilocybin mushrooms grown on the bodies of the dead could expand as rapidly as the church did, but the supply of the more difficult to find *Amanita*

*Figure 4.1.*
*An example of an* Amanita muscaria *mushroom*

*muscaria,* which grows in the wild, was fairly limited. This very likely had serious consequences over time.

In the centuries before the Christian Church began actively to discourage the use of the true blood and flesh of Christ along with the real fellowship of the Corpus Christi, the lack of some ingredients—like the hard-to-find *Amanita muscaria* mushrooms—may have adversely affected the cohesiveness of the overall church. The churches that relied on only psilocybin mushrooms and perhaps such substitutes for *Amanita* as cannabis, opium, or other plants might have encouraged a divisive theology that rejected not only the authority of Rome but any other authority, too. It was probably this growing tendency toward contentiousness and quarreling that eventually forced the Roman church to reject the original Corpus Christi in favor of ordinary (that is, non-hallucinogenic) bread and wine. Many churches had already instituted a policy of separating the Agape Feast from the free meals for the poor. It was only a matter of restricting the true Eucharist to smaller and smaller groups. Soon, only the priests had access, and eventually not even the priests could gain access to the true Eucharist.

This was similar to the situation that Jesus had complained about almost six centuries earlier in his attacks on the Jerusalem priests: "But woe to you, scribes and Pharisees, hypocrites, because you shut off the kingdom of heaven from people; for you do not enter in yourselves, nor do you allow those who are entering to go in" (Matthew 23:13).

Just as the Jerusalem Temple had earlier rejected sacred food and sacred oils, the Church of Rome eventually came to reject them ("You do not enter in yourselves"), and the Church of Rome prevented other churches from entering the kingdom by using the power of the Roman Empire to crush any heretics who might want to use the Eucharist to experience the kingdom of heaven and gain divine knowledge.

Once the Church of Rome decided to abandon necromantic foods and ointments the true history of the early church was suppressed, and the use of these ointments was made heretical. Eventually, once Roman Christianity became the official religion of the Empire, this policy of suppressing the original Eucharist led to the extermination of all the heretical and Gnostic Christians by Roman armies at the end of the sixth century. Even as the Roman Empire in the West began to collapse, the church extended its religious authority all across Europe. Over time the Church of Rome continued to gain strength, and in the thirteenth century Pope Innocent III had the full cooperation of the French king when he ordered his crusade against the heretic Cathar Christians in southern France.*

Despite the fact that the Cathar religion was destroyed in France, the influence of these old necromantic foods and cannibalistic rites continued to persist. The Cathar beliefs no doubt inspired the legends of the Holy Grail. As Clark Heinrich and other scholars have maintained, the strangely compelling mythology of the Holy Grail appeared in France like a mushroom in the night.† The Grail legends are based on the spiritual teachings and folklore surrounding the use of hallucinogenic mushrooms in secret religious rites. There are many incidents in the Grail legends that point to the old Christian cult of the dead, and the Grail authors revel in the strange supernatural powers of the Sangre Sancte and the Corpus Christi.

At this point in history, the use of hallucinogenic ointments and food went underground but continued to be widespread in many parts of Europe long after the Cathars had disappeared. Carlo Ginzburg's *Ecstasies: Deciphering the Witches' Sabbath* presents compelling evidence that such practices continued in Europe, but outside the Catholic faith. The use of these foods and oils was, from this point on, ascribed to witchcraft and necromancy.

Church officials actively pursued anything that smelled of heresy,

---

*Perhaps ironically Irenaeus in *Against Heresies* writes: "Besides those, however, among these heretics who are Simonians, and of whom we have already spoken, a multitude of Gnostics have sprung up, and have been manifested like mushrooms growing out of the ground" (Irenaeus 1:29:1).

†See Clark Heinrich's book on this topic. It's not an accident that the mythology of the Holy Grail originated in southern France, lands once possessed by the heretical Cathars. Several authors have already suggested that lost Cathar myths inspired the Grail literature.

and the confessions forced from heretics and witches often included facts mixed with a few gruesome details that were probably invented by the prisoners to satisfy the sadism of the judges. In 1022, for example, a group of heretics was burned in Orleans, France. One of these heretics claimed that he "carried with him the ashes of a dead child: whoever ate of them immediately became a member of the sect" (Ginzburg 1991, p. 75). The idea that we could eat human remains, even in the form of ashes, and immediately become a believer in the sect suggests that this idea was commonly held at the time. Even though the account confuses necromantic food and ashes, it suggests a connection to the food and ointments used by the apostle John and his followers. Perhaps this story is merely the echo of a much older belief in the power of a magical food to grant us a direct knowledge of the supernatural.

The confession of literal cannibalism by this heretic, then, probably disguises ritual cannibalism and the use of hallucinogenic mushrooms. As Carlo Ginzburg observes, the witches who were brought to trial often made confessions that conformed to the expectations of the Inquisitor. At the same time few of the witches were likely to describe what they were really up to. Eating human flesh was considered normal for a witch, but eating mushrooms grown on a corpse, well . . . what Inquisitor would believe it? At the same time the nature of these confessions confirms that many people believed a magic drink or a witch's ointment could bestow a secret knowledge or a vision of the supernatural world.

In a case cited by Italian historian Carlo Ginzburg, a young man claims to have drunk a potion from a skin flask given him when he was initiated into a sect of witches. His story of initiation into the group is quite remarkable. The young man tells that after drinking from the flask, he "had all of a sudden the sensation of receiving and preserving within himself the image of our [witches] art, and the principle rituals of our sect" (1991, p. 307; see also Sidky 1997, pp. 36, 212). This story is probably reliable, because the young man was not under arrest and his story is conveyed as a personal account of his own experience. Did this young man drink a magic potion that had the power to bestow spiritual knowledge, much like the ointment described in the Christian Epistle 1 John many centuries earlier?

These stories of witchcraft in Europe point to a belief among the local people (and the Inquisitors) that magical potions and ointments actually existed. This absolute belief in the power of magical foods and ointments to convey secret knowledge is a reflection of the magical ointment described by John. The stories of these magical foods and ointments continued to persist in Europe in spite of the best efforts of the Catholic Church to suppress the witchcraft cults.

For instance, the use of magical ointments was well known in medieval Europe, and these ointments probably contained a wide variety of hallucinogens, narcotics, and other drugs. The idea that witches could use magical potions and ointments to cast spells was common even into the eighteenth century. It was also understood that witches sought to acquire cadavers in order to work their magic. In *The Incorruptible Flesh,* Italian historian Piero Camporesi describes how European witches practiced the act of anointing with necromantic ointments—ointments derived from corpses. According to Camporesi, the practice of anointing with magical oils was a common part of witchcraft: "The image of the anointed body appears and reappears almost obsessively in the context of necromantic medicine (witches anoint themselves and stun themselves with vapours from oil)" (1988, p. 161).

According to contemporary accounts, some of these magical ointments were used by witches also to give themselves the power of flight (or at least the illusion of being transported across great distances). Witches anointed themselves and then traveled astride broomsticks to attend their Sabbath. At the witches' Sabbath there were often dances and banquets—much like the rites of the Hebrew Marzeah Feast—but in the minds of the Inquisitors these occult rites also included sexual orgies and invocations of demonic spirits.

In examining stories of the witches' Sabbath, historian Carlo Ginzburg states that medieval witches were typically found to have an ointment that gave them visions of flying. In the conclusion of his book Ginzburg suggests that the use of hallucinogenic *Amanita muscaria* might account for these visions (1991, p. 306). Further, he notes that witchcraft trials were particularly common in the Alps, the Jura, and the Pyrenees mountains—all regions that are home to this species of mushroom. It's probably not a coincidence that the Pyrenees were also the home of the heretic Cathars and, later on, Father Saunière, whose funeral in 1917 leads us back to where we began.

The town of Rennes-le-Château in southern France is where Father Bérenger Saunière decided to be buried in accordance with the rites of the Cathars. As we have seen, the red tassels removed from his vestments may have symbolized the reddish-tinged psylocibe mushrooms that once adorned the bodies of those who had already died in Christ. They are the "blessed dead" referred to in Revelation. These hallucinogenic mushrooms were used with *Amanita muscaria* mushrooms to create a powerful vision of the afterlife. In spite of centuries of repression, the sacred red and white imagery is still powerful today, as we see in the funeral of Pope John Paul II, whose burial vestments are striking combinations of red and white, much like the colorful cap of *Amanita muscaria*.

✠

**Note:** As I was completing work on this book, I came across a documentary film called *Exploring the Da Vinci Code: Henry Lincoln's Guide to Rennes-le-Château* (2005). The film is essentially a traveler's guide to the area around the town of Rennes-le-Château. In this documentary Henry Lincoln—the man who first discovered some of the mysteries surrounding Father Bérenger Saunière and his odd little church—explores some of the unusual religious sites in the area.

At the end of the film Lincoln presents some images of a place located on the hillside above Rennes-le-Château. On the map it's called the "Camp Grand," or the Great Camp. According to his book *The Holy Place,* Lincoln found this camp in 1990 while exploring the local area for filming this documentary. This small place, located on a mountainous hillside, has hundreds of stone huts, which Lincoln calls beehive-shaped structures. The purpose for building these hundreds of stone huts is a mystery, as is the reason for having so many small stone huts all together on the same hillside. The huts were clearly not designed as living spaces, because they have no chimneys or any way to vent fires. Lincoln tells us, "Most were clearly and easily identifiable as stone buildings, erected to last, each containing one small room with a doorway and, invariably a narrow window. Some were square, some were rectangular, some circular, some ovoid. Each had a beautifully and skillfully constructed dry-stone domed roof" (2004, p. 152).

According to Lincoln's book, a historian who examined photos of Camp Grand described the buildings as resembling Neolithic beehive burial chambers.* Perhaps, though, what Henry Lincoln has discovered on this hillside is the most important secret of Rennes-le-Château. The existence of the Great Camp demonstrates that thousands of years ago this area was a major religious center for a cult of the dead. These stone huts probably served the same purpose as the ancient stone burial chambers already discovered on the island of Crete. This holy place in the mountains of France is truly a lost world—a secret and very special site for making elixirs used by the cults of the dead in their most important religious rites.

The existence of Camp Grand is evidence that the people

---

*Not many people are aware of the fact that there are similar sites with the same stone, beehive-shaped tombs on the island of Crete. Other sites are just across the mountains in Spain, on the western slope of the Pyrenees. This strongly suggests ancient contact between the Minoans of Crete (or the Mycenaean Greeks) and this part of southeastern Spain, much like the connection that may have existed between southwestern France and Egypt.

of Rennes-le-Château once gathered *Amanita muscaria* here, a hallucinogenic mushroom that is found only in the higher altitudes of mountain ranges (like the Pyrenees). These bright red and white mushrooms were probably used in concert with the mushrooms grown on a corpse, which were likely a reddish-tinged variety of psilocybin mushroom, similar to a *Psilocybe fimetaria* or *Psilocybe cubensis.**

---

*There are dozens of varieties of Psilocybe mushroom and recently a bright red variety was discovered, growing in the San Francisco area, named *Psilocybe Cyanofriscosa*. No one knows where this variety originated. See an image of this mushroom, along with some nice specimens of *Amanita muscaria,* at https://mycotopia.net/forums/wild-mushrooming-field-forest/60886-cyanofriscosa-cyanescens-amanitas-11-19-2009-1-a.html.

## PART TWO

# Your Own Personal Jesus

*Reach out and touch faith*
*Your own Personal Jesus*
*Someone to hear your prayers*
*Someone who cares*
*Your own Personal Jesus*
*Someone to hear your prayers*
*Someone who's there*

DEPECHE MODE, "PERSONAL JESUS"

# 5

# Cults of the Dead in the Modern World

In the modern world, as in past ages, our relationship to death is an overriding force in both our individual lives and society as a whole. Death stands like a silent partner behind all our religious ideas and social constructions. Humanity's effort to escape or delay death has been a springboard for the arts, sciences, and virtually all our aspirations as a species. As we enter the twenty-first century our primary obsession has shifted from our mortality to finding ways to cheat the aging process. We spend billions of dollars each year on cosmetic surgery, diets, exercise equipment, and other ways to look young. These vast sums exceed by far what we now spend on funerals and gravestones. Yet ultimately all our efforts to escape old age and death must fail. In the end we go back to thinking about death and our existence (if any) that follows after death.

Our bookstores are filled with books that try to show us how to think about death. Books such as Elisabeth Kübler-Ross's *On Death and Dying* and Mitch Albom's *Five People You Meet in Heaven* remain popular. The vast majority of these books approach death from a mystical and supernatural perspective. By contemplating heaven we try to ignore the gritty reality of death. Luckily we are abetted by the fact that our postmodern corpses are safely hidden somewhere behind the stainless-steel doors of the funeral home.* Like the first-century Hebrews, we are a bit necrophobic; we prefer to avoid any direct contact with the dead, as if they are somehow dangerous or contagious.

This wasn't always the case. In the ancient world death was necessarily a part of people's everyday lives—mainly because it was so prevalent. It was nearly impossible for people to get away from death, or to get away from the dead bodies—human and animal—that piled up around them. For the people of the ancient world, handling dead bodies was a part of ordinary, everyday life. Death and disease were everywhere. To make matters worse, people died of diseases whose causes and progression were far beyond their ability to understand. Many died of highly communicable diseases. To most people the plagues that moved across Europe probably seemed to be, in their own brutal way, simply an unusual overabundance of death.

It's important to understand that in the ancient world there were two prevalent ways of thinking about life and death. First, there was the pragmatic, life-centered approach typical of the early Greeks. Second, there was the view, common among the Egyptians, that this life is only a stepping-stone to a more important existence, an eternity in the heaven created by their god.

Many people in the ancient world felt a tough realism about death that usually was quite straightforward. Both the ancient Greeks and the earliest Hebrews, for example, had a life-centered understanding— that is, they did not believe in a heaven. Instead, they believed that after death there was only a ghostly spirit existence in the underworld. The Greeks called this place Hades, and the Hebrews called it Sheol

---

*On the other hand, the popularity of TV programs such as *CSI* shows that there is still a desire for realism concerning the dead, even if it's the fake realism of computer-generated imagery and trick photography.

(Larson 1977, p. 24). Preparing the dead was also straightforward. In the classical era the Greeks believed the corpse must be covered only with dirt, and a coin must be placed in its mouth to pay the boatman of the underworld. These acts accomplished all that was necessary for the spirit to reach the land of the dead.* The passage from life into death for the Greeks was simple and uncomplicated.

Unlike the early Greeks and Hebrews, the Egyptians believed that the dead must have a complex and elaborate ritual in order to reach the heaven ruled by the god Osiris. The ancient Egyptians saw a person's death as the doorway to either a grim and ghostly existence on earth or a heavenly existence in a beautiful Oz-like world ruled by Osiris. This Egyptian heaven, called Tuat, was envisioned as a much more pleasant version of our lives here on earth. The priests of Osiris regularly prayed to the gods to provide food and drink to the dead in this heavenly world. For the Egyptians the belief in a pleasant supernatural existence was just as powerful and compelling as any modern ideas about heaven.†

The Egyptian religion celebrated death in some obsessive ways. The Egyptians exalted the cadaver with a series of complex rites, offerings, and prayers as the deceased progressed toward achieving a heavenly existence. They treated the corpse not as a carcass full of corruption but as something more important. The corpse had to be ritually prepared— this preparation was necessary for attaining eternal life. The desire for a pleasant afterlife spread, over time, to include the lower classes. The pharaohs had been buried with elaborate mystical rites in enormous stone tombs, but as Egypt fell first to the Greeks and then the Romans,

---

*The Greek play *Antigone* gives a clear-cut idea of how the Greeks felt about death and the afterlife. An angry King Creon decrees that his enemy will be left unburied: "You shall leave him without burial; you shall watch him / chewed up by birds and dogs and violated . . ." (Sophocles, *Antigone,* lines 205–6). This is a serious punishment, because without proper burial, the deceased can't go to the underworld. The major action of the play focuses on the dead man's sister, Antigone, who defies Creon and risks her own life in order to cover her brother's corpse with dirt.

†According to E. A. Wallis Budge, the educated Greeks and Romans could not even begin to comprehend the Egyptian obsession with death and its many rituals (see Budge 1969a, 1:viii).

even the poorest Egyptians could envision a future in Tuat, based on a minimum rite and an abridged ceremony by the Egyptian priests. It was necessary only to be buried with the appropriate rites to become an Osiris and share in his immortality. During the all-important Opening of the Mouth burial ceremony the mouth of the cadaver was pried opened with an iron tool, and in that instant the dead person was said to become like the god Osiris. The priest said, "Horus opens the mouth and eyes of the deceased as he opened the mouth and eyes of his father. He walks! He speaks! He has become immortal!"

This opportunity to become immortal like Osiris was also made available to women. After death each woman had to have a small, Osiris-styled beard glued to her chin before undergoing the burial rites for the dead.

There can be little doubt that the Egyptian cult of Isis and Osiris was the most sophisticated and advanced mushroom cult in the ancient world. Images of mushrooms are very cleverly imbedded in many Egyptian works. For example, the stele of King Apries—made to commemorate his twentieth regnal year (570 BCE)—has an enormous, stylized mushroom.* The mushroom is shown as an elaborate winged sun disk that stands over all the figures, but the feathers (representing the gills of the mushroom) and the two serpents at its base (representing the evil grubs who eat the mushroom from the base up) are indications of what this image truly represents. Like the famous eye of Horus, the images of the winged sun disk are clever, stylized images of the sacred mushroom. This image was popular all across the ancient Near East, including among the Hebrews, who called the image "the sun of righteousness" (Malachi 4:2).

Based on centuries of using hallucinogens to contact the souls in

---

*We can see the photo in Erik Hornug's *The Secret Lore of Egypt,* 10. The stele is currently in Lausanne, at the Musée Cantonal des Beaux Arts. Egyptologists call this a winged sun disk, but this identification masks the true origin of this popular icon. We can find another excellent example of this design in Budge's *Legends of the Egyptian Gods,* plate XVI.

Tuat, Egyptian priests developed an elaborate supernatural view of death, and their views slowly spread to other cultures. They influenced the worship of Dionysus, Adonis, and other savior gods all across the Near East. The Egyptians accomplished a good deal of missionary work for these ideas, and eventually even the pragmatic Greeks became more mystical in their views (according to Nilsson, from about 500 BCE on). The process accelerated after Alexander the Great conquered the Persian Empire, and Greece was suddenly exposed to a wide range of cultures and religions, including the Egyptian cult of Isis and Osiris.

In the centuries after Egypt fell to the army of Alexander (in 332–31 BCE) the religion of Isis and Osiris became more evangelical. Egyptian priests sent missionaries all across the Near East. Over time the elaborate mysticism of the Egyptians spread across the Mediterranean world, and eventually the Egyptian concept of death overwhelmed that of most of the other cultures in the ancient Mediterranean. The historian Diodorus Siculus, writing in about 59 BCE in *Bibliotheca Historica,* attributes the origin of certain Greek rites to Egyptian sources.

> For the rite of Osiris is the same as that of Dionysus and that of Isis very similar to that of Demeter, the names alone having been interchanged; and the punishments in Hades of the unrighteous, the Fields of the Righteous, and the fantastic conceptions, current among the many—which are figments of the imagination—all these were introduced by Orpheus in imitation of the Egyptian funeral customs. (I, 96, 5)

By the first century BCE even the hard-nosed realism of the Hebrews (already diluted with Babylonian ideas) began to fall victim to these mystical ideas. In time most of the ancient world embraced the idea of a future life filled with happiness and pleasure, which often stood in sharp contrast to the poverty and squalor of daily life.

In Egypt the idea of a blessed life in a heaven ruled by Osiris had started very early on, and these ideas gave birth to complex religious practices. Over many centuries the Egyptians turned their fascination with death into a complex set of rites and ceremonies, and the tombs of the pharaohs were practically cathedrals devoted to the worship of death. Today the pyramids dot the landscape of Egypt, enormous stone monuments to the ancient obsession with death and the world beyond. To most modern scholars, ancient Egypt was "a land dominated by the thought of death" (Lang 1996, 2:106). It would be hard to find another society so completely obsessed with death and with performing the rites necessary for crossing over to the Osirian heaven.

The earliest evidence suggests that the Egyptian religion first began as a form of ancestor worship.* Although daily life was focused on the immediate need for good harvests, the Egyptians spent much of their spare time in the performance of various religious rites that were concerned with providing food and drink for the dead. Prayers were directed toward the gods so that the gods would provide the dead ancestors with food, water, and even air to breathe. The Egyptians were worried about this provision, because they believed that a spirit that did not get food from the gods was doomed to wander the earth. These spirits would become the ghostly beings that eat whatever filth they can find lying on the ground.†

The Egyptians depended on the god Osiris to provide them with food in both this life and the next. In one of their prayers they ask that Osiris provide these things for their ancestors, saying, "They live on thy breath, they subsist on the flesh of thy body" (Frazer 1961, p. 113). From this prayer we can see that a kind of supernatural cannibalism was involved. Only those who died as believers in the god Osiris were fed from his body in the afterlife.‡ This idea was reflected in some of the Egyptian religious practices. For example, wheat grown in the Nile Valley was imagined as growing directly from Osiris's body. Archaeologists

---

*This is a commonly held view (see Vulliamy 1997, p. 65).

†The ancient Egyptians would have no trouble sympathizing with the plight of the ghost of Jacob Marley from Charles Dickens' *A Christmas Carol*.

‡The prayer "Give us this day our daily bread" is very likely based on this sentiment (Matthew 6:11).

have found many small clay pots shaped like Osiris's body. The Egyptians used these for growing a few sprigs of wheat as a religious token (much like today's popular Chia Pets).

In some ways this attitude toward the body of their god is not very different from the view of medieval Christians toward the body of Christ. A number of priests and nuns claimed to have survived for years by eating only the Host. These ideas were carried over into the mythology of Renaissance art. In later religious paintings, including several famous illustrations by Albrecht Durer (1471–1528), we can often see individuals gathering Christ's blood in cups. Similarly, Donatello's sculpture "Blood of Christ" shows angels catching Christ's blood in a chalice. In the legend of the Holy Grail this cup filled with Christ's blood miraculously provided food and drink for all those who were in its presence, much as Christ fed the masses on fish and bread that was multiplied by his supernatural power. The religious idea of a god as a supernatural buffet is never far removed from the images of eating the god's body.

# 6

✠

# Hebrew and Christian Ointments

Many other religions in addition to the Egyptian religion used fats and fluids taken from corpses. The fluids were used to make an unguent (salve or balm) that could be applied to the lips of the dead, but its use was not limited to the dead and dying. According to famed Egyptologist Sir J. Gardner Wilkinson, the Egyptians applied the balm by "moistening the ring finger of the left hand with various sweet ointments" and then applying the balm (1878, p. 420).

Among the Hebrews a special "oil of gladness" was used to anoint the dead in a last unction. Wilkinson notes that this kind of anointing was common "in Egypt, no less than Judaea" (1878, p. 363). Early on in their history the Hebrews almost certainly added bodily fluids to their holy oils, following the Egyptian practice; but they probably stopped using bodily fluids early in the post-exile period (586 BCE–210 CE), when the old Mosaic/Egyptian rites fell out of favor. Yet in the post-exile period their "oil of gladness" almost certainly still contained a powerful mixture of drugs, including cannabis, which in Genesis is called "Kaneh Bosem," according to the official recipe for making this holy oil.* These special oils were considered vital to the dying believer by providing physical comfort and perhaps a vision that would guide him in the next world.

The Hebrew priests were very specific about the oil's ingredients and its use in rites. By the time the Book of Exodus was compiled in the post-exile period, the use of some holy ointments was already limited to the priesthood. We can glean this from Exodus 30:31–33: "You shall speak to the sons of Israel, saying, 'This shall be a holy anointing oil to Me throughout your generations. It shall not be poured on anyone's body, nor shall you make *any* like it in the same proportions; it is holy, *and* it shall be holy to you. Whoever shall mix *any* like it or whoever puts any of it on a layman shall be cut off from his people.'"

The word translated as *layman* carries the sense of "stranger" or "outsider," though this passage came to be interpreted by the priests as meaning that anyone who is not a priest of Yahweh must not be anointed with this special oil. In any case, this passage in Exodus demands that any unauthorized person be punished for making similar oils or applying it to anyone. To most of us the punishment seems extreme unless the sacred oil is more than just oil. Obviously it must contain some very special ingredients.

The act of anointing a dying person with ordinary oils would have been a pointless ritual of little real physical or medicinal benefit to the dying aside from whatever psychological consolation it provided to the believer. But a special oil, heavily spiked with cannabis, could benefit a dying person by relieving physical suffering. Further, when hallucinogens were added to the oil, the anointing could also provide a powerful vision of the afterlife. We also know that, like the Hebrews, the early Christians practiced a similar anointing ointment probably derived from early Hebrew and Egyptian recipes. The powerful supernatural qualities of this Christian ointment were endorsed by an early Chris-

---

*The recipe for this oil is found in Exodus 30:23–25.

tian apologist, Minucius Felix (150?–270? BCE), who claimed that the Christians of his time anointed their dead and dying with a special unguent.*

The same holy balm was almost certainly applied to the lips of the living—that is, to people who were being initiated into the most holy and secret beliefs of the Christian cult. This practice was common to both pagans and Christians. Further, we know that the practice of anointing the lips with a supernatural unguent persisted in the Christian Church for several centuries, at least to the time of the emperor Constantine. A contemporary of Constantine, Julius Firmicus describes applying an unguent to the lips of Christians while comparing it to a similar balm used by the pagans. According to Firmicus the balm used by the pagans is "no better than grease," while the balm used by Christians is made with "an immortal composition." This statement, of course, raises the question: What immortal ingredients are in this ointment?

After praising the supernatural qualities of the Christian ointment, Firmicus quickly offers an odd statement: "This ointment frees the decaying limbs of mankind from the snares of death, so that when the first man is buried, straightway from the same person another man may be born in happier case. And to explain this more manifestly, we must unfold the mysteries of the Sacred Scriptures" (Firmicus 1970, p. 94). This passage hints at how Christians transmitted the sacred flesh of Jesus from one generation to the next. Much like the Egyptians, who were using in their sacred ointments the decaying fluids taken from the bodies of dead, the Christians were doing something unusual. Many people today might read the passage as simply a metaphorical description of the deceased being born into eternal life, but because this idea of death as a doorway to heaven was commonly held at the time by many

---

*See *Octavius* 12:6, likely written in the second century, between 166 and 198. Mary Magdalene poured perfumed oil upon the body of Christ in what was, essentially, a funerary rite similar to the anointing of the dead. Clearly, the anointing with sacred oils was of no value at all to someone who was already dead, unless the oil was necessary for the process of "germination" as the Egyptians expressly described it in their liturgy.

pagans, including the Egyptians, it would hardly need to be explained or described as one of the great "mysteries of the sacred scriptures."

Perhaps Firmicus is hinting at the real mystery: when a Christian dies his decaying flesh and bodily fluids provided the means for others to be redeemed. Firmicus understood that some spiritual quality was transferred from the dead to the living and that the sacred ointment was vital to the process; but this was also a sacred mystery passed on in secret rites, and it could not be written down except for vague allusions such as in this passage. The secret of the Christian ointments was that they were made with hallucinogenic mushrooms grown on the cadavers of the Christians themselves. This is what Firmicus means when he says, "when the first man is buried, straightway from the same person another man may be born in happier case." The body of the dead provided the sacred food and ointments that were used on those that came after him as followers of the Christ.

Firmicus then proceeds to quote from Psalms 45:2–8, which begins "grace is poured into thy lips" and ends with "thy God hath anointed thee with the oil of gladness." Firmicus uses the quote to make his meaning clear, at least to other initiated Christians. Obviously, Firmicus associated the ointment used by Christians in his time (fourth century) with the oil of gladness used by the early Hebrews during the time the Psalms were written. Anyone reading this passage from Firmicus would assume that the Christian ointment was the same as the oil of gladness used to consecrate Hebrew kings and priests, and it was also similar to the notable Balm of Gilead that the Christian authors often compare to Christ (based on Jeremiah 8:22).

Did the Hebrew holy oil, however, include human bodily fluids? We know that the ancient Hebrews used sacred oils and unguents in their most important rituals. W. Robertson Smith, in his highly regarded text *The Religion of the Semites,* states that the unction or unguents were originally made from the fat of a sacrificial victim.* Sir James Frazer agrees and further suggests that when a king was anointed, "the application of

_____

*Later in Jewish history other oils were substituted for the fat (Smith 1956, p. 383).

the holy oil to his head was believed to impart to him directly a portion of the divine spirit" (1961, p. 21). In the early Semitic cult of the dead this spiritual power was derived from the sacrificed victim, who was now identified with the god. When Moses arrived in Palestine, his people very likely tried to prohibit human sacrifice among both the early Semitic tribes and Canaanites in favor of the Egyptian practice, which called for animal sacrifices. Yet the actual source of the oil's power was in the use of cannabis and hallucinogens that were added to the sacred oil.

Were hallucinogens—particularly hallucinogenic mushrooms—used to make an ointment used by the apostles and the earliest Christians? We can find the answer to this question in the Christian scriptures.

The earliest Christians firmly believed in the supernatural powers of their holy salves and unguents. The Epistle called 1 John plainly states that a new Christian who has had his lips anointed with the unction has an immediate knowledge of Christ and requires no other teaching (2:27). According to John, "ye have an unction from the Holy One, and ye know all things" (2:20 KJV). We can compare John's statement to that of Aristeo Matais, a Zapotec mushroom shaman who lives in southern Mexico. Aristeo says that after eating the sacred mushrooms the spirits of the mushroom made him a shaman. "Then all the spirits come, all the Virgins, all the Saints. Then you *know* and are a *menjak*. From that moment the mushroom teaches you all things" (Wasson 1980, 47). Other shamans echo this sentiment. The mushroom can "teach and also show pretty things or, if the person is evil, the mushrooms can show them serpents and blood and other evil things" (Escalante 2007, p. 34). This instantaneous knowledge is derived from the mushroom, and it's clearly the same kind of Gnostic experience described by John, who firmly believed in the power of anointing to convey a direct experience of Christ. With this vision came a supernatural knowledge.*

---

*The unguent, or unction, is the oil of consecration, or the Chrism. According to Marvin Vincent, in *Word Studies in the New Testament,* this is the unction: "The word means that with which the anointing is performed—The Unguent or the Ointment as it is used in 1 John 2:20 and 2:27." (See also Vincent 1984, 2:338 and Allegro 1970, p. 56.)

This vision of Christ was not limited to John and his followers. It seems likely that the apostle Paul also received his vision—a direct experience of the risen Lord—while on the road to Damascus, and in much the same way. Further, Paul considered his spiritual knowledge of Christ to place him in a more intimate relationship with the divine. After all, Peter and the others had only known Christ in the flesh, while Paul's direct experience of Christ was a divine and supernatural knowledge that sustained him throughout the rest of his life and through many physical ordeals.* Whether Paul's vision came from sacred oils or from sacred food or drink is impossible to say, but Paul's devotion to the Agape Feast is evidence of his understanding of the role of sacred food in conveying the gifts of the Spirit.

Modern Christians believe that Paul and many of the first Christians had a direct supernatural experience of Christ. Sacred anointing oils were widely used in the early church for several centuries (Acts 8:14–17). On numerous occasions during the first three centuries of church history, the rite for anointing of a new bishop was delayed because the right kind of oil was not available, which seems suspicious, because all kinds of oil—including many precious oils—were easily available in any city large enough to have a bishop. If, as some might suggest, this holy oil was no more than oil from a balsam tree, then why delay the anointing? Perhaps the oil was not merely symbolic, and the anointing of the Holy Spirit was not mere ritual, as modern theologians tend to suggest.

The anointing in Christ was a real experience and not a purely symbolic act. This is also the opinion of Hippolytus of Rome, which he expresses while writing about the Hebrew scriptural figure of Susannah.

---

*Like John and Paul the demigod Hercules claimed to have gained knowledge of the divine through a vision. When Hercules is initiated into the greater mysteries at Eleusis in Greece he claims that he does not need to be initiated because he already had a vision of the goddess when he descended into Hades (Shelley 1995, p. 94). Euripides shows in his play *Hercules* that because of his vision of the divine, this heroic demigod was able to conquer death and return from Hades (Euripides 1884, p. 613).

But what were these unguents, but the commandments of the holy Word? And what was the oil, but the power of the Holy Spirit, with which believers are anointed as with ointment after the layer of washing? All these things were figuratively represented in the blessed Susannah, for our sakes, that we who now believe on God might not regard the things that are done now in the Church as strange, but believe them all to have been set forth in figure by the patriarchs of old. . . . (commentary on Daniel 6:18)

The act of anointing was considered vital in the early church. For example, the Gospel of Philip says, "The Chrism (or anointing) is superior to baptism, for it is from the word *chrism* that we are called Christians" (Gospel of Philip 74:12–21; Robinson 1988, p. 153). Similarly, Theophilus of Antioch (in about 181 CE) states, "Are you unwilling to be anointed with the Oil of God? Wherefore we are called Christians on this account, because we are anointed with the oil of God" ("To Autolycus," 1:12).

In his essay "On Baptism," Tertullian makes it clear that anointing follows baptism and that they are both literal, rather than symbolic events.

After this, when we have issued from the font, we are thoroughly anointed with a blessed unction—a practice derived from the old discipline, wherein on entering the priesthood, they were wont to be anointed with oil from a horn, ever since Aaron was anointed by Moses. Whence Aaron is called "Christ" from the "chrism" which is "the unction" which, when made spiritual, furnished an appropriate name to the Lord, because He was "anointed" with the Spirit by God the Father; as written in the Acts: "For truly they were gathered together in this city against Thy Holy Son whom Thou hast anointed." Thus, too, in our case, the unction runs carnally [on the body] but profits spiritually; in the same way as the act of baptism itself too is carnal, in that we are plunged in water, but the effect spiritual, in that we are freed from sins. (ca. 206 CE)

After baptism cleans the soul, the anointing seals the Holy Spirit within. This is why Jesus was called the "horn of salvation" (Luke 1:69), for he was the source of the anointing, just like the sacred horn used to carry the anointing oil in the time of King David.

The various rivalries among pagans and several Christian sects were still going on in 255 CE, when Cyprian wrote:

> It is also necessary that he should be anointed who is baptized; so that, having received the chrism, that is, the anointing, he may be anointed of God, and have in him the grace of Christ. Further, it is the Eucharist whence the baptized are anointed with the oil sanctified on the altar. But he cannot sanctify the creature of oil, who has neither an altar nor a church; whence also there can be no spiritual anointing among heretics, since it is manifest that the oil cannot be sanctified nor the Eucharist celebrated at all among them. But we ought to know and remember that it is written, "Let not the oil of a sinner anoint my head," which the Holy Spirit before forewarned in the Psalms, lest any one going out of the way and wandering from the path of truth should be anointed by heretics and adversaries of Christ." (Cyprian 69–70:2)

Here, Cyprian is concerned that some Christians are anointed with a false unction. Only sacred oils made from the body of the dead who is truly in Christ and has Christ in him can provide the correct immortal ingredients for sacred food and oils. Cyprian's letter suggests that he was battling both pagans and some Christian sects. Cyprian insists on the importance of the official anointing of a true Christian Church.

The similar composition and function of both the pagan and Christian ointments was not all they had in common. In addition, early on there was an ongoing competition between the various pagan communions and the Christian Agape Feast, or Love Feast. During the first few centuries of the Christian Church, the early church fathers engaged in a series of running battles with pagan church leaders. Frequently, these conflicts surrounded their competing forms of the Eucharist. The competition between the Christian communion and the pagan communion was intense, and some people partook of both ritual meals. This practice is condemned by Paul when he says, "You cannot drink the cup of the Lord and the cup of demons; you cannot partake of the table of the Lord and the table of demons" (1 Corinthians 10:21).

The competition between Christians and pagans is also clearly reflected in the writings of the early church father Ignatius (?–108 CE). He was concerned about Christians who took the Christian Eucharist and also took communion with pagans. In his *Epistle to the Trallians* (Book 6) he says, "I exhort you therefore—no, not I, but the love of Jesus Christ: partake of Christian food exclusively; abstain from plants of alien growth, that is, heresy. Heretics weave Jesus Christ into their web—to win our confidence, just like persons who administer a deadly drug mixed with honeyed wine, which the unsuspecting gladly take— and with baneful relish they swallow death!"

Similarly, in his Epistle to the Philadelphians (3:1–4:1) he says, "Abstain from noxious herbs, which are not the husbandry of Jesus Christ, because they are not the planting of the Father. Be ye careful therefore to observe one Eucharist for there is one flesh of our Lord Jesus Christ and one cup unto union in His blood."

Ignatius frequently uses images that involve herbs, plants, and growing things—knowing that some of his readers understood the barely disguised meaning of his words. This imagery permeates the documents of the early church. For example, the Didache, one of the oldest writings of the Christian Church, states, "We give thanks to You, our Father, for the life and knowledge that You made known to us through Jesus, Your Servant. Glory to You forever. As this broken bread was scattered over the hills and was brought together becoming one, so gather Your Church from the ends of the earth into Your kingdom, for You have all power and glory forever through Jesus Christ" (Didache, chapter 9; see also Rordorf 1978, p. 2).

In addition to the surface meaning, it's very likely that "this broken bread" that "was scattered over the hills" is a reference to hallucinogenic mushrooms and other plants that were gathered from the mountainous areas of Palestine and used in making sacred food. This so-called bread that is scattered across the mountains appears often in later Jewish and Christian mystical literature. Jesus was often associated with plants and growing things. Indeed, one of the first sacred titles applied to Jesus in the early church was the "Plant of Renown" based on his identification with the plant of Ezekiel 34:29.*

It's likely that Christians and pagans shared an advanced and highly specific knowledge of hallucinogenic plants that were added to the Eucharist and had the power to give initiates a direct experience of the divine. Even when ancient religious practices were suppressed, the religious idea continued to echo down through history—though often in a distorted and corrupted form. For example, the religious use of human fat and bodily fluids persisted into the medieval era. In *The Incorruptible Flesh,* Piero Camporesi describes how the Catholic Church used the corpses of various saints to demonstrate the miraculous. For example, the corpse of Beatrice d'Este was washed on an annual basis, and "this fluid and the impregnated cotton rags with which the holy body had been washed and wiped were distributed to hospitals" (1988, p. 10). The water was believed to have acquired healing powers. Later on, in 1501, the nuns of the Eremite monastery added the fluids used in washing Beatrice's corpse to the barrels of wine in their cellar. According to Camporesi, "The wine thus 'laced' with sap from the incorrupt bones and flesh of Beatrice were used to calm the fermentation of the wine" (1988, p. 8). The liquid was supposed to prevent spoilage, which the nuns viewed as both a spiritual and material condition. As Camporesi suggests, the idea of adding bodily fluids from a corpse to the wine suggests the influence of Egyptian ideas about using corpses as a source of supernatural power: "*Homo Homini salus:* human beings were a source

---

*"And I will raise up for them a plant of renown, and they shall be no more consumed with hunger in the land, neither bear the shame of the heathen any more" (KJV).

of precious medicament for their fellows, both dead and living, by providing excrements and other by-products of the body" (1988, p. 11).

In both the ancient Egyptian and medieval Christian faith the corpse of a saintly person provided oils and unguents to benefit both the living and the dead. This belief continued for centuries, even after the church had abandoned sacred oils made from the dead.

# 7

# Hallucinations
## as
## History

In *Bread of Dreams* the Italian scholar Piero Camporesi claims
that in early modern Europe (late fifteenth to eighteenth centuries) the lower classes lived in a state of nearly constant hallucina-
tion, because the poor were victims of a food supply contaminated
by hallucinogenic herbs and molds and because of their own deliberate use of opium and alcohol. In some cases they consumed
bread made from grain infected with ergot fungus, capable of creating hallucinogenic visions similar to those caused by LSD. In
other cases the hallucinations were caused by folk remedies and witches'
potions.

It seems then that early modern Europe was simply awash in hallucinations, and many hallucinogens had dangerous side effects. The
side effects of ergot poisoning, for example, could be a hideous and
disfiguring rotting away of the flesh, much like leprosy. Some medical

texts refer to the condition as "mummification of the extremities."*
Because medical science could not yet explain these afflictions, people
believed that supernatural forces caused these diseases. Often people
came to believe that witches were attacking them.

For many centuries the effect of these hallucinations was a popular obsession with the supernatural and with witches and evil spirits.
Among poor people the fear of supernatural forces was nearly universal,
and their obsessions were easily manipulated by the religious authorities
into a constant and almost hysterical fear of demonic influences. Under
these conditions a series of witch hunts were inevitable, and the church
seized the opportunity by creating the holy office of the Inquisition in
1478. The Inquisition hunted and destroyed witches along with many
heretics whom the Inquisitors arrested, tortured, and burned at the
stake. The definition of a heretic included, of course, anyone who could
not prove that he was a devout Catholic and anyone who was discovered
to have experienced visions.†

The witch trials that took place in Salem, Massachusetts, in 1692,
exemplify what can happen when a community believes it's under supernatural attack. Some scholars argue that a heavy rainfall that year led
to the growth of ergot on the wheat. When the wheat was baked into
bread and eaten, it caused hallucinations, madness, and even death. The
local authorities set up the infamous witchcraft trials and proceeded to
arrest and try anyone who was suspected of being a witch. At first the

---

*A similar epidemic of ergot poisoning took place in a small French village in 1951. The
victims described hallucinations of animals and other delusions, including the belief that
they could fly. Several people fell from the windows of upper stories (Fuller p. 277). If
we assume that a similar ergot-based ointment was available in ancient times, we might
explain the death of Simon Magus. Simon tried to buy the Holy Spirit possessed by
the apostle Peter. Shortly after, he fell from a tower and was killed (Acts 8:9–24). We
also know that European witches possessed a flying ointment, and a similar ointment
probably existed in ancient times.

†The Inquisition was also active in the Americas, wiping out most of the mushroom
cults, some of which managed to survive into the twentieth century only in remote
mountainous areas.

arrests were limited to women who were accused of practicing magic. Later the authorities used the trials to prosecute wealthy farmers, execute them, and then seize their property. The social causes for this sudden religious panic are complex, and many historians have examined both the origins and the end of the panic. Some scholars suggest that after the infected grain was used up (the rainfall the next year was normal), the hallucinations ceased. The trials ended soon after.

Because people did not understand brain chemistry or how hallucinogens function, they always gave these experiences a supernatural or religious interpretation. To them the drug-induced vision was very real. It fact, the vision was probably felt as more real than ordinary experiences. Although the source of the vision might be interpreted as either demonic or divine, there was no question that the vision must be treated as conveying a spiritual message.

# 8

✠

# Plants from the Bodies
# of the Gods

A great deal of research has been done over the past twenty years on the role that naturally occurring hallucinogens play in our religious history. Some of the best studies include Richard Schultes's *Plants of the Gods: Their Sacred, Healing, and Hallucinogenic Powers,* Jim DeKorne's *Psychedelic Shamanism,* and R. Gordon Wasson's *Persephone's Quest: Entheogens and the Origins of Religion.* These studies suggest several possible candidates for the plants that were used in ancient religious cults, including belladonna, Syrian rue (*Peganum harmala*), fly agaric mushrooms (*Amanita muscaria*), and a dozen different species of psilocybin mushrooms. The use of hallucinogenic mushrooms is particularly ancient, as shown by the recent discovery in a cave in northern Africa of several wall paintings that are at least seven thousand years old. These paintings include one that depicts a man holding what appears to be a handful of psilocybin mushrooms.

These cave paintings, found in Tassili, Algeria, also show mushroom-headed people dancing as part of a religious ritual. Although most of the cave paintings are naturalistic, these dancing men have strangely elongated, mushroom-shaped heads. Yet even more interesting than the painting of the dancing men is another painting of a man whose body is covered with small mushrooms. The mushrooms are usually explained as symbolic images and the painting has been described as a mushroom priest experiencing a mushroom-induced vision. In actuality this picture is fairly realistic, and the image more likely represents a corpse on which mushrooms are growing.* It's a foreshadowing of the later (and numerous) images of the god Osiris with plants growing from his body, images that were created a few thousand years later in nearby Egypt.

Sacred plants have always been part of the worship of the ancient gods. In *The Divine Origin of the Craft of the Herbalist,* Sir Wallis Budge states, "The religious and magical writings of the great nations of antiquity . . . contain abundant evidence that these primitive peoples believed that the first beings who possessed a knowledge of plants and their healing properties were the gods themselves." More important,

> They further thought that the substances of plants were parts and parcels of the substances of which the persons of the gods were composed, and that the juices of plants were exudations or effluxes from them likewise. Some of the ancients thought that certain curative plants and herbs contained portions of the souls or spirits of the gods and spirits that were benevolent to man and that poisonous plants were the abodes of evil spirits. . . . (1997, p. 1)

Ancient peoples clearly believed that some medicinal plants came directly from the bodies of the gods. For example, it was thought that the nart tree came from the blood of Osiris, myrrh came from the tears of Horus, the cedar tree came from the blood of Gebban, and a power-

---

*The shaman also wears a beelike mask, which is significant given the fact that mushrooms can easily be preserved in honey. We can note too that in the Greco-Roman period children were sometimes buried in pots filled with honey (Budge 1997, p. 25). In addition, we know that the body of Alexander the Great may have been preserved in white honey when he was buried in Egypt.

ful herb that some believed could render a soldier invincible grew from the blood of Prometheus (Valerius Flaccus 7:355–70). Not to be outdone by the pagans, Christian writers claimed that a balsam tree grew from the water used by Mary to wash the body of Jesus when he was an infant; it was believed that the tree sprang up from the child's sweat.* The sweat from the Egyptian gods seems to have been particularly fertile; the plants that grew from their sweat were the same plants used in burial rites to reanimate or resurrect the dead.

Wonderful medicinal plants grew from the bodies of the gods, and the healing powers of these plants came directly from the spirits of the gods. The plants contained either good or evil spirits, because of their divine origin; but however the process is explained, many ancient peoples believed that the bodies of the gods were the source of divine plants, usually plants with supernatural power to do good or to cause harm.

Even more interesting is the fact that the old gods often gave birth to new gods—but not through the normal sexual method. Instead, the younger gods were born from parts of the bodies of the older gods. The goddess Athena, for example, was born from the forehead of Zeus, and the god Dionysus was born from his thigh. This belief led the Roman comedian Lucian to exclaim, "Zeus gets pregnant all over his body!" Similarly, the Egyptian gods frequently gave birth from various body parts, including, for example, Thoth, who was born from the forehead of Set.†

---

*According to Budge, balsam oil was used as the oil of consecration (1997, p. 23). The most precious type of balsam oil was the Balm of Gilead. See also chapter 8 of *The First Gospel of the Infancy of Jesus Christ.* Peoples in southern Mexico believe that mushrooms spring up from where Jesus spit or where Jesus's blood fell to the ground (Benitez 2007, p. 87).

†According to one Irish tradition, Jesus was born from the crown of the Virgin's head (Lang 1996, 2:137). These new gods were, like the sacred plants, born from the bodies of the old gods. This idea is clearly presented in Erik Hornug's comment on the Egyptian god Osiris: "The characters and . . . the action itself are derived from the myth of Osiris: after his death, a king, in the process of decaying (the *nigredo,* the 'black condition'), engenders the heir in whom he will live again" (2001, p. 39). Furthermore, during the rite the deceased affirms, "I have come that I might behold Osiris, that I might live at his side, that I might rot at his side" (2001, p. 39). This is how the new gods were born from the body of the old gods who were dried out and blackened with age. Through contact with his corpse, the worshippers who died with Osiris also shared in this renewal.

The ancient god Set himself was, like the Hindu god Indra and even the Buddha, born from his mother's side (Lang 1996, 2:137).

Stories about the birth of these new gods often suggest that they overthrew the old gods. The replacement of old gods with new gods may represent a natural process. Once the corpse of the old god was exhausted and its fertility was used up, it was probably necessary to begin growing sacred mushrooms on the corpse of a younger and more vital god. Although the Greeks and Egyptians developed several rites for maintaining and extending the vitality and fertility of the dead god, inevitably the god's body was exhausted and was replaced by the body of a younger god.

The process is suggested not only in Greek and Egyptian mythology but also in the ancient religion of India. The great folklorist Andrew Lang notes that "some passages in the Rig Veda imply that the reigning deities were successors of others who had previously existed." In mythology the replacement of the old god with a new god is often attributed to parricide. The Greek god Zeus overthrows his father, Kronos, while he is drunk on the sacred mead. Ironically, Kronos had earlier attacked his own father, Uranus, and castrated him. This act of castration also suggests the act of removing the sacred mushrooms from the divine corpse. The Hindu god Indra also kills his father "for the purpose of stealing and drinking the soma, to which he was very partial" (Lang 1996, 2:163). Soma, as we will see, is the Aryan name for a drink made with sacred mushrooms. The Greeks called it ambrosia, or "the food of the gods."*

---

*Soma is, according to R. Gordon Wasson, the pressed juice of the mushroom mixed with milk (Wasson 1978, p. 81). See also Spess 2000, p. 87.

# 9

⊕

# Signs of the Cult of the Dead

Many of the great Western religious traditions—Egyptian, Hebrew, Christian, Greek, and Indian—include several religious icons that likely represent the sacred mushroom. Further, each of these religions has at least one image that embodies the idea that the sacred mushroom was grown on the body or corpse of the gods/man. The mushroom itself is sometimes represented by a female goddess in the form of a bird that rests on a corpse. The bird stands with its wings outstretched, thus resembling the outstretched cap of the mushroom, and the bird's feathers easily suggest the winged gills of the mushroom.*

In Egypt, a common religious symbol was the corpse of Osiris lying prone in his tomb with his wife, Isis, in the form of a hawk perched on his pelvis. The icon was explained as the goddess Isis conceiving her son Horus by copulating with the corpse of Osiris. Frazer describes a typical Egyptian statue showing how Isis and Osiris conceived their son Horus.

---

*For a full discussion of bird/mushroom imagery, see Heinrich 1995, pp. 101, 132.

At the four corners of the bier are perched four hawks, representing the four children of Horus, each with their father's banner, keeping watch over the dead god, as they kept watch over the four corners of the world. A fifth hawk seems to have been perched on the middle of the body of Osiris, but it had been broken off before the tomb was discovered in recent years, for only the bird's claws remain in position. . . . The scene represented is unquestionably the impregnation of Isis in the form of a hawk by the dead Osiris. . . . (1961, 2:20)

This display is probably not an accident or coincidence. The child Horus, conceived in this manner from the corpse of the dead god, was clearly the embodiment of the sacred mushroom grown on a corpse. The famous talisman the Eye of Horus, shown as a disk-shaped eye resting on a stem, represented more specifically the sacred mushroom itself. Egyptian art includes many mushroom images, which are skillfully masked as, for example, a canopy, a parasol, or a bird. The famous Egyptian ankh is also a symbol for the mushroom. As a symbol of the divine power, the ankh itself also suggests the shape of the Christian cross.

In Greek lore there are likewise many symbols similar to the Egyptian eye of Horus that could be used to convey the mystery of the sacred mushroom, including the Medusa, golden apples, and the Golden Fleece.* Yet the most famous representation of the dying god is the Greek myth of Prometheus. The popular image of Prometheus chained to a mountain is taken from the story of how he was punished by Zeus.

The legend of Prometheus is quite well known.

Once in the reign of Zeus, when gods and men were disputing with one another . . . Prometheus, with a view of deceiving Zeus, cut up a bull and divided it into two parts: he wrapped up the best parts and the intes-

---

*Each of these symbols is intimately linked to the mushroom. The golden apples are the mushrooms growing under a tree and having the appearance of apples. Medusa with her serpent hair is used to represent the ill effects that can come from eating mushrooms. The Golden Fleece is the shaggy hide used to filter the mushroom juice—so that the fleece is stained a golden color.

tines in the skin, and at the top he placed the stomach, which is one of the worst parts, while the second heap consisted of the bones covered with fat. When Zeus pointed out to him how badly he had made the division, Prometheus desired him to choose, but Zeus . . . chose the heap of bones covered with the fat. ("Prometheus" 1851, 2:711)*

After Zeus discovers the trick, he becomes so furious that he withholds the gift of fire from humanity. Prometheus later steals fire and gives it to humankind. As a result he is punished by Zeus: Prometheus is chained to a cliff. Each day an eagle tears out his liver, and each night the immortal's liver grows back, only to be eaten again the next day. Prometheus is thus exposed on a mountain peak to suffer for offending the gods.

The story of Prometheus and his punishment touches on other aspects of Minoan rites. All educated Greeks were familiar with the story that Prometheus had been chained to a rock, where he was held immobile while the eagle of Zeus ate his liver. The iconic image of Prometheus chained to a mountain while the eagle perched on his body was a familiar religious icon to the ancient Greeks, and the image finds its way fairly often into both Greek art and literature. Interestingly, this story suggests how the Minoans disposed of the leftover skins of those who were killed as part of a human sacrifice: their skins were nailed to rocks at one of the holy mountain peaks on Crete and left for the eagles as their meal.† The sight of "the bird of Jove" eating from these human skins was probably the original inspiration for the story of Prometheus and his punishment by Jove (Zeus).

In Hebrew legend the icon for the corpse of God is suggested by

---

*The Prometheus legend helps to explain how a sacrificed bull's hide could become "the portion of Zeus" and be hung on a post and revered as a sacred object.

†The famous cave of Zeus is located at one of these mountain sanctuaries on Crete. Citing Psalms 103:5, St. Ambrose in his "On the Sacraments" (2:7) compares the person who eats the body of Christ (Eucharist) to the eagle eating carrion. This bizarre idea may be based on the Greek idea of Jove's eagle eating the body of Prometheus. This idea was significant enough that Alberic of Monte Cassino cited it in his famous "Libellus" (Radding and Newton 2003, p. 129).

the design of the Ark of the Covenant. The Ark is frequently shown as a coffin-shaped box and on it rest two birdlike seraphim, their wings outstretched over the box. It's likely that the representation of the Ark is simply a variation on the Isis/Osiris image; the sacred hawks are replaced by seraphim perched on the coffin of the dead God. The similarity of the Ark to the coffin of Osiris is obvious, and other scholars have commented on this resemblance (see, for example, Hall 1928, p. 134).

In the Christian religion the icon for the sacred corpse was altered somewhat, becoming the Christian cross—which was probably adapted from the much older Egyptian ankh. The later and more detailed crucifix was the subtle joining of the cross and the corpse of the tortured god. Just as Prometheus was nailed to the mountain, Jesus was nailed to the cross. As Sir James Frazer demonstrates in *The Golden Bough*, the dying god is found in many pagan religions. Included in the Christian image is, typically, a dove, which appears to replace the hawk of Isis as a Christian icon. Many crucifixes include a dove hovering over the center of the cross, and the dove has now become another symbol for Christ in his spirit form.

The Egyptian image of Isis lamenting over the corpse of Osiris has been replaced by that of the Virgin Mary holding the corpse of Jesus, as seen, for example, in Michelangelo's statue *The Pieta* (Frazer 1961, 1:257). In fact, art historians have noted that every artistic rendering of the Madonna with Jesus could just as easily be interpreted as either Isis's discovery of the corpse of Osiris or Isis holding the baby Horus. (There are numerous Madonna and Child paintings like this.) According to many historians, this substitution of Mary for Isis reflects the historical development of the Christian Church as it took over many pagan temples: during the first few centuries of the Christian era, when the Christian Church was appropriating abandoned pagan temples, it was common for images of Isis and her infant son Horus to be re-identified as the Virgin Mary and the infant Jesus.*

---

*The significance of the sacred infant may lie with something inherent in mushroom cults. For example, in southern Mexico the mushroom is often called *el nino,* as if it was a child (Ravicz 2007, p. 51).

The symbol of a bird standing on a corpse was very common in northern Europe.* It's demonstrated in Celtic lore by the legend of the hero Cù Chulainn, who is killed in battle, and a raven/crow goddess perches on his corpse. In the famous sculpture by Oliver Shepherd, the raven/crow is perched on Cù Chulainn's shoulder much as the raven is often shown standing on the shoulder of the Norse god Odin. Although the most ancient versions of the legend are not specific about where the goddess stands, there are several popular Celtic mythic figures of a man with a bird on his shoulder that speaks into his ear. For example, a gigantic stone relief found in Sault (in Vaucluse, France) depicts a man with a raven talking in his ear (Ross 52). This suggests another important aspect of the sacred mushroom: a source of wisdom or gnosis.† According to Donald Mackenzie, "Dark and melancholy birds were evidently regarded as forms of the spirits of darksome Hades. They were, it would seem, associated from an early period with a sepulchral cult" (1995, p. 191).

The use of bird imagery is pervasive in mushroom-based religions.‡ One reason is the fact that the large cap of a fully grown *Amanita muscaria* often twists into a bird shape with the gills exposed, like feathers (Heinrich 1995, p. 45). The association between birds and the sacred mushroom appears quite often in mythology. The gods often took the form of birds in order to steal soma, or ambrosia, or food of the gods.

---

*Gartz suggests that in addition to *Amanita muscaria*, *Psilocybe semilanceata* was used by the Celts and the Nordic cultures and even as far south as the alpine valleys of northern Italy where, not coincidentally, the Inquisition was very active in exterminating witches and heretics (Gartz 1995, pp. 10–11).

†In the Christian era the familiar pagan icons of a man with a bird on his shoulder may have been re-identified as St. Francis of Assisi. In the far north a raven/oracle was often associated with the Norse god Odin. A bird associated with wisdom, ravens are also noteworthy as the only birds that will eat the *Amanita muscaria* mushroom. In Norse mythology the eye of Odin and spear of Odin may also have once been powerful talismans that represented the mushroom, because they appear to resemble similar Egyptian icons.

‡This is true not only in the Old World but also in the Americas, where the Mazatec word for "bird" is also used for the hallucinogenic mushroom *Mexicana* (Akers 2007, p. 9). Bird/mushroom shapes are also suggested by the images of the Winged Isis (Arthur 2000, p. 51) or the Winged Scarab (p. 42).

The Norse god Odin took the form of a bird in order to steal the mead of Suttung, and Indra took the form of a hawk to get soma.* Similarly, the eagle of Zeus brought ambrosia from the mountains, where it grew. In addition, it's not a coincidence that the same eagle of Zeus tears out the liver of Prometheus. As is the case in so many myths, "The sacred plant was brought to men from the sky or from a mountain by a hawk" (Lang 1996, 2:137). Interestingly, *Amanita muscaria* typically grows only in the mountains.

Important here is the portrayal of a human corpse (representing the god) and the sacred mushroom (in the form of a bird) that is growing from his body. As we have seen, this is the main symbol of many of the cults of the dead. The initiates of the cult understood what the image was meant to represent, whatever form the myth assumed.

*See, for example, Lang 1996, 2:170.

# 10

⊹

# Immortality

Another important icon of the sacred plant is the sacred tree, also known as the Tree of Life, or the Tree of Knowledge. Robert Graves, in *Hebrew Myths: The Book of Genesis,* first suggests that the symbol of the sacred tree in Eden actually represents the sacred mushroom. Graves corresponded with R. Gordon Wasson, a retired banker who had developed a strong interest in mushrooms a few years earlier. Wasson had begun studying the mythology of India, while Graves investigated stories from Greek mythology and the Hebrew scriptures, looking for evidence of the sacred mushroom. Their work was further augmented and expanded by the biblical scholar and author John Marco Allegro in *The Sacred Mushroom and the Cross.* Allegro identifies the sacred mushroom as *Amanita muscaria* and explores the extensive linguistic evidence for Christianity as a mushroom cult.

In fact, *Amanita muscaria* grows only in the mountains and only under a few species of conifer trees, because it apparently needs nutrients provided by these specific trees. The mushrooms, then, are often found growing in "fairy rings" where dead trees once stood. In Greek lore the mushrooms grow under a sacred tree and are identified as the apples

111

of the tree. In several Greek myths the mushrooms are called golden apples, because their appearance is like apples that have fallen from the tree and, like ordinary apples, the mushrooms are a bright red or golden yellow color (Ruck, Staples, and Heinrich 2001, p. 117). Apples appear frequently in European literature as symbols of immortality. All across Europe the symbol of the sacred tree points to or represents a "paradise of delights and many wonderful gardens filled with herbs laden with manna and other magical plants" (Camporesi 1988, p. 190).

In *Food of the Gods,* Terence McKenna discusses the Tree of Knowledge as described in the book of Genesis. McKenna's analysis suggests that there is really only one tree in the Garden of Eden; though biblical scholars seem to think that there are two trees—the Tree of Life and the Tree of the Knowledge of Good and Evil—in fact, they are the same tree. McKenna is able to resolve several confusing passages in the Genesis story by recognizing this fact.

The mistake of assuming there are two trees comes quite naturally from the sacred mushroom's two very important functions: the first was the power to grant a person the gift of discernment, also called the knowledge of good and evil. McKenna points out the second even more important function: bestowing immortality. Although we think of immortality in terms of a heavenly existence after death, many ancient legends report stories of how the gods achieved immortality in terms of living forever here on earth. Usually this immortality was bestowed on them as the result of drinking the sacred mead, called many different names in different cultures all across Europe and the Near East.

This idea is expressed in the Persian mythology of ancient Iraq, where the drink haoma bestows immortality.* According to mycologist Adrian Morgan:

> The Persians' earliest surviving religious text, the *Avesta,* is of a late date, written down in the third or fourth century CE. The *Avesta* mentions a magical drink called "haoma," which derived from a

---

*Also called soma in the ancient texts of the Rig Veda.

plant of the same name. As in the case with soma, the written references are so distanced by time from their sources that the identity of the original haoma was forgotten. Myths of the haoma stated that it was yellow, grew on the tops of mountains, and was brought by "the birds of heaven." Like soma, it gave strength to gods and men and imbued the deities with immortality. By the will of the god Vohu-Mana, the spirit of goodness and lord of creatures, haoma was imbued with the power to heal. (1995, p. 111)

The divine drink haoma (or soma) was the same as the Greek ambrosia, and it has its counterpart in many other supernatural foods (Wasson 1980, 148). So great was their power that eventually even the food containers became sacred. In the legend of the Holy Grail the Grail king is able to live forever simply by gazing on the Grail cup, which once contained the sacred blood of Christ.

The sacred haoma plant also had the power to transfer the essence of a person into the body of another. Morgan continues his description by explaining how the soul of Zoroaster was placed in his father's body when his father ate a haoma plant.

Later traditions maintained that the unborn soul of the prophet/ saint Zoroaster (Zarathustra) resided in a haoma plant and took physical form when his future father, a priest, consumed it. In the events to come at the end of the world, the haoma that will give eternal life to the resurrected dead will spring from the blood of a bull slaughtered by Mithra. (1995, p. 111)

Whether or not we accept the idea that the spirit of Zoroaster is eaten in this manner, the story does illustrate the ancient belief that a soul can be contained in a plant and transferred to the person who eats it. The story further points to the sacred bull as the source of the soma/ hamoa plant. This odd story takes on a new significance in the bull worship of ancient Crete.

*Figure 10.1. Side view of bull's head rhyton with the horns and ears restored*

*Figure 10.2. A late Hittite example of a ritual vessel from a tomb near Ain Tab.*

As with several other legends, including the legend of St. George, the soul or spirit of the dead can be transferred to the living by means of eating the sacred plant that grows from the corpse. This is no different from consuming the bread and wine of the Last Supper. The body of Jesus Christ is eaten, and his spirit is absorbed into the bodies of his followers. This notion is repeated in many Christian and pagan stories. For example, according to one of the more peculiar legends of St. George, he is executed for committing a crime, and his body is cremated and his ashes scattered. Over time, an apple tree grows on the ground where his body's ashes were sown. Some years later a virgin eats one of the apples that fell from this same tree. She later gives birth to a baby boy, who proclaims to his astonished family, "I am George, and I have been born a second time"* (Howey 2005, p. 182).

---

*According to the great Victorian scholar John Ruskin, the name "George" has the same derivation as the word "gorgon" and suggests a connection to the story of Perseus and the Medusa. As a famous dragon slayer, St. George has a strong resemblence to Perseus (Ruskin 2009, p. 162).

These stories hint at an ancient technique by which an individual could attain immortality, or at least a continuing existence here on earth: he could pass on as a living spirit or a Holy Spirit that lives on in the bodies of those who consume his body or who consume a plant grown from his corpse. This is the reality, the true origin of the ancient rite that lives on today as the Christian Eucharist. Among the earliest Christians it was proclaimed that the initiate has the Christ within him as a living spirit. The spirit or ghost of Christ is eaten by his followers so that through his death he becomes a living part of each of them.

Dozens of legends about the sacred food were popular in the ancient world: soma (India), hamoa (Persia), manna (Palestine), ambrosia (Greece), and the maat plant of ancient Egypt. The Egyptian maat plant had remarkable powers, including the ability to transfer the soul or essence of Osiris to his followers. According to Budge,

> As the god and judge of the dead he [Osiris] dwelt in a portion of the Tuat or Underworld, and the souls of the beatified dead spent their time there in the cultivation of the wonderful Maat plant. The plant or shrub was a form of the body of Osiris, and his followers ate it and lived upon it. It maintained their lives, and because they ate the body of their god, they became one with him and, like him, lived for ever. (1997, p. 12)

In Christian lore the Eucharist is transformed into the body of Christ—at least in the official theology of the Roman Catholic Church. We can note that in both heretical Christianity and in the popular imagination the blood of Christ transfers some of its miraculous power to the Holy Grail—supposedly the cup used at the Last Supper. The Grail appears in numerous medieval poems and is attached to the legend of King Arthur. It supposedly has the power to produce food magically, enough to feed a room full of people (just as Jesus did with the loaves and fishes). The Grail can also heal wounds and grant physical immortality. The magical association persists even today, as we can see in the film *Indiana Jones and the Last Crusade* (1989). In this story the Grail has the magic power to both preserve life and heal near-fatal injuries. But drinking the water of life from an impure vessel can be fatal.

Studying the ancient cults of the dead is important to us even today, because much of their mythological material has spilled over into popular culture. For example, the cult's imagery has found its way into all three of the Indiana Jones films. In *Raiders of the Lost Ark* (1981) it is the Ark of the Covenant, and in *Indiana Jones and the Temple of Doom* (1984) it's the blood of Kali. In the film *Indiana Jones and the Last Crusade* (1989) it's the Holy Grail, which, after twenty centuries of use, has gained the power to transform plain water into a potent drink.

Somebody needs to wash that cup more often.*

---

*"As part of dried mushroom material, psilocybin is a remarkably durable substance. A sample of desiccated mushrooms dated 1869 from a Finnish herbarium was still found to contain 0.014 percent of psilocybin" (Gartz 1996, p. 27). It takes as little as 0.25 gram of dried *Psilocybe cubensis* to glean results.

# PART THREE

# Sweeney Todd among the Nightingales

*Oh give me Greeks, Good Luck, Give me Ulysses*
*Or one of his Greek breed. I'll take them living*
*To eat them naked-raw, their lungs, their livers,*
*To wet my poor dry throat with their sweet blood*
*To tear them gently and to taste their gooseflesh*
*Still trembling as I close my teeth. Oh Glory!*

CYCLOPS, OVID, *METAMORPHOSES*
(TRANSLATION BY HORACE GREGORY)

# 11

# The Cult of the Dead in Greece

Most people today like to think of the ancient Greeks as a group of warrior philosophers, much like the Spartans in the film *300* (2006) starring Gerard Butler and a cast of well-tanned and physically unblemished male specimens. Other people might imagine the Greeks looking perhaps a bit more scarred and sweaty, like Brad Pitt in the film *Troy* (2004). Or some people may prefer their Greeks to look both dirty and ethereal, like Sam Worthington and Liam Neeson in *Clash of the Titans* (2010). Still others prefer to imagine the Greeks as being lower class, like the characters from the television series *Hercules: The Legendary Journeys* (1995–1999). Personally, I still enjoy the Italian "sword and sandal" movies that were popular in the 1950s.

Until recently the ancient Greeks were primarily remembered for their many intellectual accomplishments and not so much for their fighting skills. Although we may enjoy viewing the lovely walled villages and rural hamlets set in a lush green, mountainous landscape of *Xena: Warrior Princess* (1995–2001), in reality the ancient Greeks lived in a harsh and more brutal environment. Their daily lives were often a painful struggle to survive. Even while contemplating Pythagorean mathematics and inventing democracy, they lived in a culture heavily grounded in the ancient religious rites of their remote ancestors. As much as we might admire the sweep and grandeur of Homer's great epic poems, the *Iliad* and *Odyssey,* we must keep in mind that they have their origins in a culture filled with bloodshed, superstition, and revenge. Similarly, when we look at the later achievements of Greek literature, we must keep in mind that the art of Greek drama developed directly out of much earlier religious rites and ceremonies. Many of the ideas and attitudes found in classical Greek drama can be traced back to the Greek cult of the dead, which sprang forth from the older rites of the ancient Minoan cult of the dead. The Minoans originated on the island kingdom of Crete, and they strongly influenced the culture of Greece, including its religious ideas, from before 1600 BCE. There were also strong influences coming from the Egyptian cult of the dead, active in nearby Thrace and elsewhere from sometime before 1200 BCE (Larson 1977, p. 40). The later Greek mystery religions were essentially the red-headed stepchildren of the much older civilizations of Crete and Egypt.

During the classical age (fourth and fifth century BCE), which we admire so much today, professional actors wore masks made of fine linen, but in the earlier religious rites of the cult of the dead the same masks had a much more unusual purpose. According to Lewis Paton's *Spiritism and the Cult of the Dead in Antiquity,* the Greek rites of the dead included a role for priests, who wore masks at funerals to impersonate the dead (2003, p. 75). And it seems likely that the masks were of soft leather, rather than linen. Yet even this grim detail is still fairly mild compared to the violent rites that date from before the beginning of classical Greece. We know, for example, that the rites of Dionysus apparently included bloody religious rituals. These violent rites are described in Euripides's *The Bacchae* (405 BCE). In his play a group of women caught in the throes of Dionysian ecstasy wander the woods when they seize King Pentheus, tear him to pieces, and eat his flesh. This violent death is justified in the play as his punishment for dishonoring the god Dionysus by spying on the women. These violent images remained popular into the classical age, and we can find in Greek art and everyday artifacts the image of a young man being seized by the Bacchae and torn limb from limb.* This violent theme runs through much of Greek and Egyptian mythology, as Dionysus had himself been torn apart by the Titans, just as the god Osiris was killed and dismembered by his enemies.

The death of Orpheus was also a popular subject in Greek art. Just as King Pentheus was captured and torn apart by the Bacchae, the musician Orpheus was captured and killed by the Bacchae because he refused to honor their god, Dionysus. As the author of the *Orphic Hymns,* Orpheus was considered a prophet, and he was the center of his own cult in both Greece and in Thrace, where he was honored as part of the Orphic rites. Some scholars, including Sir James Frazer, have pointed out that the Orphic rites were similar to those of the early Christians, but in spite of the resemblances, it's hard to say if there was any direct influence on early Christianity (Herrero de Jáuregui 2010, p. 1*ff*). Orpheus had some connection to rites for the dead too, and many Greek funeral artifacts have inscriptions that appear to be derived from Orphic beliefs.

Apparently some of the very early Greek religious rites were almost as bloody as the later Aztec sacrificial rites in Mexico. Although the Greeks did not achieve the quantitative numbers of hearts plucked from chests that the Aztecs did, certainly the Greek rites were more violent than we would like to believe. But modern research on these ancient Greek cults leads us to just such a conclusion.

There has been a good deal of vigorous debate over whether the

---

*For example, we can see this image in "Pentheus Torn Apart by Agave and Ino," an Attic red-figure *lekanis* (cosmetics bowl) lid dating from 450–425 BCE, which is currently displayed in the Louvre. This image seems to suggest that the face cream in the cosmetics bowl (an everyday artifact with this image) included an ingredient associated with the death of Pentheus. Perhaps it would have made more sense, however, to have Psyche or Persephone on the lid, especially because, according to the Greek legend, Persephone possessed a powerful beauty ointment that was used by the gods.

early Greeks engaged in human sacrifice on a regular basis.* Historical evidence suggests that the later Greeks occasionally engaged in human sacrifice in times of social upheaval, just as the Romans did several centuries later. Although we seem to have no trouble with the idea that the Egyptian, African, and Middle Eastern (that is, dark-skinned) cultures engaged in human sacrifice, we admire the Greeks too much to accept that they engaged in this practice. We could accept that the Romans did—especially because, in many people's estimation, they crucified Jesus—but the practice seems brutish for the Greeks.

Many historians agree that human sacrifice was common throughout the ancient world. The Greeks were no exception. For example, the Greek leader Agamemnon sacrificed his daughter Iphigenia. Some of the later Greek versions of this story are fairly similar to the biblical story of the sacrifice of Isaac, because the goddess Artemis (Diana) replaces the girl with a deer (or goat) at the last moment, thus sparing the girl's life. By the time Homer began reciting the lines of the *Iliad,* in about the eighth century BCE, the Greeks were already far enough removed from the practice of human sacrifice to consider Agamemnon's sacrifice to be perhaps a bit too old school for their tastes, and there is no mention of the practice in the *Iliad.* Certainly the popular story of the Greek hero Theseus killing the monstrous half-human/half-bull Minotaur suggests that the Greeks of the classical age had come to disapprove of human sacrifice. This was especially true when young Greek men and women were taken as captives to Crete to be sacrificed to the

---

*The extent to which the Greeks engaged in human sacrifice is still a disputed matter. See, for example, Dennis D. Hughes, *Human Sacrifice in Ancient Greece,* London: Routledge, 1991. We do know, however, that in 480 BCE Themistocles sacrificed three Persian captives to Dionysus. Human scapegoats called *pharmakoi* were expelled yearly from Greek cities, and, according to some authors, they were killed: on Mount Lykaion children were sacrificed and consumed by worshippers. Many other texts report human sacrifices performed regularly during emergencies such as war and plague. This appears to be the case on Crete, when the aftershocks from an earthquake were instrumental in the collapse of a temple during the sacrifice of a young man in about 1700 BCE.

Minotaur.* By the beginning of classical Greece the practice of human sacrifice was, for the most part, long over. Yet many animal sacrifices, including the sacrifice of bulls, still continued.

In fact the early Greeks often wore the skins of religious sacrifices. Wearing the skins of sacrificed animals was quite common in the ancient world, and spotted panther skins were especially valued, particularly in Egypt (Wilkinson 1878, p. 361). The mottled colors of the panther, like the pied cowhide of the sacred bull, seemed to suggest a particular image, just as the description of the many-eyed giant—the all-seeing Argos of the Hundred Eyes—conveyed a certain mental picture, which, for the Greeks, became an idée fixe. The Greek word for "All-seeing" (*panoptes*) suggests the image of a mythic being whose head was dotted with many eyes, but it also implies the power to see beyond ordinary reality (Evans 1914, p. 11). The giant Argos kills the bull that ravages Arcadia and then clothes himself in its skin. Argos also kills a serpent creature that is half nymph and half speckled snake, the Echidna. Several scholars, including Carl Ruck, have noted that the giant Argos appears to have some mythological connection to the spotted *Amanita muscaria*, whose bright red cap covered with white specks may explain the fascination that the Greeks (among others) had for all such spotted, mottled, dappled, freckled, pied, stippled, and speckled creatures and plants, both real and imagined.

The study of hallucinogenic plants and their relationship to these ancient religious rites first began more than fifty years ago through a series of articles written by R. Gordon Wasson. While writing a book on mushrooms in 1956, Wasson and his wife, Valentina, traveled to southern Mexico to investigate stories about a still-existing mushroom cult. Once there, they met a genuine mushroom shaman, Maria Sabina. Maria

---

*According to legend, the city of Athens was forced annually to send nine young men and women to Crete as a tribute or tax for the death of one of King Minos's children. Theseus went as part of the group sent to Crete to be sacrificed, and on the journey he managed to slay the Minotaur in the labyrinth. In Greek legend the killing of the Minotaur also implied the destruction of the Minoan empire. The heroic story of Theseus and the Minotaur was probably meant to explain and justify the collapse of Minoan culture and the corresponding rise of Greek civilization. The legend of the Minotaur may also be derived from an era when the Minoans shifted from sacrificing men to using bulls.

was persuaded to let the Wassons participate in a sacred mushroom ceremony. The Wassons' experiences in Mexico were later reported in a May 13, 1957, article in *Life* magazine, and the story drew the interest of many scholars worldwide. The Wassons also coauthored the book *Mushrooms, Russia and History* (1957), which examines the role of mushrooms in Western culture. Shortly before the book was published, Valentina's health began to fail, and she died in 1958. Wasson went on to write several books on his own about the religious use of sacred mushrooms in ancient Mesoamerica, Greece, and India.

During this same time period, R. Gordon Wasson corresponded with the famous British novelist and scholar Robert Graves, who had a long-standing interest in Greek literature and mythology. Graves was the author of two seminal books on mythology: *The Greek Myths* and *The White Goddess.* He had already begun corresponding with Wasson in the early 1950s, sharing information about mushrooms and ancient religions. Graves was intrigued with Wasson's work on hallucinogenic mushrooms in Mexico. His interest became especially intense when he discovered that ancient Greek art and literature included numerous references to mushroom lore. This remarkable discovery is outlined in his essay "Centaurs' Food," which appears in his book *Food for Centaurs.* In this essay Robert Graves uses mushroom lore to answer three questions that as a historian had long puzzled him.

1. What food did the centaurs eat?
2. By what name was Dionysus known to the Maenads?
3. What lies behind the story of Samson and the three hundred foxes he set loose among the Philistine cornfields?

As Graves began exploring mushroom lore, the answer to these three questions became suddenly clear. They came directly out of the use of Greek word associations for mushrooms. For Graves this was an earth-shaking discovery. In time, Graves also became convinced that the so-called fruit of the Tree of Life described in Genesis was in fact a reference to *Amanita muscaria.* The description of the mushroom as an apple came about because these bright red or golden-colored mushrooms often grow under trees, and from a distance they look like apples that have fallen from the tree.*

Graves strongly encouraged R. Gordon Wasson to broaden his investigation of the use of hallucinogenic mushrooms to include ancient Greece. In time Wasson produced two books dealing with hallucinogenic plants in Greek mythology. *The Road to Eleusis: Unveiling the Secrets of the Mysteries* and *Persephone's Quest: Entheogens and the Origins of Religion* were major steps forward in understanding the origins of Greek mythology in prehistoric mushroom cults.

Hallucinogenic mushrooms may have dominated early Greek culture, but they were not the sole drug used in Greece. By the beginnings of the Greek classical age wine was much more popular, and the pouring of libations of wine was often included in religious rites. Like many ancient societies, by the fifth century BCE the Greeks had largely relegated the mushroom to a minor role in their religious rites, relying instead on a sacred wine probably laced with opium and other drugs.[†]

In *The Road to Eleusis,* Wasson presents the case that ergot, a rust or parasite that grows on wheat, was the main ingredient in a hallucinogenic drink used in the Greek mystery religion at Eleusis.[‡] Ergot contains a primitive chemical compound very similar to LSD. Wasson believed that the ergot-based drink was provided to worshippers at Eleusis just

---

*The golden apples are a euphemism for the mushroom in Greek mythology (see Graves 1964, 81). Graves's views might also have been influenced by references to the Tree of Life in the Jewish mystical book the *Zohar,* in which the sacred mushroom is evoked. Later in his career Graves backed away from this identification of the Tree of Life, at least as it was presented in Genesis. The vicious attacks on biblical scholar John Allegro in the 1970s may have influenced Graves in this decision.

†This transformation from matriarchal mushroom societies to patriarchal wine societies was a widespread phenomenon all across the Mediterranean world. The matriarchal society of Crete has been explored in several books, including C. S. Barnes's *In Search of the Lost Feminine: Decoding the Myths that Radically Reshaped Civilization.*

‡In *The Mystery of Manna: The Psychedelic Sacrament of the Bible,* Dan Merkur made the argument that Hebrew manna was derived from ergot.

before they viewed the religious ceremony.* The ceremony at Eleusis was a ritual to initiate people into the secrets of the mysteries. After consuming the spiked drink the initiates witnessed a sacred play based on the goddess Persephone's visit to the underworld. In a separate ritual, which took place in the spring, the initiates witnessed a play in which Persephone returns from the underworld. The second play was essentially a resurrection play.† Evidently, among the Greeks the ritual use of hallucinogens was tied directly to ideas about life, death, and immortality. Like the other cults of the dead, the Greeks used hallucinogens to contact the divine. How the Greeks thought about death, and what came after, was shaped by these shared visions of the spirit world.

The exact nature of the mysteries has been unknown to historians for almost two thousand years. By carefully examining the historical record, however, it seems clear that some kind of hallucinogen was essential to the initiation rites of the mysteries. One clue to this is a trial that took place in 415 BCE for a prominent Greek politician accused of revealing the secrets of the mysteries to non-initiates. The profanation of the mysteries was a serious crime to the Greeks, who were very protective of these rites. According to Wasson and others, it seems likely that this particular crime involved using hallucinogens as recreational drugs, outside of their proper religious use. This was a famous scandal among the ancient Greeks, although the exact nature of the offense is only hinted at by contemporary accounts. Yet as Wasson demonstrates in *The Road to Eleusis,* the material and linguistic evidence for the use of some kind of hallucinogenic drink in the mysteries is substantial.‡

---

*In humid climates accidental poisoning with ergot was probably frequent. Evidently the Greeks discovered how to use ergot safely by employing a simple water-filtering process.
†Although a hallucinogenic drink was used in the initiation rituals, Wasson believed that there was still another separate mystery rite at Eleusis that used the sacred mushroom (Wasson 1978, p. 118). For a detailed description of the public ceremony of the mysteries, see Wilkinson 1878, p. 389*ff.* See also Kennedy 85.
‡See McKenna 1992, p. 130*ff.* Several scholars have studied the role of hallucinogenic plants in the mysteries of Eleusis, including most recently Carl A. Ruck.

# 12

The Goddesses of Crete

Acorrect understanding of the Greek mysteries requires that we first understand the much older civilization of ancient Crete, an island kingdom located in the Mediterranean, south of Greece.* The island of Crete was the home of the legendary King Minos and the fabulous labyrinth of the Minotaur. The people of ancient Crete, called the Minoans, were a major civilization more than a thousand years before the first flowering of classical Greece. Long before the birth of the Greek city-states, the Minoans dominated the eastern Mediterranean, including the mainland culture of Mycenae (preclassical Greece). Their cultural and economic influence probably reached as far west as Spain. Both ancient and modern historians agree that the Minoans were the people who originally created the sacred rites of the Greek mysteries. From the writings of the later Greeks, we know that the major elements of the Greek mystery religions began in Crete. This is shown, for example, by

---

*Minoan history was divided by Sir Arthur Evans into three periods that include the whole of the Bronze Age: Early Minoan (ca. 3000–2200 BCE), Middle Minoan (ca. 2200–1500 BCE), and Late Minoan (ca. 1500–1000 BCE).

the fact that two major Greek gods, Zeus and Dionysus, were (according to Greek legends) born on Crete.

In *Minoan Civilization,* Stylianos Alexiou, curator of the Archaeological Museum in Heraklion, devotes a chapter to examining the cult of the dead as it existed in ancient Crete. He considers the goddess worshipped by the Minoans to be, at least in part, a dying goddess (perhaps like the Egyptian god Osiris) or a goddess who ruled over the dead (again, like Osiris). In spite of the fact that we have not yet learned how to decipher the Linear A script, the oldest writing used by the Minoans, the sheer number of grave artifacts left behind is staggering, and they give us a great deal of information about life in ancient Crete (1969, p. 115). These artifacts, combined with other sources, have given us at least a limited understanding of Minoan culture. It seems that Minoan religion was heavily invested in the experience of ecstatic sensations and especially the ecstatic worship associated with altered states of consciousness (Morris and Peatfield 2002, p. 107). Psilocybin mushrooms were probably grown on Crete, as argued by Terence McKenna and other scholars who have identified ancient Crete as a culture dominated by mushroom worship. In addition to using psilocybin mushrooms, the Minoans had easy access to the hallucinogenic *Amanita muscaria,* which still grow in the mountains of southern Crete. This area is where the famous cave of Zeus is located, a religious mountain sanctuary used for thousands of years (Russell 1998, p. 160).

We also know that the Minoans grew large amounts of opium. According to historian Karl Kerenyi in his book *Dionysos,* the use of opium was common in Crete. There is evidence that the opium was smoked, but it could also have been added to oils and ointments, which could have a medicinal or religious use. A small statue of the Minoan woman, called "goddess of the poppies" and dating from about 1300 BCE, was discovered in the sanctuary of Gazi, Crete, together with a simple smoking pipe. The statue wears a crown of three opium poppies. In ancient times opium was also mixed with poison hemlock to relieve pain in those who were dying. Opium was taken for a wide variety of medical problems, and its religious use goes back several thousand years.

In *Minoans: Life in Bronze Age Crete,* scholar Rodney Castleden argues that opium use was prevalent in Minoan society and strongly influenced Minoan religious ideas (1990, pp. 142–44). The Minoans of Crete may have brought the religious use of opium and other drugs to mainland Greece along with the rites of the mysteries (p. 24). Recent evidence suggests too that the Minoans of ancient Crete not only used opium themselves but also exported it throughout the Mediterranean region (Tubb 1998, p. 72). In fact, ancient shipping records (written in the later Linear B script) suggest that specially prepared and refined opium-based ointments and liquors were a major export for the Minoans. Small jars and larger containers from Crete that are noted for their uniquely beautiful designs have been found all over the Mediterranean, including in Egypt (Russell 1998, p. 104*ff.*). The illustrations and designs on Minoan pottery show that many of these pots often held "entheogens and anodynes like bearded barley, opium poppies and the psychoactive bulbs: lilies, hyacinths and saffron" (Russell 1998, p. 40). Similar jars from mainland Greece have been found as far north as the Balkans and Russia.

In his book on Minoan prehistory, Leonard R. Palmer puzzles over why the Minoans exported their ointments and creams—all products made from plant oils—to the mainland of Greece when these very same plants could be grown and processed locally and much more cheaply by the Greeks themselves: "The question arises what was the interest of the mainland in importing such products from Crete when they were busy manufacturing them from their own staple products. As we have seen there was no lack of oil from the Peloponnese . . ." (1962, p. 109).

Palmer suggests that the oils and unguents from Crete had a powerful religious significance. He also believes that the newly translated Minoan unguent texts may hold the key to the mystery. In these texts he finds that Crete's sacred oils and unguents were labeled WA, derived from the word *wanax,* which signifies "king" or "ruler" and is a religious reference to a young Minoan god who is probably similar to Adonis and also to the Greek god Dionysus (1962, p. 232). Thanks to an archaeological discovery in 1979 there is now proof that young men were sacrificed in religious rites on Crete. Indeed, that WA label may refer to the products of these human sacrifices in the form of liquids taken from the bodies of the dead. It seems these Minoan sacred oils and salves were no ordinary unguents. Instead, they were specially prepared for religious uses, which is why they carried the WA label. These powerful unguents also contained some mysterious ingredient labeled MA, which had some religious function (p. 121).

It seems likely that the Minoans were also quite familiar with several varieties of psilocybin mushrooms. Like the Egyptians, they developed an efficient system for growing these on the flesh of the dead. The Egyptians used a somewhat different technique, which we will see later, but in addition to growing mushrooms on the dead, the ancient Minoans had an unusual technique for adding mushrooms to fermented honey in a ritualized process that began with a human sacrifice.

In the ancient world both human and animal sacrifices were quite common. In Sir James Frazer's *The Golden Bough* human sacrifice is recorded abundantly all over the ancient world. In most cases human sacrifice was preferred over animal sacrifice, because humans were considered more valuable to the gods. Dedicating a human as the sacred victim was more pleasing and therefore more appropriate as a gift to honor the gods. Over time, however, as we have seen, ancient civilizations began to reform their religious rites and substitute animals for humans. They also justified this substitution by pointing to religious stories that supported the value of animal sacrifices. Among the Hebrews, for example, the story of the binding of Isaac supports this idea. Yahweh directs Abraham to sacrifice his only child. But an angel interrupts Abraham while he is raising his knife to his son, Isaac.* The angel suggests that Yahweh will gladly accept a substitute (in this case a ram that Yahweh has provided) in place of the human sacrifice (Genesis

---

*The destruction of the Minotaur may be similar to the sacrifice of Isaac as a mythic justification for ending human sacrifices on Greece.

22). Through the centuries Abraham's willingness to sacrifice his only son has been interpreted and reinterpreted many ways in both Jewish and Christian theology.

Eventually the Greeks also rejected human sacrifice, but the situation was far more complex for the Minoans. Even though the sacrificial victims changed from men to bulls, the rites probably remained fairly similar; and we can learn a good deal about Minoan human sacrifices, based on how the Minoans performed their later bull sacrifices. This may seem speculative, but the chapter "Awakening of the Bees" presents evidence that supports this theory of human sacrifice on Crete.

Based on what we know about bull sacrifices in Minoan religion, the sacrifice of a human began with the selection of the young man to be sacrificed. More than likely he was a strong physical specimen who had proved himself adept in bull jumping and perhaps other athletic competitions. It was also likely that his skin was unscarred and unblemished. A bad case of boils, worms, or perhaps even acne or hemorrhoids might disqualify a young man as a candidate for sacrifice. He might also be disqualified for being morally impure, because only a person who was spiritually upright could be sacrificed.

It seems likely that a candidate for sacrifice should be virginal, although this concept probably had a loose application in Minoan culture. Many religions have pondered the idea of virtue in terms of what moral and physical virtues were acceptable to the god(s). Although human sacrifice may have been fairly common in the very beginnings of Minoan civilization, it's more than likely that near the end of their civilization it had been reduced to an annual event.*

The shift from sacrificing men to the regular sacrifice of bulls probably began early in the Minoan history, perhaps as early as 2700 BCE, but the bull sacrifices continued to have all the rites and ceremony that originated with the human sacrifice. For the sake of convenience we

---

*The Minoan festival of the dead was probably similar to the later Athenian celebration called the Anthesteria.

will call the man sacrifice Promethean and the bull Dionysian. In either case the divine nature of the sacrificial victim was recognized by the community and honored. The young man selected for sacrifice was essentially the god Prometheus for the length of the festival.

Once the young man was appointed to be the sacrifice, he was fed a mash consisting of a mixture of psilocybin mushrooms along with a few *Amanita muscaria*. Then the young man was bound with ropes, essentially trussed up in much the same manner as we see in numerous Minoan images in which a young bull is bound and lying on a table-like surface (Nilsson 1970, p. 230, fig. 113). This much we can discern from a 1979 archaeological discovery in which the body of a young man, trussed and placed on a table, had been sacrificed by a priestess and two male attendants. They were all killed when the roof collapsed, probably because of aftershocks from the earthquake that struck Crete in about 1700 BCE.*

In a typical sacrifice the priestess who presided over the rite probably waited until the young man began to show the effects of his meal of mushrooms. At this point he was killed, probably in a manner that did the least possible damage to his skin. Then, his major bodily orifices—nose, mouth, eyes, ears, and also the anus and foreskin—were sealed with wax and sewn shut with leather sutures; and then his body was placed in a cool, dry area for about forty to fifty days. During this time his flesh would liquefy and mix with the mushrooms.†

At the end of this time the sutures in the mouth were cut and a mixture of liquefied flesh and mushrooms was drawn off to be added

---

*Y. Sakellarakis and E. Sapouna-Sakellarakis, "Drama of Death in a Minoan Temple," *National Geographic* 2, no. 159 (1981): 205–22. See also the websites http://projectsx .dartmouth.edu/classics/history/bronze_age/lessons/les/15.html and http://ok-arts .blogspot.com/2006/10/minoan-painting.html.

†Because human skin does not have the strength of cowhide, a body was probably netted, much like a ham, to avoid rupture and spillage of the liquefied flesh (see Matthew 9:17). A small-gauge fishing net would serve this purpose, and fishing nets were easy to find in fishing communities such as those on Crete, as in the old Greek expression "There is no shortage of fishing nets in Gennesaret."

to several large jars (*pithoi*) of raw honey.* The liquefied flesh helped in the fermentation of the raw honey and the mushrooms added a bite to the finished mead. This spiked mead was used in religious rites and also exported to Egypt and other countries, along with sacred oils. While making their sacred ointments the Minoans likely added mushrooms directly to the oils, or the mushrooms were pressed along with the olives (or other plants) when these plants were used to make oils.†

Discovering this process has taken a considerable amount of detective work, but there is evidence in Greek literature and folklore and in Minoan artifacts to support the theory of this process. This technique for making sacred mead appears to be limited to Crete and perhaps Mycenean Greece, but the ideas that were born from this practice appear to have filtered to Egypt, Palestine, and parts of Europe. The Egyptians appear to have rejected the use of human sacrifice from fairly early on in their history, probably from the beginning of the Old Kingdom (2650 BCE), but at the same time they embraced the practice of growing mushrooms on and in the bodies of the dead.

The Minoans, on the other hand, probably continued the practice of human sacrifices, right up until their civilization was overwhelmed by invaders in about the fifteenth century BCE. A massive earthquake had compromised their defenses, and they were conquered by mainland Greeks and later engulfed by the Dorian migrations. We can assume that the more common use of bull sacrifices to make the sacred mead also ended with this collapse. After the end of Minoan civilization the people of Crete probably continued to produce and export cheaper commercial mead spiked with hallucinogenic mushrooms and opium, but this drink no longer had the powerful

---

*This process may be suggested by one of the few images of a Minoan funeral rite found on a sarcophagus of limestone shaped like a chest, which has been assigned to a period prior to 1400 BCE. Found at the Aghia Triadha site, the sarcophagus shows some kind of fluid being poured into a large jar, apparently a ritual vessel, which may contain raw honey.

†In ancient Egypt the god of the winepress also served a funeral function as the one who pressed the mushrooms. Dried mushrooms were hydrated and then pressed.

religious significance that had been established in previous centuries.

As we have seen, it's likely that earlier in their history the Minoans specialized in exporting jugs of sacred mead (honey wine) laced with hallucinogenic mushrooms.* This wine was probably the infamous Greek wine (*trimma*) mentioned by several ancient Greek writers. Trimma was so powerful that it had to be heavily diluted with water before it could be drunk. Likely this was the same wine used to drug the gigantic Cyclops in Homer's *Odyssey*. Although Greek authors stated that trimma had to be diluted with water at a ratio of 1:10, according to Homer's story the honey sweet wine given to the Cyclops was diluted at a ratio of 1 part wine to 20 parts water (Hillman 2008, p. 105). It seems probable that this Greek legend of the Cyclops is itself derived from ancient mushroom lore, in all likelihood from a story about stealing the magic plants from the chthonic gods (much like the English fairy tale "Jack and the Beanstalk" or the Viking myth of Odin stealing the sacred mead from the giants).

At the dawn of the Minoan civilization, before 3000 BCE, the sacred mushroom added to fermented honey or wine was the guiding force for Minoan religious ideas. The production of exotic wines was also very likely important to the economic exchange system of the Minoan civilization early on in its history. Aside from its beautiful artwork, sacred wines and holy oils were the only products of Crete that could command high prices in the marketplaces of Egypt, Palestine, Asia Minor, and Mycenaean Greece.†

In *Food of the Gods,* Terence McKenna presents a great deal of

---

*In Europe the use and export of hallucinogenic mushrooms is limited not to the distant past, but survived into the twentieth century, as related by R. Gordon Wasson (1980, p. 43). "Professor Marija Gimbutas, the renowned Lithuanian historian, has reported to us on the contemporary use of *Amanita muscaria* (i.e., 'Soma') in the remote parts of Lithuania at wedding feasts and the like when the mushrooms were mixed with vodka. We know, too, that the Lithuanians used to export quantities of *A. muscaria* to the Lapps in the Far North for use in their shamanic practices." In nearby Latvia the port city of Salacgriva has the image of an upside-down anchor on its official flag, suggesting a mushroom shape. Latvia is today a major exporter of *Amanita muscaria*.

†See Castleden 1990, p. 116*ff*. for a discussion of Minoan trade. We can note that the Philistines were also influenced by Minoan trade and culture (Dothan 1992).

evidence for the ritual use of hallucinogens in ancient Crete. McKenna also believes that the material remains of the Minoan civilization provide us with an excellent example of what a typical mushroom society would look like if it were allowed to develop fully as an advanced civilization. For McKenna even the structure of the Minoan palaces suggests an obsession with mushroomlike shapes.

The Minoan goddess's most popular symbols—bees, cow horns, sacred doves, the golden double ax—are all images that were derived directly from worship of the sacred mushroom.* A curious observer might wonder why the Minoans incorporated bees and cattle into their art and religious icons. The odd beehive designs they used in building their tombs has never been adequately explained. One easy connection is of course that bees make honey, and mushrooms are easily preserved in honey. In addition, according to some modern sources, psilocybin mushrooms are often eaten with honey as part of religious rites in southern Mexico (Benitez 2007, pp. 83–84). In modern Europe connoisseurs still consume psilocybin mushrooms mixed into jars of honey, sometimes called "blue honey" or "mushroom honey." Yet, in addition to the usefulness of honey, perhaps the bee was an important symbol for other reasons: the bee was part of a larger and complex set of religious symbols tied to the Minoan's most important rites, which included both human and animal sacrifices.†

---

*Doves were later associated with Adonis, and the double ax was itself a symbol of the mushroom. The ax as a symbol also plays a significant role in Egyptian iconography. It's probably not an accident that the Egyptian *wedjet* (and also Thor's hammer) were often made from carnelian, a reddish stone (red was associated with the cap of *Amanita muscaria*). These stone necklaces were popular both in Egypt and in the Norse lands. We might also see that some Egyptian and Minoan jewelry suggest a mushroom shape. See, for example, Castleden 1990, figs. 1 and 6.

†Bees have played a significant role in European literature, from Shakespeare's "Where the bee sucks, there suck I," to Sylvia Plath's bee poems, and bees have often been linked to death. For example, Jean Genet's *Funeral Rites* laments the death of Jean Decarnin: "I am his tomb. The earth is nothing. Dead. Staves and orchards issue from my mouth. His. Perfume my chest, which is wide, wide open. A greengage plum swells his silence. The bees escape from his eyes, from his sockets where the liquid pupils have flowed from under the flaccid eyelids. To eat a youngster shot on the barricades, to devour a young hero, is no easy thing."

Over the centuries the goddess-based religions that used the sacred mushroom were replaced by religions based on drinking ordinary wine or beer, which was easy and cheap to produce. This shift from mushroom cults to alcohol-based religions repeated itself throughout history as invaders who had patriarchal, alcohol-based religions conquered the old mushroom-based societies. We can see this process in Bronze Age Greece and in Egypt during the Old Kingdom, where emphasis shifted from the female goddesses to the male gods.

In *Food of the Gods,* however, Terence McKenna suggests that the Minoan civilization of ancient Crete managed to avoid being conquered by invaders until after 1700 BCE, fairly late in its history. The main military advantage of the northern invaders over the local cultures in mainland Greece and Egypt was the knowledge of how to use horses in battle. Yet horses were not a significant advantage in attacking an island such as Crete. The Minoan civilization was a maritime power much like modern Great Britain. It could easily have survived long after mainland cultures had been invaded and conquered (Nilsson 1970, p. 19). Ancient Crete probably possessed a significant navy; and it would have been very difficult to invade and conquer by ship.* Only when the Minoan civilization was already in serious political decline was it finally conquered by invaders.

Several books by archaeologist Marija Gimbutas point to the ancient worship of a great mother throughout most of prehistoric Europe. The female goddesses of Crete are only some examples of this popular religious idea. In some cases—in ancient Crete and in many parts of Europe and the Near East—goddess worship was associated with the ritual sacrifice of bulls.† Several frescos in Minoan palaces show young people leaping into the air, grabbing a charging bull by the horns, and

---

*This was proved again in WWII, when the Nazis sacrificed hundreds of paratroopers in order to take Crete from the Cretans and their British allies. The losses were so great that the Nazis never again tried a paratroop attack on this scale.

†Bull sacrifice was, for example, important in the Neolithic town of Çatalhüyük in Turkey, which has only recently been explored and excavated (Balter 2005, p. 176).

finally somersaulting over the bull's head and onto its back. This dangerous performance was probably part of a religious ceremony dedicated to the Minoan goddess. This particular aspect of Minoan society was reflected in a very distinctive style of art, which included a great deal of horn-shaped architectural ornaments and design. Several other artistic motifs of the Minoans are similar to those of the other ancient goddess-based societies of prehistoric Europe.* Symbols of a female goddess persisted right up to the final collapse of Minoan civilization. According to British archaeologist Jacquetta Hawkes, "At the dead end of Minoan civilization the goddess still keeps the horns, doves, the double ax" (1968, p. 51).

Other religious images from Minos include the sacrifice of bulls, the sacred tree, and also the golden bee.† Even more interesting are the amazing statues and images of the goddess, including the famous statue of a goddess holding two serpents, as if she were subduing the powers of evil.‡ This goddess is probably related to the Egyptian goddess Heka, who is often shown holding two serpents, one in each hand. This image suggests both the magic power of Ra's words, which can overcome the

---

*A comparison of Minoan art in Hawkes's book and the art in Maria Gimbutas's book *The Goddesses and Gods of Old Europe, 6500–3500: Myths and Cult Images* reveals a remarkable similarity. For example, an eight-thousand-year-old cult vessel from Yugoslavia depicts two bird-headed snakes guarding a ritual bowl (Gimbutas 1982, p. 101). Bird and snake imagery predominated in several mushroom cults, including the Egyptian and the Mayan religions. For example, the Mexican god Quetzalcoatl (represented as a feathered serpent) clearly represents the combination of the snake and the quetzal bird into one powerful image, as does the popular symbol of an eagle holding a snake, which was adopted as the official coat of arms for Mexico. The mushroom cults believed that the bird and the snake represent the forces of good and evil, and the two creatures are oddly mixed in many symbols, as in Matthew 10:16, "be ye, therefore, wise as serpents, and harmless as doves" (KJV).

†This recalls the cave painting of the Neolithic bee shaman found in Algeria. See also Ruck, Staples, and Heinrich 2001, pp. 71–76.

‡This image was usurped by patriarchal religion, as in, for example, the legend of Hercules from the Greek mainland, where, as the divine child, he is said to have crushed the two serpents sent by Hera to kill him (Russell 1998, p. 163). In Catholic iconography the same idea is suggested by the image of the Virgin Mary crushing the head of the serpent.

*Figure 12.1. Rhytons in the shape of bulls with acrobatic performers,
from Early Minoan Ossuaries, Messarà, Crete*

power of poison, and Heka's own power to subdue the evil represented
by the snakes (Budge 1969a, 2:131).

Modern historians often refer to the Minoan goddess as the snake
goddess, but this simply may be one aspect of her role as goddess of the
dead (Alexiou 1969, p. 78). Clay objects in the form of votive honey-
combs and honey cakes were used in rites to honor her. To the Minoans
her serpent aspect was not threatening, because her power was primarily the ability to subdue or control the evil of the serpents.* To be
more specific, the goddess had the magic power to protect her followers
from the ill effects that might come from drinking sacred honey mead.
The spiked mead made in Crete was very powerful, and precautions
were made to avoid these evil effects, which, depending on the drugs

*More recently historians have backed away from calling her the snake goddess, because
there is some question about whether the woman is a goddess or simply a priestess (perhaps with a fondness for snakes). Also, snakes appear to have been popular as pets in
ancient Crete. We must call her something.

used, could range from serious depression to a deadly case of gangrene. Magic images and spells were written on the inside of ceremonial cups to protect the worshipper from these dangerous side effects (Alexiou 1969, p. 108). Similarly, the Hebrew scriptures describe Moses as crafting the Brazen Serpent to overcome the dangerous effects of snakebite. This story is founded on the idea that those who looked upon or gave due worship to the icon of the bronze serpent (snakes represented the chthonic underworld) would not be harmed by the evil poison—including the poison that lives in the dregs at the bottom of the sacred cup.

The power to ward off the evil that might befall someone who drinks the sacred wine (or mead) is also alluded to in Christ's pronouncement: "And these signs shall follow them that believe; In my name shall they cast out devils; they shall speak with new tongues; They shall take up serpents; and if they drink any deadly thing, it shall not hurt them" (Mark 16:17–18).

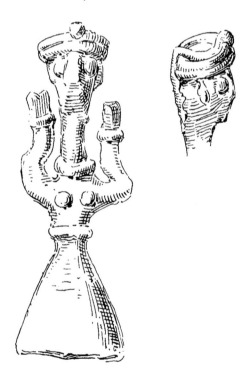

*Figure 12.2. A small leaden image of the snake goddess*

Like the early Christians, the followers of the snake goddess could take up serpents—meaning they were immune from evil—and could drink any deadly mixture without fearing the harmful side effects of the mushroom, which could be very severe.* This is why images of serpents such as that of Medusa with serpents in her hair and other mushroom-related symbols were frequently inscribed on the inside of ritual cups (Castleden 1990, p. 145). Even today we use the caduceus—a mix of bird and serpent imagery—as the symbol for the profession of medicine, suggesting the physicians' power to ward off evil. The caduceus is often associated with Asclepius, the god of medicine. His daughter Hygieia, the goddess of medicine, is often depicted on Greek and Roman coins feeding a serpent. Her worship might be derived from the serpent goddess of Crete. The caduceus itself dates back to about 4000 BCE when, according to the famous Orientalist Dr. William Hayes Ward (1835–1916), it was a Babylonian symbol for the serpent god.

Study of these cults from Crete and Greece is important to understanding the religious environment of the Roman Empire in the first century. Although the Greeks probably had little, if any, direct contact with the Hebrew cult of the dead, they were certainly responsible for the later Hellenistic culture in Europe and Asia Minor. When the apostle Paul began his evangelical mission to convert the pagans he entered a culture that was already strongly molded by Greek religious ideas. Many of the attitudes of the Christian cult of the dead fit well with the existing Hellenized culture, and Paul's evangelical mission was easier because of the similarities between Christianity and the Greek mystery religions.

The Roman historian Plutarch (46–120 CE) claimed in *Table Talk* that there was no difference between early Judaism and the public rites of the cult of Dionysus. Unfortunately the part of his essay that

---

*Clark Heinrich experienced a severe depression during a bad mushroom trip that he describes in his book as like being in a living hell. The symbolism of the serpents and doves is found in the Gospels of Thomas (39b, 88.7–10), Matthew 10:16, and Ignatius 2:2; and the Gospel of the Nazarenes 7. The symbol of the Holy Grail is also likely based on the fact that it was used to drink the new wine without suffering harm.

presents his evidence for this no longer survives (Hillman 2008, p. 103), but it's obvious to us today that the similarities between these various religions—which all sprang from the ancient cult of the dead—are striking and deserve further investigation.

It is certainly worth examining the remains of the Greek cult of the dead for clues to a variety of events and details in the Hebrew scriptures and Christian scriptures that are otherwise strange or obscure in meaning.

# 13

# Minoan Graves

Most of what we have discovered so far about Minoan religion may seem unusual compared to later religious practices in Greece and Rome. Yet another aspect of Minoan religion is much more peculiar, at least compared to the information nineteenth-century historians thought they knew about Mediterranean cultures. Archaeologists have found that the people of ancient Crete had some odd burial rites compared to those of other cultures.

If the Minoan civilization of ancient Crete was based on mushroom worship, then we might expect that this would have been reflected in the Minoans' burial practices. The earliest Minoans seem to have gone out of their way to keep the corpses of their dead near at hand. In this they are different from modern societies, which hide corpses in steel-reinforced concrete vaults. In today's complex technological world, except for brief mourning ceremonies, the corpse is disposed of quickly, never to be seen again.

Minoan funeral practices were different from those of other cultures. Minoans had peculiarly designed tombs called *toloi* or *tholos* tombs. These large tombs were rounded structures built with stone walls and a domed roof (perhaps made of clay bricks). They resemble old European round barns made of stone and brick. Over the centuries all of the domed roofs have collapsed and disappeared, leaving behind only the round stone walls. The circular walls of dozens of these ancient tombs dot the rural landscape of modern Crete. Similar burial structures have been found as far away as Spain and even Scotland, though often they get little public attention, because they are located in remote, rural areas.

Unlike the members of most other cultures, the Minoans built their tombs within close proximity to their settlements. Generally the tholos tombs were built to face east, and the settlements were usually positioned either north or south of the tomb. In this way the villagers could keep an eye on the tomb, but someone standing in the doorway of the tomb could not see the settlement. A person standing in the doorway of the tomb could, however, see the rising sun each morning. These rounded stone tombs were essentially "collective tombs used for the repeated burials (often hundreds in number) of a whole community" (Hood 1960, p. 168). As we will see, the Minoan mortuary practices were fairly basic. Essentially a corpse was taken to the tomb, its flesh was stripped off and placed in the central round structure, and the smaller bones were crushed and charred. The larger bones and the rendered flesh were often stored in the main part of the structure.

Keith Branigan, probably the foremost scholar on the Minoan tholos tombs, describes them as round stone structures with a single door that leads into a single square antechamber or a complex of antechambers attached to the larger central round structure of the tomb. These tholos tombs were used to house human remains, which were likely placed there for a certain period of time, then later removed.* Some of the tombs show evidence of continuous use for as much as a thousand years (Hood 1960, p. 169). Some of these existing tholos tombs date from as early as the Neolithic era (8000–5000 BCE).

---

*Similar tombs have been found in Scandinavia, Catalonia, and the Pyrenees (see Piggott 1953, p. 141). Interestingly, the Pyrenees Mountains already figure in this book as the home of the heretical Cathars.

Archaeologists have discovered that the tombs were used for the selective storage of skulls and the charring and grinding of bones. Yet they served another purpose: according to Branigan, "In addition there is a good case for recognizing that the cemetery sites were the focus of rituals which took place outside the tombs, some of which was not of an explicitly or exclusively funerary nature" (1998, p. 13).

Branigan suggests that the antechambers were often set up with a table, cups, and other household materials useful for eating and drinking, and the areas outside the tomb were often paved, as if for dancing. It appears that the tholos tombs were used as places for celebrations.* It seems likely that the local community used the tombs as sites for public ceremonies, which were probably not very different from the Day of the Dead celebrations held in Mexico today.†

We know very little about these celebrations, but we might assume that they were similar to funerary feasts (Marzeah) common in Palestine and other nearby Near Eastern cultures.‡ Another scholar, Leonard R. Palmer, suggests that the Minoan festival of the dead was probably similar to the later Athenian All Souls Day celebration called the Anthesteria. The structure of the Greek Anthesteria festival, which took place centuries later in Athens, may give us clues to the nature of the earlier Minoan festival. According to Professor Palmer, "The first day was 'the Opening of the Pithoi' (jars), the broaching of the new wine. One of our tablets bears a date formula which had already been interpreted 'New Wine.' The second day of the Anthesteria was taken up by a sacred marriage. After the Sacred wedding followed drinking

---

*Feasts were held in honor of the dead in both Greece and Egypt. It was common to have these feasts at the tomb (see also Evans 1914, pp. 11–12). It may seem odd to use a tomb as a place to have parties. On the other hand, many modern horror films are based on the premise that teenagers like to hang around graveyards, mortuaries, and haunted houses. Historically, the only cultures that we know of whose members spent time in graveyards were the Christians of Rome or perhaps the witch cults of Europe.

†In the Matlatzinca lexicon, from the highlands of central Mexico, the word *chohui* means both "mushroom" and "fiesta" (Akers 2007, p. 29).

‡See, for example, Marvin H. Pope, "A Divine Banquet at Ugarit," for some intriguing ideas.

and revelry. Finally the last day was devoted to the festival of the dead" (1962, p. 126).

The opening of the jars of new wine was a necessary first step before the wedding of the deities, probably Dionysus and the goddess of the Minoans. The wedding celebration was followed with a festival for the dead during which people could make contact with the dead by eating sacred foods. The closest modern parallel to this funeral celebration is an Irish wake, in which the life of the deceased is celebrated with drinking and dancing.

Yannis Hamilkis's paper "Eating the Dead: Mortuary Feasting and the Politics of Memory in the Aegean Bronze Age Societies" suggests that Minoan ritual burials included the consumption of narcotics (1998, p. 122). It seems likely that opium was used at these feasts, because it was commonly grown in Crete. Many of the tholos tombs also show signs of being used for ceremonies that involve drinking; many cups and other vessels have been discovered in the tombs, along with ceremonial knives. According to Castleden, "In a pillar crypt . . . at Knossos, 200 small conical offering cups were found, still containing remains of vegetable matter" (1990, p. 149). These cups could have been used for a ceremonial beverage or perhaps to hold some kind of finger food. Ceremonial cups have been "found crammed in large numbers into outer chambers of tombs" (Branigan 1998, p. 21). Further, the evidence for dancing is substantial, including Minoan artwork representing dancers.

A ring-shaped vessel from Kourtes was found in a Minoan burial place. It comprises six juglike shapes connected by several dancing women, all in a circle.* The vessel obviously has some funereal function, but it's practically unusable for liquids, because the small jugs or cups were attached to each other. It seems possible that the wide neck of the vessel might have been used to hold some kind of food (Nilsson

---

*The dancing figures are also significant. According to Dan Russell, it was through the rite of dancing with ghosts that the fertility of the earth was restored (1998, p. 136). These dancers are similar to dancers of the Neolithic cave paintings found at Tassili, Algeria (see also Alexiou 1969, p. 98 for similar linked containers, called *kernoi*).

1970, p. 138, fig. 48), perhaps small cakes that included opium or other psychoactive ingredients.

Many centuries later the mainland Greeks commonly placed a small cake in the mouth of the deceased. This cake was intended for Cerberus, the guard dog of the lower realm. The small cake is known to have contained "soporiferous herbs to put the dog to sleep" (Wilkinson 1878, 3:459). Certainly, we know that opium can have a powerful soporific quality, as do some hallucinogenic mushrooms.

In a similar rite, which persisted into late antiquity, the Greeks typically placed a coin in the mouth of the deceased so that he or she could pay the boatman Charon to be ferried over the river Styx. The act of placing an object in the mouth of the deceased is important in both Greek and Egyptian religions. In Egypt this action was part of a funerary rite known as the Opening of the Mouth ceremony.* It was also common in early Christian funeral services to place the Eucharist in the mouth of a corpse. This practice continued for more than three hundred years in churches all across northern Africa and Europe until the Christian bishops created rules forbidding it.

One of the leaders in the effort to end the practice of feeding the Eucharist to the dead was the famous bishop St. Augustine. According to Jensen:

> By the end of the fourth century, St. Augustine made additional efforts at reform through absorbing the funeral feasts into the overall structure of the church. The funeral rites were moved into the church and linked directly to the cult of the saints, while using the

---

*According to Budge, this rite for the Opening of the Mouth included a series of offerings accompanied by the liturgy, as in ". . . the Eye of Horus hath been presented unto thee, and with it the god passeth; I brought it unto thee, place thou it in thy mouth," and "unto thee, and with it the god passeth; I brought it unto thee, place thou it in thy mouth . . . the *shaku* cakes of Osiris have been presented unto thee, the *shaku* from the top of the breast of Horus, of his body hast thou taken to thy mouth." In the main act an iron tool is used to open the corpse's mouth, and the deceased is declared to be immortal (1994, p. 158).

sacred foods was discouraged. A council of African bishops forbade a celebration of the eucharist in the presence of a corpse, specifically prohibiting the practice of putting the consecrated bread into its mouth. (2008, p. 134)

The Christian rite, probably similar to the Egyptian Opening of the Mouth rite, ended within the Christian Church in Europe a short time earlier; and thanks to St. Augustine, with the passage of new rules, the North African churches were also prohibited from the practice of including corpses in the celebration of the Mass.

The Egyptian and Christian funeral rites were elaborate compared to the more pragmatic practices of the Minoans of Crete. The earliest Minoans had their own ideas about how best to harvest the flesh of their dead relatives. The flint knives found in Minoan tombs are described as ceremonial, because they show little sign of use (and are therefore probably not personal knives belonging to the deceased). Archaeologists have found stone blades, many of which are still quite sharp and could easily have been used to cut flesh from bone. The flayed flesh was then likely placed in the large central area of the round tholos tombs. The flaying of skin and flesh also had important implications for later Greek mythology, including the story of Marsyas, who is flayed alive by Apollo. Like Prometheus, Marsyas is punished by the gods for his hubris.

Based on recent archaeological discoveries we know that the Minoans probably began by placing their corpses in the outer chamber of the tholos tomb. Once the body had been dismembered, the remaining flesh was scraped away with obsidian knives. The small bones were crushed and the larger bones were sometimes charred or burned. The flesh was then stored in the large circular tomb. There is an important similarity between the practices of the Minoans and those of the Egyptians:* both

---

*Unlike Egyptian sarcophagi, Minoan *larnakes* (a type of small closed coffin; a box or ash chest often used as a container for human remains in ancient Greece) usually had a series of holes drilled in the bottom perhaps to allow bodily fluids to drain off or tissues to desiccate. The Neolithic people of Çatalhüyük in Turkey may have used a process similar to the Minoans (Balter 2005, p. 287).

seem to have kept the corpse close at hand in an effort to maintain a con-nection to the decaying flesh—and perhaps to gain access to the halluci-nogenic mushrooms that grew on the flesh. The Minoans were different from most societies in that they used a single large communal tomb to house their dead, while the Egyptians typically used a great deal of care in preparing each of the bodies of their dead.*

Although their funereal practices had a similar purpose, the Egyp-tians and the Minoans couldn't be more different in their views of life and the afterlife. According to Karl Kerenyi, the people of ancient Crete were almost unique in their attitude toward death.

> In Crete artists did not give substance to the world of the dead through an abstract of the world of the living, nor did they immor-talize proud deeds or state a humble claim for divine attention in the temples of the gods. Here and here alone (in contrast to Egypt and the Near East) the human bid for timelessness was disregarded in the most complete acceptance of the grace of life the world has ever known. (1996, p. 10)

The religion of ancient Crete did not include the idea of indi-vidual immortality. No doubt the Minoans viewed the Egyptians and their obsession with personal immortality as vulgar and unseemly. Instead, the people of ancient Crete seem to have focused on celebrat-ing life and living—dancing, playing, singing, eating and drinking, all activities that focus on life rather than death (Dietrich 1997, p. 20).

There are, however, significant similarities between the two cultures regarding death practices. Like the Egyptians, the ancient Greeks also used oils and unguents to prepare their corpses (Cavanagh 1998, p. 106). This concern for handling the bodies of the dead and for using the proper burial ceremonies was reflected centuries later in classical Greek literature, including, for example, the preparation of Hector's corpse in the *Iliad* and in the plays of Sophocles, especially

---

*In Palestine rock tombs were easily accessible for this purpose.

*Antigone* (as we have already seen) and *Oedipus at Colonus*.* In spite of their minor differences, the Egyptians' and Greeks' intense concern with proper rites for the dead has a certain natural logic if we assume that their goal was to maintain contact with the bodies of the dead.

With the passage of time the Egyptians built ever larger tombs, culminating in the Great Pyramid of Cheops. Similarly, over the centuries the Minoans built larger tombs, some of the largest located on the mainland of Greece. These Mycenaean tombs are often called "beehive tombs" because of their design. According to Sinclair Hood, "Tombs of this type, with corbelled stone vaults sunk in the ground and approached by long entrance passages (dromoi), seem to appear for the first time in the Aegean about 1600 BCE, and reach their finest and grandest expression on the Mainland of Greece in the two centuries between 1500 and 1300 BCE" (1960, p. 166). Hood goes on to say that we can suppose that the design of these enormous beehive-style graves on the mainland was derived from the smaller, rounded Minoan tombs found in Crete.

Human sacrifice probably became infrequent on Crete, used only during regularly scheduled festivals to celebrate the fertility of the earth or occasionally resorted to in times of great social upheaval or distress, such as during a natural disaster (the earthquake of 1700 BCE, for example). This shift happened as their society moved to a more frequent use of animal sacrifices, especially bulls. At the same time the Minoans continued to use the bodies of their own dead ancestors as a source for growing hallucinogenic mushrooms that were then incorporated into sacred oils and sacred food. Using human cadavers for this purpose was a regular social practice, although it sometimes

---

*In *Antigone*, as we have seen, the proper burial of a corpse is the action around which the tragedy is built. In *Oedipus at Colonus* the burial of Oedipus's corpse near the city of Athens is the basis for the later ascendancy of Athens as the center of Greek culture. Like the Minoans, the leaders of Athens want the corpse nearby. In the play the Greeks believe his grave has a magical power.

slowly fell out of favor, as it did in Palestine from about the eighth century BCE.

Even so, the theology that came out of this ancient practice continued to cascade down through the centuries, and the idea of the community of the "blessed dead" was a powerful influence on later religious ideas and practices.

# 14

# Eating the Dead

In the absence of a historical record, what can we determine about the tholos tombs of ancient Crete? What was the process used in preparing the dead? Thanks to the work of Sinclair Hood and other archaeologists we have a very good idea of what the Minoans did. Yet why would the Minoans bury their dead in this way?

The Minoan burial rites, as we have seen, are certainly far removed from the elaborate funereal ceremonies of the Egyptians. Yet these religious rites were probably practical and functional—at least from the standpoint of the people of ancient Crete. Why then did the Minoans engage in these rituals?

One theory suggests that, like the Egyptians, the Minoans had a mushroom-based religion that depended on creating and maintaining a supply of the sacred mushrooms used in their religious rites; by growing these mushrooms on human flesh, they maintained both a spiritual and physical connection to the dead. In this theory the tholos tombs were a convenient place to harvest the human flesh needed to grow the mushrooms. The flesh was scraped from the bones and placed in a central vault. The small bones were crushed to serve as a kind of bone meal fertilizer. On a regular basis the tholos tombs had to be cleaned out, primarily because the presence of decaying flesh over long periods of time could lead to a buildup of dangerous toxins that might harm the mushroom crop. The tombs show evidence of being cleaned on a regular basis, and fire was likely used to destroy leftover remains "in order to make room for new arrivals" (Alexiou 1969, p. 17).

It's probably not an accident that the Greek word *sarcophagus* means, literally, "flesh devouring." In this case the tholos tomb was a place where human flesh was quite literally consumed by the sacred mushrooms. As we have seen, these mushrooms in turn were used in the sacred foods and oils prepared for a public funeral feast similar to the modern Mexican Day of the Dead festival.*

Based on the evidence of archaeology, history, and the literary remains of the ancient Greeks and Egyptians, the scenario described above is what we may believe. The ancient cult of the dead may have originated in North Africa and spread throughout the Mediterranean world and across Europe. Many historians agree that the cult spread even as far as the British Isles. For example, according to John W. Hedges, a tomb found in Orkney, Scotland, contains the remains of humans who were defleshed and their bones placed in a central pit. This stone tomb is similar in design to the tholos tombs of Crete. Interestingly, archaeologists also found the bones of eagles in the Scottish tomb, mixed in with the human remains. We know that the eagle, the bird of Jove, is an important symbol in Greek myth; and it seems likely that these carrion-eating birds were also revered by the ancient cults of the dead. In several of the Greek myths, for example, the eagle carries the food of the gods down from the mountains. More

---

*According to Piero Camporesi, "The conservation of flesh from deterioration, by the lengthy process of salting, hanging and smoking, belonged to a culture in which the active presence of the deceased, the prolongation of his memory, the attempt to keep at bay annihilation and pulverization, went hand in hand with a feeling for life's slow unraveling and a collective search for longevity, not only of the flesh, but also of memory and experience" (1988, p. 181). Although he writes about medieval Italy, this notion seems quite relevant to the Minoan idea of death.

important, as we have seen, the eagle plays a central role in the Greek legend of Prometheus.

According to the *Merriam-Webster Dictionary,* the cult of the dead is "a ritualistic system of veneration, honor, and propitiation of the spirits of dead ancestors for the purpose of avoiding evil consequences and securing good fortune." There are many varieties of this cult worldwide, including those in China and in the New World. The focus of this book is, however, specifically on the Indo-European cult that was widespread across the Mediterranean, Near East, and Europe, reaching probably as far north as Sweden. It evolved into many complex and ingenious varieties, including Egyptian, Minoan, Greek, Celtic, Norse, and no doubt smaller and more localized varieties. The evidence suggests that many of these Indo-European cults of the dead made use of human cadavers in order to grow hallucinogenic mushrooms, most likely a variety (or several varieties) of psilocybin mushrooms. This practice was supplemented by gathering *Amanita muscaria* from mountainous areas to enhance the visionary qualities of the psilocybin mushrooms. In order to maintain an adequate supply of *Amanita* mushrooms, the Minoan and Egyptian civilizations may have searched far afield to gather a regular supply, including contact with the peoples who inhabited the Balkan mountains of Greece and Thrace and even establishing colonies among the natives of the Pyrenees. The Minoan ships probably also brought large amounts of raw honey from Iona (famous in ancient times for its honey) and the cities along the southern coast of Asia Minor (modern Turkey). This would include the city of Tarsus, which was a major center for bull worship in ancient times.

Although evidence for the practice of growing mushrooms on the dead is significant over much of the Indo-European world, there appears to be another practice that may have been specific to ancient Crete: the practice of sacrificing young men in order to create a mixture of liquefied flesh and mushrooms that could be added to raw honey to help it ferment into sacred mead. This is not to say that other nations did not perform human sacrifices or did not perform this particular rite for fermenting honey. Rather, it's possible that Egypt learned of this distinctly Minoan rite before the collapse of Minoan civilization, or word of this practice may have been carried to Egypt by later refugees from Crete. We can't be sure whether the Mycenaean Greeks practiced this rite, but they certainly passed on to the classical Greeks and the Romans the knowledge of a special rite that involved sacrificing humans, and later on, young bulls. The Romans called this sacrificial rite "The Awakening of the Bees." Indeed, the idea of human sacrifice is linked to a whole complex of religious ideas—such as righteousness, purity, and prophecy—which were important in both Greece and Egypt and also to the Hebrew cult of the dead.

Although the Hebrew cult of the dead was largely suppressed by the Yahweh cult after the return from the Babylonian captivity (in the years after 538 BCE), the old Hebrew cult of the dead and the popular Marzeah feast continued to persist—even against the tide of the Jerusalem Temple's "Yahweh-only" reforms—and the Hebrew cult of the dead was eventually resurrected in the guise of the early Christian Church. The religious ideas about the Blessed Dead that had originated with the Hebrew cult—and were reinforced by Egyptian and Hellenic influences—became the main religious doctrines of the early Christian Church; and they remained powerful ideas even after church authorities ended the use of hallucinogens in sacred foods and oils several centuries later. The Church of Rome proceeded to create "the cult of the saints" in the fourth century to carry on the popular notions inherited from the Hebrew cult of the dead. The tithes and gifts that once were given to honor the blessed dead were now diverted to benefit individual bishops and to churches that were closely tied to the official Roman church hierarchy.

In order to chart fully the practice of human sacrifice and the bull sacrifice that came after it, we must examine more fully the Minoan cult of the dead.

# 15

# The Horns of Consecration
# and the Double Ax

## THE HORNS OF CONSECRATION

Little is known about the Minoan religion except for the religious icons used in worship. Among these are the horns of consecration, the double ax, and various bird and serpent images (Nilsson 1970, pp. 82, 110, 396). Early archaeologists describe several images of women as the dove goddess and the serpent goddess, although we can assume only that they are goddesses from the frequent appearance of their images at Minoan religious sites.*

---

*An ancient emblem found in Palermo, Sicily, depicts a Greek gorgon, like the infamous Medusa, who has serpents for her hair. In this image, however, the Gorgon also has wings on her head, like the god Hermes (Elworthy 1986, p. 290*ff.*, fig. 133). This emblem suggests that the Greeks sometimes combined bird and serpent imagery much the way the Egyptians did. Scholars have been able to deduce that in the earliest Greek religion the serpents apparently represent the chthonic (underworld) deities and the birds probably represent the epiphany of the gods (Nilsson 1970, pp. 332, 334). A bird image on a bowl might then mean that the contents of the bowl helped to produce a spiritual epiphany. An image of a serpent might be a magical symbol on the bowl that could protect the user from evil.

Because the Minoan artists did not try to portray individual people, these pictures might simply represent ordinary priestesses performing their daily rituals.

Many Minoan homes included a room containing religious icons, including the horns of consecration. These replicas of cow's horns were perhaps used to consecrate religious objects placed between the horns in order to achieve some religious end.

The horns of consecration were made of stucco or a similar material, and they were modeled to resemble cow horns. Some scholars suggest that in the earliest form of their religion the Minoans must have used real cow horns or possibly the entire skull as an important part of their sacred rites (Nilsson 1970, p. 185). Only in the later stages of their history would they have replaced the cow horns with a stucco replica. This is really not much different from our own practice of using a small plaster or plastic crucifix to represent the religious concept of the Roman cross. That stucco cow horns were a prominent symbol in Minoan rituals points to the veneration of cattle in much the same way the Old Kingdom Egyptians and the early Hebrews displayed stone replicas of cow horns on their altars and in their temples.*

Even more interesting: it's possible that the ancient Minoans buried dead cattle in the earth with only the horns exposed, much the way they were buried in ancient Egypt and even as late as the nineteenth century in central Africa. It's possible that the stucco horns, used as religious icons by the Minoans, may actually have represented the exposed horns of a buried bull. The burial of cattle in the ground with their horns exposed in this way points to an ancient practice described more fully in the chapter "Awakening of the Bees."

The association between cattle and hallucinogenic mushrooms is common. Psilocybin mushrooms are frequently found growing in cow

---

*Animal hides were also used in Minoan rituals. In several gold rings that have survived, odd-looking genii are depicted wearing what appear to be animal hides in religious ceremonies (Castleden 1990, p. 139). During the Old Kingdom in Egypt several people in the ritual wore panther hides, but centuries later it was only the *sem* priest who could wear a panther hide during the Egyptian ritual for the dead (Nilsson 1970, p. 158).

dung (which helps to explain why cows are sacred in India). Based on Egyptian burial practices, it's possible that some types of hallucinogenic mushroom were also grown on the cadavers of sacred cattle, sheep, and other animals. Very likely the ancient Egyptians used this practice on humans, too. At least this is strongly suggested by the mortuary rituals that are described in ancient Egyptian religious texts, including the Egyptian Book of the Dead. As the two most advanced civilizations in the Mediterranean, the Minoans and the ancient Egyptians were familiar with each other's religious practices. Later we will look at the specific way the Minoans prepared human and animal cadavers as the first step to producing sacred mead.

## THE DOUBLE AX

The double ax was perhaps even more prominent in ancient Crete than the horns of consecration, examples having been found in sacred caves and at other religious sites, although they vary widely in shape and size, from tiny axes only a few inches tall to a large rough-hewn example that looks as though it could actually have been used as an ax. Some scholars suggest that the double ax may represent a special sacred ax used to kill sacrificial animals, but it seems unlikely that this alone could account for its widespread use as a symbol. The axes are found frequently inside tholos tombs (Nilsson 1970, p. 196), yet almost all of them are too small to have any useful function in the process of defleshing cadavers, and many of the axes have four blades, making them almost completely unusable as cutting instruments.

Why did the Minoans use the double ax as a religious symbol perhaps more prominent than any other? The solution to this question is more obvious when we compare the double ax to the famous Norse religious symbol Thor's hammer.*

---

*The ax also appears frequently in Celtic lore, in which there is association between the hammer and the cauldron or pot, "perhaps as symbols of death and resurrection" (Green 1997, p. 58). The pot may represent the famous Irish cauldron of resurrection. We also often see the hammer and wine barrel in Celtic mythology (p. 39).

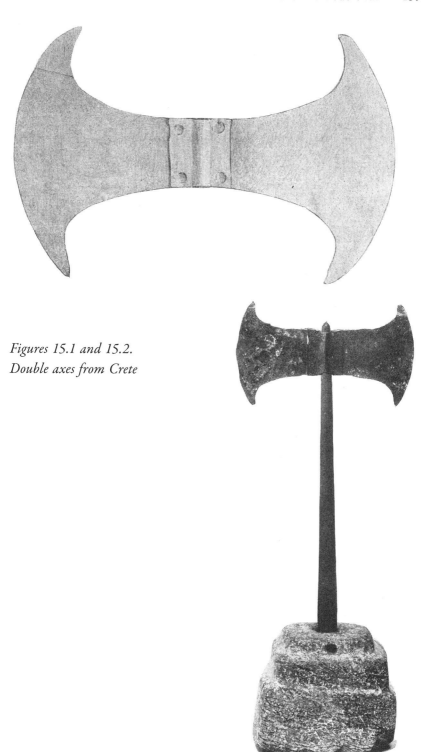

*Figures 15.1 and 15.2.*
*Double axes from Crete*

In his classic study *The Thunderweapon in Religion and Folklore,* Christopher Blinkenberg relates Thor's hammer to the double ax of the Minoans.* Like the double ax and many other thunder weapons in ancient mythology, Thor's hammer has a wide range of powers and magical associations. For example, the Greek historian Plutarch insists that thunder caused the appearance of mushrooms, a widely held belief among first-century Greeks and Romans. Yet it wasn't until R. Gordon Wasson began his study of mushroom folklore in the 1950s that the connection between thunder and mushrooms was explained.

Anthropologists have long been aware that many cultures believed thunder and lightning caused the growth of mushrooms.[†] The association between mushrooms and thunder and lightning was little more than an interesting aside to most folklorists until the Mexican shaman Maria Sabina made explicit the connection between thunder and the gestation of hallucinogenic mushrooms, which seem to appear magically after a thunderstorm.[‡] We can note too that in southern Mexico it's believed that a man who is struck by lightning will become an herbalist and mushroom shaman (Escalante and Lopez 2007, p. 33).

Among the Vikings the symbol of Thor's hammer was as popular as the Christian cross is today. The Viking thunder god Thor was probably the most popular deity in Norse religion, much like Hercules was to

---

*Blinkenberg's identification of the double ax as a thunder weapon may be inspired by the similarity of the Minoan altar and the altar to Thor. The Egyptian god Ptah also wielded a hammer (Mackenzie 1995, p. 171).

†This is true throughout the world. In European and Near Eastern cultures, the lore may have originated with the Aryans. In many cultures eating a thunder mushroom or a magic apple can, it's believed, cause a woman to conceive (see, for example, Elwin 1991, p. 294). Mayan mythology includes an odd variation on this theme: a severed head becomes the fruit of a calabash tree and later impregnates a woman (Gillette 1997, p. 32).

‡The mushrooms spring forth in places where the earth is struck by lightning. In truth, the mushrooms spring up around certain species of evergreen, and when the tree is dead and gone (whether or not it's hit by lightning), there are "fairy rings" of mushrooms where the tree once stood.

the Greeks.* Many stories were told of Thor's strength and courage, not to mention his ability to drink enormous amounts of liquor. (Indeed, a popular brand of spiced vodka today is called Thor's Hammer.) If we look up "Thor's hammer" on the Internet we find many images of the tool, including many replicas of jewelry found in Viking graves and treasure troves. Yet many of the necklace pendants called Thor's hammer actually don't look much like a hammer at all. The Vikings used hammers often, and they used a special long-handled war hammer in battle. They obviously knew how a hammer was supposed to look, so why does Thor's hammer have such an odd shape?

Many pieces of Viking jewelry described as Thor's hammer have been found in graves. The small hammer was likely worn hanging upside down, probably as a necklace with a piece of leather thong that passed through a hole at the end of the handle's shaft. The handle of the hammer is usually fairly short, and the head of the hammer is often ornately designed—covered with dots, which may represent eyes—and the hammer's head is rather large when we compare it to the short handle. Yet if Thor's hammer was meant to represent a Viking battle hammer, why don't the religious icons (jewelry) look more like actual hammers?

We already know that the Vikings had easy access to *Amanita muscaria,* which grow in the cedar-covered mountains of Sweden and Norway. Beginning with Swedish professor Samuel Ödman in 1784, scholars have suggested that the Vikings used these mushrooms in their religious rituals. We can imagine that the Vikings gathered mushrooms during the fall season and then hung them upside down, threads or thin leather thongs piercing the stem, in order to dry them for later use. The

---

*Dan Russell suggests that the symbol of Hercules's club was also a type of golden bough (1998, p. 158). The famous Golden Bough (popularized in Sir James George Frazer's classic study of mythology) was an important symbol in the ancient world. In fact, the sacred bough was originally nothing more than the limb where the hide of a sacrificed animal was displayed (like the famous Golden Fleece). Yet we should not underestimate the importance of this object, because the sacred bough became a religious substitute for the sacred fleece itself, much as the Holy Grail was venerated as a substitute for the blood of Christ.

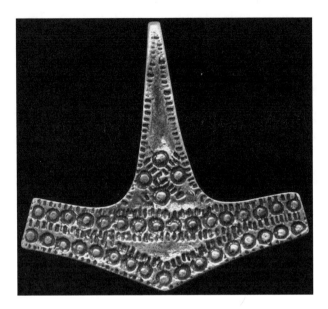

*Figure 15.3. A necklace with the upside-down icon of Thor's hammer*

image of the mushroom hanging upside down was likely the inspiration for Thor's hammer. The white spots on the red mushroom cap probably became the dots or eyes that appear frequently on the head of the hammer.*

In its most ancient form Thor's hammer was the means by which the god would become intoxicated (or get hammered). As a thunder god, Thor had power over storms and lightning, and (like other thunder gods) he was viewed as the source and creator of the mushrooms that were produced by lightning bolts and thunder.† Yet this is not the only possible connection between Thor and sacred mushrooms. According to Blinkenberg's *The Thunderweapon in Religion and Folklore,* Thor

---

*Beings with many eyes are common in folklore, including Greek, as we have seen. For example, the many-eyed Argos was associated with sacred mushrooms (Ruck, Staples, and Heinrich 2001, pp. 53–54). Eventually, like the Aryan mushroom god Soma, Thor's magic hammer took on a personality and identity of its own: Mjolnir.

†Nilsson suggests a comparison between the Minoan ax and the thunder weapon of Zeus (1970, p. 114). See Russell (1998, p. 143) for a discussion of mushrooms and lightning. We can note that the Vikings believed the god Ymer produced underworld beings from his sweat and evil demons came from his feet. We have seen similar notions in Egyptian mythology: the sweat of Set and the evil worms/serpents who live at the base of the Eye of Horus. These were sometimes produced by the effluxes or liquids taken from corpses.

also had a special relationship with the dead. He is their protector, and symbols of his hammer appear frequently on Viking tombstones (1987, p. 22). On a related note, Thor used his magic hammer to consecrate the funeral pyre of the dead god Balder. Clearly, like the Egyptians and the Minoans, the Vikings had a highly developed cult of the dead in which Thor was a prominent deity (Ellis 1968, p. 99*ff.*).

The hammer as a lightning weapon motif appears frequently in various religions from Mexico to India and from Norway to the Middle East. Some examples of Thor's hammer also include a raven motif, which implies a connection to Thor's father, Odin, who sacrificed his eye to gain possession of supernatural wisdom.* It's likely that Odin himself had ties to mushroom worship, for some representations of Odin's spear, Gungnir, resemble either a standing mushroom or a sacred tree.

Like Thor's hammer, the double ax of the Minoans probably represented the sacred mushroom. The symmetrical shape of the ax and its extremely elongated and curved blades strongly suggest the general shape of a mushroom cap.† Its use was purely ritual, and, like Thor's hammer, its shape resembles a mushroom rather than any useful form of ax.

Based on their artifacts, in Minoan religious rites a tiny double-ax figure was often inserted into a small hole between the horns of consecration. In addition to the horns of consecration, in Minoan art there are numerous images of a bull's head, and they are often linked by vegetative images.‡ The vegetable nature of the double ax is implied in

---

*Ravens appear frequently as symbols of magical knowledge, or gnosis. In Arab mythology, for example, the raven of Paradise instructs Cain on how to bury his brother, Abel, which suggests a mortuary connection too, as does the raven perched on the corpse of the Celtic hero Cù Chulainn. In Arabic lore the raven of Paradise guides the wife of Kanuh to the cave where her husband sleeps, which leads to the conception of the prophet Salih (Stetkevych 1996, p. 19).

†The effort to represent a mushroom in two-dimensional form may have resulted in the creation of the double-ax image. Some of these ritual axes had four blades, which is even more suggestive of a mushroom or plant shape (see also Alexiou 1969, pp. 91–92). A related symbol is a cross placed on the forehead of a bull's skull (p. 96).

‡Looking at all of these beautifully shaped rhyton vases, shaped like a bull's head, it is easy to imagine them saying MA (or "Moo").

*Figure 15.4. Bull's head rhyton of inlaid steatite, Little Palace, Knossos*

Minoan artwork. Dan Russell states, "Thousands of bull-head images have been recovered from Neolithic to Iron Age levels. They are consistently shown sprouting transformed shamans and magical plants, many with holes between the horns for the insertion of the stem of the sacramental plant itself" (1998, p. 39).

This may suggest that in their rites the Minoans grew mushrooms on the corpses of bulls, and they later recalled this fact through ritually placing the tiny double ax between the horns of consecration.* Likely the double ax was a symbol connected to the worship of cattle and the sacred plants that grow on them.† In this sense, the double ax is related

---

*This is no more peculiar than putting flowers on a grave or tombstone.

†Although not from Crete, a gold ring from Mycenaen Greece shows a sacred plant growing out of the back of a ram (Russell 1998, p. 174). Similar images in later Christian art depict a cross growing out of a sheep.

to the sacred ankh of the Egyptians (Nilsson 1970, pp. 207*ff.*, 275, 208).

Among the other articles on the typical Minoan altar, which included examples of the horns of consecration and the double ax, was a set of small cups sitting on a tray. Because some of them are attached to a tray or a pottery ring, they were doubtless difficult to use in drinking liquids.* Perhaps these cups were used to hold some kind of food consumed in the religious rites. Minoan altars often had a shallow indented area that was not suited for drinking liquids. Again, some kind of finger food, such as mushrooms, was likely consumed from this indentation.†

Similarly, Minoan bowls included what archaeologists call bird's nest bowls and smaller salt and pepper bowls that have unusual shapes and are frequently found in tombs (Nilsson 1970, p. 142*ff.*). Many are similar to Egyptian bowls and are funereal in nature. Their odd shapes would severely limit their usefulness as ordinary food utensils.‡

Did the Minoans use hallucinogenic mushrooms in their religious rituals? The tiny cups and oddly shaped bowls, the shallow indentations on their altars, and the prominent display of the double ax and the horns of consecration suggest they did.

Did the early Christians also have a symbol like the Minoan symbols that represent mushrooms? Some scholars suggest that the crucifix itself is a symbol of the mushroom. Yet the cross did not become the foremost symbol of the Christian Church until several centuries had passed; the crucifix was not commonly used until the fifth century.

---

*It's also possible that the Minoans may have ingested a powerful brew made from ergot, the parasitic rust that grows on wheat and barley, a practice later continued in ancient Greece where it became part of the rituals of Eleusis (Russell 1998, pp. 42, 128). Scholars generally agree that the rites of Eleusis originated on Crete; thus it was likely the Minoans who originally discovered that a hallucinogenic drink could be made from rust. Perhaps the shape of these cups was related to a process for making the drink safe for consumption.

†See Nilsson 1970, pp. 93, 107, 122*ff.* Nilsson believes that the general design of these altars may have originated with the early dynastic Egyptian tables of offering (p. 135).

‡Even the famous high-necked and high-handled libation jugs may have been used to carry something other than liquids. This is suggested by images on several seal stones (Nilsson 1970, p. 149).

Instead, in the catacombs of Rome the Christians typically used a fish symbol (Ichthys) or paintings of plates of fish and bread, probably representing the miracle of the loaves and fishes, or they used as a symbol images of the Eucharist (or Lord's Supper).

Another popular symbol was the anchor. According to historian B. M. Billon, "The oldest and one of the most common Christian ideographs is the anchor" (1976, p. 25). Yet an anchor seems out of place as a religious icon. Certainly it's hard to find biblical support for using an anchor as a religious symbol.* Furthermore there is nothing in the Christian scriptures to account for its popularity over several other symbols that certainly had much stronger biblical associations, such as perhaps a fishing net.

On the other hand, the Christian anchor is fairly similar in shape to Thor's hammer. The similarity of both the anchor and the hammer to an upside-down mushroom is perhaps the only reason for the anchor to become an early symbol for the Christian faith. This idea is supported by the connection between the anchor and images of legendary Medusa, who also has strong associations with mushroom lore.[†]

Several ancient coins such as the Apollonia Pontika minted in Thrace have Medusa's head on one side and an oddly rounded upside down anchor on the other.[‡] This association between Medusa's head

---

*The anchor was a symbol of the Seleucid empire. It might be possible, based on a Roman amulet design, that the anchor may be phallic in nature (see Elworthy 1986, p. 154, fig. 42). The fish is often described as a female symbol. The medieval combination of anchors and dolphins is also rather suspicious: many of the dolphins look like serpents, and the images suggest a Brazen Serpent, rather than a dolphin, hanging from the crosspiece of the anchor.

†See Ruck, Staples, and Heinrich 2001, pp. 41–45.

‡The letter *A* shows that the anchor is indeed upside down. See, for example, the Greek coin, Apollonia Pontika, from Thrace, Type 6 drachm (3.4g), ca. 450–400 BCE. Thrace was a major religious center for the Dionysus cult that strongly influenced the religion of Greece (Kennedy 87). Ironically, in 1999 a large quantity of alleged forgeries of Apollonia Pontika drachms were sold at the New York International Numismatic Convention. Sometimes called the New York Hoard, these apparently faked coins depicted anchors that actually resembled real anchors. In addition, the gorgon faces were more distorted and fantastic in appearance, in a way that is uncharacteristic of ancient art.

*Figure 15.5. Apollonia Pontika from Thrace with the anchor shown on the left and the Medusa, Gorgon face, shown on the right*

and the anchor symbol seems rather strange unless the anchor is actually a symbolic representation of a mushroom.

This idea is further supported by the fact that these anchors don't really look very much like anchors. In fact, the anchors on these Thracian coins have a wavy, wing shape that might be said to resemble the cap of a large mushroom. The images from the coin appear to merge vaguely anchorlike characteristics and the outline of a mushroom shape. It might seem strange that the people of Thrace included an upside-down anchor on their coins, but most Americans can't explain the symbolism of the eye on the pyramid that appears on the U.S. one dollar bill.

Based on the idea of the apostles as fishers of men, the anchor symbol might have been adopted by the first Christians as an image that both reveals and hides the secrets of the cult of Jesus. Over the centuries, as the Christian priesthood shifted its emphasis away from the sacred food and toward exalting the sufferings of Christ on the cross, the Christian anchor was largely abandoned as a religious symbol. Except for its presence as a logo in antiquarian books, the anchor is almost completely forgotten as one of the most important symbols of early Christianity.

# 16

✠

# Awakening the Bees

Some French winemakers have a special recipe for fermenting wine. They mix raw eggs with dozens of herbs and spices to make a batter. After they put up the pulp in huge wooden barrels, they add the egg batter to help the grapes ferment into wine. The raw eggs accelerate the fermentation of the natural sugars, and the spices give the wine a special flavor. This fact about French wine may seem like a pointless bit of trivia, but in fact it's the key to understanding how the ancient Minoans prepared their sacred honey mead.

Earlier we saw how the Minoans practiced a distinct form of human sacrifice. They selected a young man to be the sacrifice and then fed him hallucinogenic mushrooms along with opium and other plants. Once he started to show the effects of the meal, they bound him, killed him, and laced shut his bodily orifices using leather sutures. His eyes, nose, mouth, anus, and perhaps his foreskin were sealed with beeswax, the loose skin was sewn shut, and his body was turned into a sealed bag of skin (Kerenyi 1996, p. 40).* After forty to fifty days the leather

---

*It seems likely that sacred oils were then applied to each orifice as a kind of funereal rite.

168

sutures holding his mouth shut were cut, and the liquefied flesh and mushrooms were drawn off and added to jars of raw honey in order to ferment the Minoan sacred mead. There is evidence that this same rite was performed later by using bulls in place of young men. This type of bull sacrifice was continued by the Greeks and perhaps by the Romans (although this may be questionable). The key to this form of sacrifice is revealed in stories about "awakening the bees"—that is, creating sacred mead.

In addition to the many double axes found on Crete, we find sacred bees as a popular religious symbol. Many examples of bee-shaped gold jewelry have been found on Crete; the symbol of the sacred bees was even more important to the Minoans than it was to the ancient Egyptians (Castleden 1990, p. 51). In *Food of the Gods,* Terence McKenna suggests that the bee was sacred to the Minoans because mushrooms could be stored in honey.* In addition, honey itself was believed to be sacred in many of the cults of the dead. This idea is conveyed in Lewis Paton's statement, "Honey appears in all parts of the Aryan world as a food sacred to the dead. In both the Greek and the Roman cults of the dead, honey appears as an essential ingredient" (2003, p. 138). Although honey is linked to the cult of the dead in many parts of the ancient world, there appears to be no compelling reason this would be so.

Some of the greatest thinkers of the ancient world were interested in fermenting honey into mead, including the Greek philosopher Aristotle and the Roman naturalist Pliny the Elder. From Pliny's writings we find that he used a kind of leather sack to ferment his honey. The leather sack was made from an "animal hide that could be tied at the neck" and similar in shape to a wineskin (Kerenyi 1996, p. 38). This

---

*The practice of storing magic mushrooms in honey is suggested by the legend of Glaukos, a son of King Minos, who, while exploring the labyrinth, fell into a pot of honey and was later resurrected by a magic herb (Russell 1998, p. 164). Honey was also used for embalming; Alexander the Great's corpse was, according to legend, immersed and preserved in white honey. It's also been suggested that the Minoans used honey to embalm their dead (Castleden 1990, p. 51). The Roman senator Pliny is said to have recommended honey for preserving bodies (Camporesi 1988, pp. 159, 181).

sack was watertight but not airtight, and it allowed for the expansion of the honey as it fermented so that the leather skin would not burst. Using an old leather sack for fermenting new wine could lead to rupture, as Jesus warns us: "No one puts new wine into old wineskins; otherwise the wine will burst the skins, and the wine is lost and the skins as well; but one puts new wine into fresh wineskins" (Mark 2:22).

Here Jesus alludes to the fact that the wineskins can rupture because of a weakness or corruption in the leather, perhaps in this case from age. In the ancient world it was a common attitude to view the physical world as a reflection of the spiritual world; both were inextricably linked.*

Both Aristotle and Pliny took the fermentation of mead seriously. They were practical fellows who were the products of a Hellenistic and materialistic worldview. Pliny had his own favorite technique for making fermented honey in a leather sack, as did many other Greeks and Romans. Yet the ancient Greeks took a much more spiritual view of mead and mead making. Karl Kerenyi has carefully examined all the existing references to sacred mead in early Greek literature. In his book *Dionysos* he suggests that not only was fermented honey (sometimes called honey beer) a popular drink in the Hellenic world but also a special form of sacred mead was essential in the religious rites of ancient

---

*For the residents of first-century Palestine this failure in the leather could be interpreted as both a physical and a spiritual corruption. In Jewish history, when evil King Herod became sick, people were able to see that his body was destroyed with worms and putrefaction (Acts 12:23). These worms were taken as the outward, visible sign of his spiritual corruption. Acts describes the death of Judas Iscariot: "With the payment he received for his wickedness, Judas bought a field; there he fell headlong, his body burst open and all his intestines spilled out" (Acts 1:18). Of course human bodies almost never burst in this way, suggesting that this story reflects the extreme evil of Judas as the betrayer of Christ. As with Herod, ancient sources suggest that evil men were often punished with worms. Acts does not say whether those who found Judas's body saw thousands of tiny worms crawling in his gut, which might have caused him to burst. His contemporaries likely interpreted Judas's bursting as a visible sign of his spiritual immorality. Both King Herod and Judas were well known as fatally flawed characters, physically and spiritually (see also Hosea 4:10).

Crete.* Kerenyi believed that many of the later Greek religious rituals associated with Dionysus as a wine god were originally sacred rites developed around the making and consumption of fermented honey (1996, p. 76). Some Greek legends claim that Dionysus invented honey, and other stories say that as an infant, before his nurses gave him milk, the baby Dionysus was held and "his lips were sprinkled with honey" (p. 31). The meaning of this obsession with honey, however, is not clear—until we understand the Minoans' equally puzzling obsession with cattle.

Bull-related symbols appear often in ancient Crete. We find numerous representations of cattle in Minoan art, including large water jars and libation vases shaped like a bull's head—called a rhyton—or sometimes the jars have the shape of a whole bull (Alexiou 1969, p. 45). While it's not unusual to revere cattle (for example, the Hebrew sacrificial altars were usually adorned with stones that were shaped to resemble a bull's horns), the extent of this worship on Crete was excessive. We have all heard of the Greek legends of the famous bull of Minos and the Minotaur, but the sheer number of cups shaped like bulls' heads, the boxes shaped like cattle, the vases with horns or illustrated with decorations of cattle, and the religious icon of the horns of consecration suggest an obsession with cattle that is unequaled in any other religion.

We have a culture in the American Southwest that is somewhat cattle obsessed. For example, the typical Texan often has a nickel-plated belt buckle depicting a bull's head, a key ring with the logo for the Texas Longhorns football team, a Ford truck with horns mounted on the hood, and the truck may even have brass balls hanging from the trailer hitch. Compared to this Texan, perhaps the ancient Egyptians from the First Dynasty run a close second (their homes were decorated with cow shapes and even

---

*The Greeks and Romans should probably not be criticized for losing the original recipe, because in a mere eighty years we have lost the recipe for making absinthe, an alcoholic drink that comes from herbs and flowers. One European company claims to have rediscovered the process, but many people are skeptical as to whether this new absinthe is much like the absinthe of the pre-WWI era.

their chairs were often carved with feet shaped to look like hooves). The Minoans, however, went well beyond both of these societies in their veneration of cattle. A painting from the tomb of the Egyptian high priest Menkheperresonb (1500–1450 BCE) shows a procession that includes two Minoan ambassadors who carry a container shaped like a bull's head. This was a gift or tribute presented along with a smaller bull figure, and both were perhaps Minoan rhyton jars that contained sacred mead.

Some of these bull-shaped cups, jars, and vases appear to have been stored in Minoan tombs along with other funereal artifacts. The key to understanding the Minoan obsession with cattle is to recognize that a bull sacrifice is a necessary first step in the process of fermenting the honey wine, the sacred mead used in the religious rites of the Minoan cult of the dead.

Much the same way that Sir Wallis Budge was surprised by the fact that the ancient Egyptians used the liquids that came from decaying corpses in their religious rites, the sacred rite for the Awakening of the Bees puzzled Karl Kerenyi. In the introduction to his earlier book on the Greek rites, *Eleusis: Archetypal Image of Mother and Daughter,* Kerenyi explains his method for reconstructing ancient Greek rites.

> Let us assume, for example, that the total context of a great ceremony of the Catholic Church, such as High Mass, has been lost. Only fragments from liturgical books and ruins of churches have been preserved. We cannot assume that the Mass has been the same from the start. The preserved fragments may date from different periods. A reconstruction can, nevertheless, be undertaken, because there is one thing we do not doubt, namely, that at every stage in its development the liturgy somehow formed a coherent whole with its own inner logic. This inner logic can be grasped even if we do not know what the liturgy as a whole was for. . . . (1991, p. xxi)

In his book on Minoan religion, *Dionysos,* Kerenyi explores the historical evidence related to the rite of Awakening the Bees. In this rite the Minoans performed the sacrifice of a young bull in order somehow to give birth to a swarm of bees. Kerenyi compiles a variety of sources from early Greece, Egypt, and Rome to try to piece together the meaning of this rite.

He is astonished by the Minoan's reverence for mead and by their "strange mythical formula or recipe for the Awakening of the Bees" (p. 38). For some reason the Romans who later came into possession of the recipe seemed to believe that it was a formula for creating real live bees, which were born (they thought) from the carcasses of dead bulls.* In adopting this idea, the Romans were continuing an old Greek religious tradition. Kerenyi suggests that the Romans did not want to question the practicality of this idea, probably for religious reasons, as if the very act of questioning it was sacrilegious (pp. 39–40).

In his book section "The Awakening of the Bees," Kerenyi brings together every reference he can find that might shed light on how the Minoans produced sacred mead. Central to this process was a rite described by the Roman author Cassianus Bassus (seventh century CE). Kerenyi writes:

> According to his instructions a cubical structure should be built with a door and three windows, each turned toward one of the four cardinal points. In this house a thirty-month-old bovine must be killed with a club, so that no blood flows and the entrails grow soft. All the openings of the body must be sealed. The animal is transformed into a sack containing its own fluids. After four weeks and ten days—roughly forty days, as in the traditional brewing of mead—grapelike clusters of bees fill the hut. All that remains of the bovine is the horns, the bones, and the skin. (pp. 40–41)

According to this Roman source, the so-called bees were produced

---

*See, for example, Plutarch's *Cleomenes:* "As oxen breed bees, putrifying horses breed hornets, and beetles rise from the carcasses of dead asses, so the humours and juices of the marrow of a man's body coagulating, produce serpents" (4:505).

from the liquefied flesh of dead bulls, but Cassianus Bassus did not understand that the Awakening of the Bees rite was simply one step in the process for making sacred mead.

The idea of turning a bull into a leather sack filled with liquefied flesh may strike us as revolting. This process was, however, an important religious ritual to the Minoans. Several gold rings found in Crete show a bull trussed and placed on a table (see, for example, Nilsson 1970, p. 230, fig. 113). The bulls shown in these images would likely have to be already dead before they were bound and placed on a table this way.* The binding ropes must have served another purpose: perhaps they helped hold together the bull's hide, which, after forty days of decomposition, was no doubt stressed with the weight of bones and liquefied flesh.† Several ropes were likely necessary to prevent the hide from rupturing. Yet why would the Minoans kill a bull, sew up all its bodily orifices, and let it rot for forty days?

It seems obvious that the recipe was not meant to be taken literally as a way to make bees. Further, why would anyone want to sacrifice a young bull in order to create bees? This ritual also seems to be related to the story of Samson, who killed a lion and then, while traveling along the same road, found bees and honey inside the lion's carcass.

There are a species of bees—vulture bees—that eat meat, but it's unlikely that the bees would make their home in a carcass itself, given the likelihood that other animals would disturb the carcass. Instead, they typically carry the meat back to their nests and store it in little wax pots. The story of a honey-filled carcass seems to suggest some other purpose, and this is the secret of Samson's riddle: "Out of the eater came forth meat, and out of the strong came forth sweetness"

---

*Zevit is also of this opinion (2001, p. 278). The use of bulls to create bees has a cultural echo in the scene in the film *District 9* (2009): the aliens used a cow carcass to lay their eggs, and in the film *Alien* (1979) and its many sequels, aliens use humans to grow their young.

†In one legend Prometheus tricks Zeus into choosing a cowhide covering bones and fat, while saving the best parts of the bull for men. As a result he is punished. The story is probably derived from this practice of bull sacrifice.

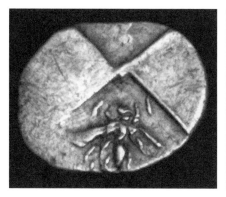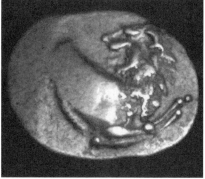

*Figure 16.1. A cherronesos coin from Thrace showing a bee on one side (left) and a lion on the other (right)*

(Judges 14:14). Some scholars have suggested that the Samson story is derived from Phoenician lore, which is possible given the close cultural ties between the Phoenicians and the Minoans.* Yet much is left unexplained.

The sacrifice of the bull clearly has nothing to do with producing literal bees. Instead, the sacrifice of a bull was necessary in order to create a gigantic leather sack, much like a wine sack. After forty days the flesh of the bull decomposed and the leather sack became a bag containing liquefied flesh and bones. This process makes sense, however, only if we assume that hallucinogenic mushrooms were fed to the bull or inserted into the body cavities before the orifices were sewn shut. At the end of forty days the Minoans had a bag of liquefied flesh and mushrooms, which could then be added to raw honey. The honey would then ferment into a powerful mushroom-spiked mead that could be used in religious rites to create visions of the afterlife. In Orphism, an ancient Greek mystery religion, sacred honey symbolized not only purification and preservation or endless life and bliss but also the secret knowledge

---

*Robert Graves has already suggested a link between mushroom lore and the Samson story. Note that the expression "a live dog is better than a dead lion" (Ecclesiastes 9:4) may have originated from the conflict between the Jerusalem Temple and the cult of the dead (Davies 1999, p. 79). See also John 6:55 for a similarity to the Samson riddle.

obtained during initiation. This spiked honey beer (or sacred mead) created the visions.*

Many centuries later the Roman author Cassianus Bassus called this rite the Awakening of the Bees. It's likely that we will never know the words the Minoans originally used to name the rite. It could just as easily be the Making of the Bee Butter. No doubt the Minoans probably meant the phrase to be metaphorical, but in fact the purpose of the rite was to create a liquid that could be used to spike the sacred mead. The Awakening of the Bees was likely a euphemism for an important religious rite that we should take seriously.

The idea that people would sacrifice a bull to make mead is hard to grasp, but this idea is strongly supported by two other legends: the story of how Orion was born and the story of how Zeus was defeated by a dragon and his body was turned into a human leather sack. The Zeus story points to a period of time when humans instead of cattle were used in this rite.

According to Karl Kerenyi, the religious ritual for the Awakening of the Bees from a dead animal is directly related to the birth story of the god Orion.† In the Greek legend a man named Hyrieus was childless, and the gods endeavored to give him a child. They did this by masturbating into a leather sack made from a bull's hide. Orion was born from the leather sack. This story is based on two puns: (1) *ourein,* meaning both "Orion" and "sack," and (2) *Hyrieus* and *hyria,* meaning "a swarm of bees" (1996, p. 42). Kerenyi believes that the leather sack contained honey and the story of Orion's birth is a description of how honey was fermented into mead. The gods added their own "seed" to the sack. Their gift was the mixture of liquefied flesh and hallucinogenic mush-

---

*In the film *The 13th Warrior* (1999), one of the Viking warriors points out that because mead is actually fermented honey, it's not prohibited by the Qur'an. In the end the thirteen Viking warriors defeat the cannibalistic skull worshippers called "eaters of the dead."
†This Awakening of the Bees ritual was performed in Greece to celebrate the festival of the early rising of Sirius. Kerenyi argues, however, that the ritual was originally an Egyptian holiday tied to the flooding of the Nile. At some point in their early history this rite was probably adopted by the Greeks and given an astronomical purpose.

rooms that, when added to raw honey, helped the fermentation process that changed the raw honey into sacred mead. For this reason the act of drinking sacred mead could lead to visions of the divine.

Any explanation of this legend about Orion must account for why the gods add their "seed" to the leather sack. Clearly something supernatural and mysterious is added to the sack. The story describes this as the seed of the gods, but it seems likely that whatever is added to the sack must be a substance that was added to the honey in order to promote and accelerate the fermentation process.

The process of creating the bees (a euphemism for the liquefied flesh and mushrooms) so that the Minoans could add this spiked mixture to fermenting honey was all part of a secret recipe.* Just as their sacred oils included some mysterious ingredient labeled MA, the Minoans also exported their sacred mead. Like their various sacred anointing oils, it was no doubt a valuable commodity used in trade with Egypt and other nations where the Minoan's mushroom-laced honey beer was appreciated. Eventually, however, the consumption of this spiked mead was later eclipsed by the popular consumption of cheaper wine, beer, and opium.

---

*Certainly this process brings to mind the way mescal, an alcoholic drink that includes a worm in the bottle, is produced. The Greek seed may have served much the same purpose as the worm at the bottom of a bottle of mescal. The ancient African and Egyptian practice of burying a bull with its horns sticking up through the ground may indicate that this was part of the fermenting process in its earliest form. Scholars suggest that this practice of burying the bull with its horns exposed is the origin of the icon the horns of consecration (Nilsson 1970, p. 187).

# 17

✠

# Zeus and the Human Sack

As we have seen, several Greek myths suggest that in the remote past humans were used instead of cattle in the Awakening of the Bees ritual. It would not be uncommon then to find humans and cattle used in similar ways in Greek art.

Branigan's *Hellas* contains two excellent photos of ritual vessels shaped like bulls' heads, one Cretan (1980, p. 46) and one Greek (p. 67). Both vessels pour from an opening in the bull's mouth, suggesting how the sacrificed bull's carcass was drained. Pouring from the bull's mouth was indeed a ritual action in Crete (Kerenyi 1996, p. 54). In imitation of this image, there are many Greek statues of animals and people identified as gods or mythic creatures that have water pouring from their mouths.*

Perhaps the process described by the Roman Cassianus Bassus was simply the first step. One bull's skin would no doubt provide enough of this mixture to spike several large jars of honey. Archaeologists have

---

*It's also quite common to have statues of lions with water coming from their mouths, suggesting a connection to Samson and the lion carcass filled with honey (Judges 14:8).

found numerous *pithoi* jars in Crete, some of which could be of the type used in this process. Once the bull's skin was emptied, the skull and hide were nailed to a tree in a holy grove or hung on a post, as the Egyptians did, or perhaps hung from the bough of a sacred tree (Alexiou 1969, p. 91).* The Minoans sometimes displayed the emptied skin on a mountain peak or other high place or sometimes on a stone pillar erected for that purpose.

The likelihood that humans were once used to create the sack for this mixture is strongly suggested by a legend about Zeus that comes to us from the southern coast of Asia Minor. Karl Kerenyi relates this story in "Mythology of the Leather Sack." Like Dionysus, Zeus was born on the island of Crete, and, like Dionysus, the baby Zeus was fed honey. Just as the rituals of Dionysus were performed in a cave on Mount Parnassus, high above Delphi, the rites of Zeus were performed in a cave on the island of Crete. According to Kerenyi, "The cave was called *Korykion antron,* 'cave of the leather sack'—the most famous of all those places in and outside the Greek world that were named after the *korykos,* the container for liquids used in fermenting honey and, as we have seen, associated with a Cretan cave of Zeus" (1996, p. 45).

Both Zeus and Dionysus are associated with the leather sack, but in one particular legend the body of Zeus himself becomes a type of leather sack. In this legend, which begins as a typical monster-slaying myth, Zeus fights a terrible dragon. He uses his lightning bolts (his thunder weapon) and later a sickle-shaped sword (often associated with the *harpe,* or small sickle used to harvest sacred plants) to attack the dragon. Unfortunately, the dragon manages to defeat Zeus and make

---

*The leftover hides and skulls were holy relics to the Egyptians and apparently also to the Minoans. The use of a sheep in sacrifices is probably the source for the legend of the Golden Fleece (Nilsson 1970, pp. 232, 347; Alexiou 1969, p. 45). The idea of using a human cadaver as a sack also found its way into the imagery of hell, reflected in several paintings by Hieronymus Bosch (1450–1516). In modern popular culture we can see this notion in such horror films as *From Dusk Till Dawn* (1996) in which a limbless body is turned into an electric guitar.

him a prisoner, and then the dragon uses the sword to cut the tendons of Zeus's hands and feet, rendering him immobile.*

Zeus is helpless, a prisoner of the dragon, and the dragon soon carries him away to Cilicia, on the coast of Asia Minor. According to Kerenyi, once the dragon arrives there, he leaves Zeus in the cave of the leather sack, "in the *Korykion antron;* he did the same with the tendons, which he hid in a bearskin. Thus he [the dragon] had not only severed the tendons, as the Greek narrator supposed or wished to suppose, but from the defeated god's body removed something that was kept in a bearskin, i.e., a leather sack" (1996, p. 48).

Kerenyi notes that the inclusion of the bearskin is clearly based on the association between bears and honey. This detail points to a time in Minoan history when bears were killed and their bodies used to make a leather sack†—probably long before bulls were used for this purpose. Yet as wild bears became harder and harder to find, it was a logical step to start sacrificing domesticated animals such as cattle and sheep. Certainly sheep were used in later Greek rites.

Cutting Zeus's tendons is an act that points directly to the practice of human sacrifice. According to John M. Robertson's study on human sacrifice, the sacrificial victim was often drugged or sometimes

---

*In the Hittite myth from the Yuzgat Tablet the supreme god declares that even if he is bound he will still conquer thanks to the power of his eye (Gaster 1961, p. 290). We can assume that the eye of the Hittite god is like the Eye of Ra, all powerful. Of course, this Hittite passion play hints at the fact that the god is a sacrifice, immobilized in order to create the eye—part of a natural biological process.

†*Bear* and *birth* have the common linguistic ancestor *bher* (Russell 1998, p. 208). That the so-called golden bees (a liquid used to spike mead or wine) were born from a leather sack made from a bear cadaver may account for the similarity. In addition, in the story "She-Camel of God" the camel is hamstrung and killed in a ritual that echoes the slaying of Dionysus and Osiris. Like *Amanita muscaria,* the she-camel is "between white and ruddy" and produces magical milk. She is slain by Qudar, "the Red One," who is then cursed (Stetkevych 1996, pp. 15–23). We can note that in Arabian lore the serpent in the Garden of Eden originally had the form of a camel (p. 55). Additionally, the name Qudar may be related to the word *qidr,* meaning "kettle" (p. 73). (See also Russell 1998, p. 110.)

even had his tendons cut as part of the religious ceremony. Rendering the sacrificial victim as pliable as possible is essential to the task of presenting a worthy and willing sacrifice for the gods. The Greeks often poured wine over the head of a sacrificial bull, which caused the bull to shake his head. This was taken as a sign that he assented to being the sacrifice. (A bull that shakes his head *no* evidently means *yes*). The Greeks also preserved the hides and horns of their sacrifices. The horns were sometimes gilded on the spot (the goldsmith stood nearby during the rite), and the hides were often presented to the priests, who preserved them as evidence that the proper sacrifices had been made (Lambert 1993, p. 296).

The story of Zeus and his defeat at the hands of the dragon is probably derived from the archaic practice of using a human sacrifice to create the leather sack. After his tendons were cut the human sacrifice, representing Zeus, was executed using precise rites, and his wounds and body orifices were sewn up, thereby turning him into a human sack. As part of the rite the human sacrifice must have been understood to be a substitution for the god Zeus. The liquefied flesh produced by this human sack became the seed of the god Zeus and could be used later in the fermentation of honey into mead.*

Though the Minoans were fairly open about their rites, the Egyptians became ever more secretive. As Dan Russell suggests, "the cult in Crete differs from the cults in Egypt and the Near East in just this

---

*One of the rituals of the mysteries included walking on Jupiter's skin, which was "the skin of a victim offered to that god" (Wilkinson 1878, 3:390). It seems likely that in the original version of the ritual the skin was in fact a human skin. The Egyptians and the Greeks shared a concern about the proper use of the skin of a sacrifice (much like the Aztecs, who wore the flayed skins of their sacrifices). In his analysis of the Greek story Karl Kerenyi also connects it to the notion that Zeus's genitalia were stolen and put in the sack. In this sense the story is similar to the Egyptian myths in which the eye of Horus is stolen or the phallus of Set is injured. In both cases a vital seed is needed to repair an injury. Ancient religious rites are typically built around an effort to repair the damage caused to the natural order as a result of harvesting grain or taking/stealing sacred fruit.

respect that provision is made for more active participation by the worshipers" (1998, p. 56). At the same time that the people of Crete were expanding and developing the use of hallucinogens, the Egyptians were likely trying to limit hallucinogens to ever smaller groups of people and also using smaller amounts of *Amanita muscaria,* which were often difficult to obtain.*

It appears likely that over time it became more difficult for the Egyptian priests to get the proper ingredients in sufficient quantities to make enough sacred food and oils for everyone who wanted to be initiated. Eventually only the royalty and the priestesses and priests of Isis and Osiris had regular access to their eucharist, while the lower classes might have access only occasionally during religious festivals, if at all.

Despite these differences, Crete and Egypt had a flourishing trade with each other as the two most advanced civilizations in the Mediterranean. According to Nilsson, "The relations with Egypt are incomparably stronger and more numerous from the oldest periods of Minoan civilization onwards, and go perhaps still further back . . . the connection with Egypt went on almost to the end of the Minoan age" (1970, p. 8).

In addition to trade and cultural relations, the Minoans and Egyptians no doubt recognized the similarity of their religious rites. Although the rites associated with the Greek mystery religions probably had their origins in Crete, it seems likely that the Egyptians were also a significant influence from the very beginnings of Greek civilization on the mainland (p. 14).

Using the rites of the mushroom from a different cultural background, the Egyptians developed a mortuary cult that became more and more elaborate over the centuries. The Minoans of Crete, however, stayed focused on the end result: creating powerful, intoxicating drinks

---

*This story ties in with what we know of the Egyptian Opening of the Mouth ceremony. Given this new insight, it may be that the story of Osiris's murder was probably also derived from an ancient rite in which the god was sacrificed for the common good and then later restored to life.

that from the beginnings of their earliest history were used in religious ceremonies.*

As their civilization went into decline, the Minoans probably began to rely on opium to strengthen their honey beer brews. A decline in their military and economic influence also made it difficult to get access to an adequate supply of *Amanita muscaria,* which grow only in mountainous areas. In addition, it seems likely that the Minoans began to shift from fermenting mead to producing a cheaper spiked wine and beer.

Some may find it hard to imagine that an ancient society—and one so far advanced culturally over the rest of Europe—could be so heavily invested in producing and exporting sacred oils, ointments, and fermented beverages. For us today, it is even more difficult to understand how the Minoans could continue to produce sacred mead when the drink relied, at least in their earliest rites, on the sacrifice of human life.†

---

*The story of the flaying of Marsyas is several steps removed from the original ritual, as is the scourging of Christ. The focus of early Christians on the blood and sweat of Jesus is clearly derived from the ancient veneration of the fluids taken from the body of the sacrificed victim. The idea persisted within the medieval church (as, for example, in the flaying of St. Bartholomew). The practice of self-flagellation persisted in medieval Europe in part because the flagellant was imitating the sacrifice and flaying of Christ's body, which was the source of divine honey. The body of Christ was imagined to "overflow with sweetness, like a beehive in Ibla, brimming with honey" (Camporesi 1988, p. 34). It is worth noting that a coin was minted in Rome in 82 BCE by L. Censorinus, with the head of Apollo and the figure of Marsyas holding an enormous wineskin, based on the statue of Marsyas in the Roman forum.

†In moral terms the closest modern parallel is the growth and export of tobacco from Virginia, or perhaps the British trade in opium in the eighteenth century. Even if the Minoans looked on life and death in a way that seems alien to us today, moral questions were likely raised, at least by the neighbors of Crete.

# 18

✠

# Dionysus and the Greek Gods

As we move from the religious practices of ancient Crete to those of mainland Greece, we find a great deal of evidence for the use of hallucinogens. Many details of Greek mythology point toward the consumption of hallucinogens in religious rites, particularly the use of psychoactive mushrooms. According to Jochen Gartz, "Mycenaean civilization began with a mushroom trip. Mushrooms were an ingredient in the ambrosia of Dionysus." He further states: "Porphyrius, the fourth-century Latin poet and contemporary of Emperor Konstantin [Constantine], knew that magic mushrooms were the children of the gods. A quasi-cannibalistic ritual, the act of eating the children of the gods, unlocked one's power to experience the truly divine" (1996, p. 7).

Today, the most comprehensive book available on the use of these sacred mushrooms in ancient Greece is *The Apples of Apollo: Pagan and Christian Mysteries of the Eucharist,* written by Carl A. P. Ruck, Blaise Daniel Staples, and Clark Heinrich. Much of this book focuses on the ancient Greeks and references to the use of *Amanita muscaria.* References to the sacred mushroom are plentiful in ancient Greek myths. Here we will only touch on these scholars' discoveries that illuminate our understanding of the ritual use of mushrooms in the early Greek cults of the dead.

So far we can draw several conclusions about the ancient Greeks and Minoans. As with many other societies in the Mediterranean region, on the mainland of Greece the early mushroom-based religions were supplanted by invaders who used alcohol (wine and beer) rather than mushrooms in their worship. We can see this shift in the career of the wine god Dionysus among the classical Greeks. Dionysus began his career on Crete as the god of sacred mead, made from fermented honey and mushrooms. Later, on the mainland of Greece, he was transformed into the god of wine. The growing popularity of Bacchus/Dionysus illustrates the shift, as Dionysus became the young god who brings the gift of wine and supplants the older mushroom gods. Yet the stories of Dionysus still retain some of the mythic content of a mushroom god and the fermented honey (mead) as a eucharistic drink in religious rituals. We must keep in mind that in the worship of Dionysus the celebrants actually ate the god.* Thus their god was both a victim and a deity, much like the Indian god Soma (Lang 1996, p. 251).

According to J. M. Robertson, during the Greek classical era the god Dionysus was the personification of beer and wine. Like the Indic god Soma, who represented divine food, the child Dionysus may have represented the divine nature of wine. Dionysus was, in some sense, the divine spirit that inhabited the wine (1911, p. 318). We should also keep in mind, however, that the wine used in the rites of Dionysus was probably more than just ordinary wine. It was very likely a heavily spiked wine called trimma, which was used in Greek

---

*In one version of the story, Dionysus is killed and eaten by Titans, but his sister is able to rescue his heart, which she gives to Zeus. He pounds the heart flat and gives it to Semele to eat (much like a Eucharist wafer), and she gives birth to Dionysus a second time (Mackenzie 1995, p. 157). This type of rebirth story, including the resurrection story of St. George and of the Egyptian god Anpu-Bata, is widespread throughout the Middle East and India (p. 158).

religious ceremonies (Shelly 1995, p. 6; Ruck, Staples, and Heinrich 2001, pp. 7, 12, 33).*

The original cult of Dionysus almost certainly had its origins in the mushroom cults of ancient Crete (Russell 1998, p. 103). Historians argue that the worship of Dionysus began on Crete, because the sacred initiation rites on Crete were open to many people, while the Dionysian initiation rites in Greece were severely restricted (Diodorus 1998–2001, 5:77). It seems likely that most of the esoteric beliefs of the Greeks had their origins in Crete, including the mysteries of Eleusis.

Even the great god Zeus was born on Crete in a cave of bees, and his nursemaids were said to have been sacred bees (Kerenyi 1996, p. 30). The cave in which Zeus was born regularly overflowed with divine blood, which, according to Kerenyi, is a reference to honey, a possession of the gods (p. 34). The theft of honey could bring terrible punishment; in one legend Zeus transforms a group of honey thieves into birds.† Clearly this story is not about stealing ordinary honey.

Kerenyi believes that the divine blood of Zeus, which overflowed from the cave, was related to this so-called honey/blood—the *divine ichor*—described in Homer's *Illiad* (Homer 1954, p. 34). The divine ichor that flowed in the veins of the gods in place of ordinary blood was yellowish, a bodily fluid that suggests honey or some mixture of honey with other fluids or perhaps even fermented honey.‡ Again, if the blood of the gods is mead, then this too points to the creation of a spiked honey beer from the "blood" taken from a human sacrifice, who

---

*We must note that there are strong similarities between the Egyptian god Osiris and several Greek gods, including Dionysus and Prometheus. All have ties to the production of the sacred food and oils.

†We can also note that the theft of honey and the transformation of the thieves into birds suggest a connection to the story of Prometheus and his theft of fire. The cave of Zeus was also noted for producing a blazing light/fire that could be seen from a distance. Prometheus was punished by the eagle of Zeus—the very same eagle that carried the food of the gods, the divine ambrosia, down from the mountaintop (Russell 1998, p. 183).

‡Ichor was also associated with the Accadian idea of the blood of trees and the yellow-red mannalike gum or resin that flows from cedar trees (Gaster 1961, p. 180). As some professional gardeners can tell you, cedar chips make an excellent host for psilocybin mushrooms.

represents the sacrificed god. The idea of ichor as fermented honey also suggests that a human "sack" was used in creating sacred mead.

According to Greek myth, Kronos castrated his father, Uranus, while Uranus was drunk on mead (Gaster 1961, p. 36). Kronos used a sacred sickle for this task, an iconic image that comes down to us today as pictures of Father Time holding a large sickle used for cutting wheat. This story parallels an Aryan myth in which Indra castrates his father in order to access the divine soma. In both cases the drink was probably a mixture of fermented honey and hallucinogens, perhaps mixed with milk. The religious importance of this drink is reflected in the *Odyssey* in which, during rituals for the dead, the priests give priority to the presentation of the *melikratos,* an intoxicating mixture of honey and milk, over the libations of sweet wine (Homer 1960, p. 37).

The religion of Dionysus was transported to mainland Greece while the Minoan civilization was at its peak. Later, as the Dorians and other invaders conquered Greece and Crete, the religious practices persisted, though with some changes. Some alterations were also strongly influenced by the Egyptians, who had developed trade with and cultural ties to Greece.

Although the first Dionysus probably originated with the Minoans of ancient Crete, the early Greek historians were convinced that Dionysus was a transplant from Egypt. According to Greek historians the Egyptian god Osiris arrived in Thrace, where he was renamed Dionysus; this took place long before the beginnings of classical Greece. Rather than create a new name, it seems more likely that the Osirian missionaries simply adopted the name of an already existing Dionysus—who was probably a Minoan god and whom they recognized as being similar to their own god, Osiris. The later Greek historian Herodotus used the names Osiris and Dionysus interchangeably, because to him they were one and the same (Larson 1977, p. 37*ff.*). Modern historians suggest that the original Dionysus cult from Crete merged with several Egyptian rites and festivals at some point before 1200 BCE.

Many ancient Greeks believed that Dionysus was just another form of Osiris, and at the end of the Mycenaean period, from 1200 to about the eighth century BCE, this may well have been at least partly true. For example, according to the Greek historian Diodorus:

> Orpheus, for instance, brought from Egypt most of his mystic cere-
> monies, the orgiastic rites that accompanied his wanderings, and his
> fabulous account of his experiences in Hades. For the rite of Osiris is
> the same as that of Dionysus, and that of Isis very similar to that of
> Demeter, the names alone having been interchanged; and the pun-
> ishments in Hades of the unrighteous, the Fields of the Righteous,
> and the fantastic conceptions, current among the many, which are
> figments of the imagination. All these were introduced by Orpheus
> in imitation of Egyptian funeral customs. (1998–2001, p. 96)

Several ancient Greek writers noticed the strong resemblance between Dionysus and Osiris. Sir J. G. Frazer summarized the evidence in his famous landmark work *The Golden Bough*.

> Herodotus found the similarity between the rites of Osiris and Dio-
> nysus so great, that he thought it impossible the latter could have
> arisen independently; they must, he supposed, have been recently
> borrowed, with slight alterations, by the Greeks from the Egyptians.
> Again, Plutarch, a very keen student of comparative religion, insists
> upon the detailed resemblance of the rites of Osiris to those of Dio-
> nysus. We cannot reject the evidence of such intelligent and trust-
> worthy witnesses on plain matters of fact . . . the resemblances of
> ritual are matters of observation. (1961, p. 127)

---

*Some scholars see all these gods as identical. For example, Donald A. Mackenzie states: "The Cretan Zeus-Dionysus links not only with Osiris, but also with Tammuz of Baby-lon, Ashur of Assyria, Attis of Phrygia, Adonis of Greece, Agni of India and his twin brother Indra, the Germanic Scef and Frey and Heimdal, and the Scottish Irish Diarmid" (1995, p. 156). R. Gordon Wasson has already identified Agni as a mushroom god, and the other gods in Mackenzie's list are also likely derived from or associated with mush-room worship. In his earliest form, the Cretan Zeus, called "the boy," resembles the dying youth Adonis/Tammuz (Castleden 1990, p. 125).

Was the religion of Dionysus directly derived from the Osirian faith? We can't say with certainty.* Greek historians seem to have believed the two religions were one and the same. The Minoans of Crete had closer contact with the Egyptians than with any other culture. They may have borrowed some of their public ritual practices from Egyptian religious rites and adapted these rites to their own use (Kerenyi 1996, p. 72).

Though some of the Greek rites of Dionysus were derived from those of Osiris, the original stories of Dionysus's birth, death, and resurrection, however similar to the story of Osiris, are different enough from the myth of Osiris that we can believe the stories about Dionysus originated with the Minoans. There may in fact have been no more difference between the religions of Osiris in Egypt and Dionysus in Greece than the difference that exists today between the Catholics and the Methodists.*

Like Osiris, Dionysus was attacked and his body was torn to pieces in both legend and as part of his sacred rites.[†] According to legend, Dionysus was captured and killed by the Titans. This act of ritual dismemberment was re-enacted as a part of the early ceremonies of the Dionysus cult. In many cases the Dionysus religion of Greece retained elements from the earlier Minoan rites, and, as we will see, Greek literature often preserves elements from the earlier, more open mushroom rites of Crete.

---

*The original rites of Dionysus on Crete, however, may have been closer to the ecstatic snake-handling holiness movement of rural Kentucky. Certainly, based on their art and pottery, we know that the Minoans did a great deal of snake handling, whereas the Egyptians feared snakes, and the cobra was a symbol of great power.
†Osiris was captured by his enemies and dismembered so that his wife, Isis, had to wander all across Egypt looking for parts of his corpse. The breaking and gathering of the loaves and fish (Mark 6:31–44) may suggest a similar legend existed among the early Hebrews.

# 19

✠

# Dionysus and Osiris Worship: Greek or Egyptian?

Although Dionysus likely originated in Crete, it seems that many of the later religious rites of Dionysus familiar to the ancient Greeks were derived from the rites of Isis and Osiris with only a few alterations. Egyptian missionaries carried the Osirian religion to the mainland of Greece early on. In order to appeal to the Greeks, Osiris was renamed after the Minoan god/boy Dionysus of Crete when the Osirian religion was first transmitted from Egypt to Greece some time before 1200 BCE. Historians believe that the religion of Dionysus came to Greece in several waves. According to Martin A. Larson, "we know that there were at least two major penetrations into Greece by his cult before 1200, and at least three far-reaching reforms of it between 1100 and 500. The cult was first introduced from Egypt by a priest named Melampus . . . possibly as early as 1300; the second invasion came directly from Thrace, may have occurred about 1200, and it is credited to Orpheus" (1977, p. 40).

Yet if it was true that the worship of Dionysus was derived from the worship of Osiris, we would expect that this belief was in a religious form that existed fairly late in Egyptian history, during the New Kingdom. By the beginning of the New Kingdom in Egypt, the worship of Isis and Osiris as a popular religion had shifted: at religious ceremonies the worshippers were given wine, perhaps laced with opium or hallucinogens. Essentially, during the time of the New Kingdom the worship of Isis and Osiris was no longer solely or even mainly a mushroom cult. The emphasis in public ceremonies had shifted to specially prepared beers and wines along with bread. In contrast, the Greek wine, called *trimma,* was probably still very potent and relied on hallucinogenic mushrooms for its effects.

Modern chemists have shown that the Greeks could not have produced a wine that was more than 14 percent alcohol (Russell 1998, p. 145). If wine was the only ingredient in trimma, the beverage would hardly need to be heavily diluted. Yet the ancient Greek authors claimed that trimma was so strong that drinking it straight was often fatal. This suggests that this type of wine had powerful drugs added either before it was fermented (which is what the evidence suggests) or before it was consumed.

Like the Egyptians, the Greeks were concerned about the ill effects of using several of these drugs; and, like the Egyptians, they identified their side effects with evil spirits. This evil might be a bad trip or it could be as serious as a slow, lingering death—like the gangrene that sometimes accompanied ergot poisoning. Perhaps the evil might be simply an overwhelming stupor and folly. As the Greek Iamblichus notes in his book *On the Mysteries,* "It is necessary, therefore, from the beginning, to divide ecstasy into two species, one which leads to a worse condition of being and fills us with stupidity and folly, but the other imparts goods which are more honorable than human temperance" (Iamblichus 1821, 3:25). As Iamblichus implies, this powerful ecstasy might sometimes lead to a vision of the divine. Many people were willing to risk the possible ill effects while trying to experience this powerful ecstasy.

Just as the Egyptians believed that the spirit of their god Osiris lived within a sacred bull, the ancient Greeks believed that Dionysus sometimes took the form of a bull (Frazer 1961, 1:123). According to Plutarch, many Greek statues depicted Dionysus in the form of a bull. In Greek lore Dionysus was born with horns on his head, much like the cow goddess Isis. Further, just as cattle were sacrificed to Osiris, sacred cattle were sacrificed to Dionysus at Delphi in secret rituals (Lang 1996, p. 248). These facts might suggest that Dionysus was simply a copy of Osiris, but perhaps it's more likely that the rites of Dionysus and Osiris influenced each other while developing along parallel lines in Crete, Greece, and Egypt.

Dionysus, like Osiris, developed out of the worship (and sacrifice) of bulls, thus Dionysus was associated with images of bulls. Dionysus has "either been developed out of, or succeeded to, the worship of a bull-totem, and had inherited his characteristic ritual" (Lang 1996, p. 252). Further, like Osiris, Dionysus was conceived as a savior god: "The sacrifice, in fact, is a sacrament, and in partaking of the victim the communicants eat their god." In the rites of Dionysus, the worshippers (bacchants) were said to have "abstained from the flesh of animals altogether" (p. 251). If, then, the worshippers are "partaking of the victim" but are not eating "the flesh of animals," then what are they eating? If not the bull's flesh directly, then perhaps they ate the *Amanita muscaria* mushrooms that the bacchants found growing in the fields; or perhaps they consumed the psilocybe mushrooms grown on the carcass of a sacred bull. The rite of the bacchants seems to combine the search for wild mushrooms with the eating of mushrooms taken from their god's flesh.

Both Dionysus and Osiris represent "the divine savior who died for mankind and whose body and blood were symbolically eaten and drunk in the Eucharist" (Larson 1977, p. 37). The rites of Dionysus were, like the rites of Osiris, intended "to make the celebrants immortal by transforming them into an essence identical to that of Dionysus" (p. 48). The Eucharist of Dionysus was understood to consist of wine, honey, water, and flour, along with various things "of an intoxicating nature" (Hislop 1945, p. 5).

We know that a eucharistic beverage was used in the Greek mysteries, but it seems clear that the Greeks had hallucinogenic ointments, too. According to Rev. Alexander Hislop, "they were also anointed with 'magical ointments' of the most powerful kind; and these ointments were the means of introducing into their bodily systems such drugs as tended to excite their imaginations and add to the power of the magical drinks they received, that they might be prepared for the visions and revelations that were to be made to them in the Mysteries" (1945, p. 166).

Rev. Hilsop also quotes Eusebe Salverte: "These unctions were exceedingly frequent in the ancient ceremonies. . . . Before consulting the oracle of Trophonius, they [the Greeks] were rubbed with oil over the whole body. This preparation certainly concurred to produce the desired vision. Before being admitted to the Mysteries of the Indian sages, Apollonius and his companion were rubbed with an oil so powerful that they felt as if bathed with fire" (p. 282).

From his writings we can see that Rev. Hilsop believes that these magical unguents, which were used to prepare an individual to see a vision of the afterlife, were also used for those who were about to visit the afterlife. The anointing of the dying, which under Catholicism came to be called Extreme Unction, was instituted to prepare the dying believer for what he was finally going to experience: death itself. In the later Catholic version of Extreme Unction, the priest says: "Through this holy unction and His most tender mercy may the Lord pardon thee whatever sins thou hast committed by thy sight, hearing, etc."*

The priest anoints the dying on several parts of the body corresponding to the various senses through which the dying would have sinned. The priest had the option, however, of anointing only the lips. Among the Greeks, Egyptians, and early Christians, this method was preferred, because it would most quickly and directly allow the drugs in the oil to enter the body of the dying person. Only later in church

---

*In Latin, *Per istam sanctam unctionem et suam piissimam misericordiam indulgeat tibi Dominus quid per visum, auditum, odoratum, gustum, tactum, deliquisti.*

history, when Extreme Unction became purely symbolic, were the sacred oils merely plain oils, with no added drugs.

Strong similarities existed between the religions of Dionysus and Osiris, especially in their followers' conceptions of death and the afterlife. Just as the Egyptians used rituals to ensure the resurrection of the dead, the followers of Dionysus had burial rituals and they sometimes placed etched gold tablets in graves to ensure that the deceased would enjoy the protection of the god in the afterlife (Cole 1993, pp. 276–77). Both Osiris worship and the worship of Dionysus had public ceremonies that imitated the secret worship services conducted for initiates.

As we've seen, like the Greek Dionysus, the Egyptian Osiris was murdered and dismembered by his enemies. Edward Carpenter tells the story.

> But he [Osiris] was betrayed by Typhon, the power of darkness, and slain and dismembered. . . . His body was placed in a box, but . . . came again to life, and, as in the cults of Mithras, Dionysus, Adonis, and others, so in the cult of Osiris, an image placed in the coffin was brought out before the worshipers and saluted with glad cries of 'Osiris is risen.' His sufferings, his death and his resurrection were enacted year by year in a great mystery-play at Abydos. (1996, p. 22)

We can note that the Greeks describe in their literature a kind of hunting rite that was part of the rituals of Dionysus. According to Greek lore, in the Dionysian hunt the Bacchae, the women who worshipped Dionysus, wandered through the woods searching for animals, which they would kill and eat with their bare hands. Yet perhaps this legend is just a cover story for a hunt for mushrooms. When these Bacchae found the mushrooms they would treat them as if they were human, and then they consumed him (the mushroom Dionysus) in the forests where they found him. R. Gordon Wasson was the first scholar to recognize that this hunt was really a mushroom hunt. According to Wasson, the Dionysus child was "the object of their hunt, who was suckled, then like a beast torn to pieces and eaten raw; his own mothers, as was often claimed, were guilty of cannibalism eating his flesh, for like mothers the women would have brought the drug into being" (Wasson 1978, p. 43).

This sacred hunt is alluded to in several Greek texts, including the famous play *The Bacchae*. The Greeks used the metaphor of cannibalism to hide the true nature of the hunt for sacred mushrooms.

# 20

# Prometheus

According to many historians the Greek god Prometheus is older than Zeus and the gods of the classical Greek pantheon. The evidence strongly suggests that a cult devoted to Prometheus was part of the most ancient Greek worship of the sacred mushroom. In this respect he was similar to Osiris. Like Osiris in Egyptian culture, Prometheus was said to have civilized the ancient Greeks. He stole fire from the gods and then sacrificed his own body to satisfy the wrath of Zeus. The details of this story cleverly hide a connection to the sacred mushroom (Alcorn 2005, p. 138). Because of the bright red color of the cap of *Amanita muscaria,* the mushroom is often identified as "fire" in religious texts. It's probably not a coincidence that in Aryan lore the god Agni, or Fire, is a symbol for the sacred mushroom. The idea that this magical fire is actually a plant is supported by the lines of the first speech of the famous Greek play *Prometheus Bound.* Prometheus is described as having stolen "a blossom of fire" from Hephaestus (Vulcan). He is also said to have stolen fire in the form of lightning, which may associate the fire with mushroom lore that explains that mushrooms are produced by lightning.

Before examining the Prometheus legend more closely we must

look at the legend of a man named Ixion, whose punishment resembles that of Prometheus. Ixion is a mortal who is condemned to be tied to a wheel (a punishment carried out by Hephaestus, the blacksmith god who bound Prometheus in chains on the side of Mount Caucasus).* It's probable that Ixion, like Prometheus, is a legend derived from the themes of mushroom worship and funereal rites. Both the Prometheus and the Ixion stories probably originated in Neolithic times. Because Prometheus is a god he could be punished for centuries before being released by Hercules, but Ixion is a mortal and therefore is doomed to be tied forever to the wheel in the underworld.

Images of Ixion are common on Greek grave materials, and these images often include both wings and serpents.† The serpents are sometimes used to tie Ixion to the wheel, or they appear elsewhere, in metalwork or stone engravings. Exactly how the wings and snakes are incorporated into the illustration is probably irrelevant; it's important to note only that images of wings and serpents are typically found in

---

*Ixion tries to seduce Hera and is punished by Zeus: he is tied to a flaming (or winged) wheel, which might be a symbol for the bright red *Amanita muscaria*. Ixion also fathers the race of centaurs by impregnating a cloud, suggesting additional mushroom connections (see Ruck, Staples, and Heinrich 2001, p. 15; Hislop 1945, p. 298). Prometheus is eventually released from his imprisonment by Hercules, who has a strong resemblance to the Norse thunder god Thor as the bearer of the thunder weapon. Prometheus is also associated with the ax (or hammer), because he is (in some tales) the god who splits Zeus's skull to release Athena, a goddess noted for her wisdom/gnosis.

†Images of Ixion are frequently found on the backs of Greek mirrors. The use of Ixion as a sacrificial victim is discussed extensively in Ruck, Staples, and Heinrich 2001. *The Apples of Apollo*. In shamanistic religions, mirrors have the power to reveal the souls of the dead (Eliade 1972, p. 154). In Aztec mythology the god Tezcatlipoca is called Lord of the Smoking Mirror, and he has a torn foot (that is replaced with a mirror), which clearly shows his similarity to various Greek heroes who have a muddy foot (Olivier 2003, p. 231*ff.*). All of this concern about the torn foot is based on ritualistic fears about tearing the mushroom out of the ground the wrong way and damaging the foot. The shaman Maria Sabina claims that tearing the mushroom's foot leads to visions of the mushroom spirits angered about their damaged foot. We can note that in the Mayan religion the god K'awil has a serpent foot that carries the power of lightning (Gillette 1997, p. 66). It's possible that Greek funerary mirrors may have been used in prophecy. Similarly, among the Celts reflective water sources may have been used this way, as seen, for example, in the film *Cold Mountain* (2003) in which an old stone well is used to see the future.

the iconography of mushroom worshippers.* The wings represent the underside of the mushroom—the feathery gills—and the serpents represent the grubs that eat the mushroom and are often associated with evil and both physical and spiritual corruption, as in the worms that corrupt people's bodies: "And they will go out and look on the dead bodies of those who rebelled against me; the worms that eat them will not die, the fire that burns them will not be quenched, and they will be loathsome to all mankind" (Isaiah 66:24). Over time the phrase "the worm that never dies" or "the undying worm" or some variation of this title came to be associated with Satan and evil.

As with other mushroom religions bird and serpent images are frequently linked in Greek myths. For example, when Perseus cuts off the snake-covered head of Medusa, the blood from her neck gives birth to the winged horse Pegasus (Ruck, Staples, and Heinrich 2001, p. 42). The image of Medusa is a common figure on Greek cups and bowls, because her magic image provided protection from the evils that might come from drinking mushroom-spiked wine or food. The apostle Paul also warned that those who were unworthy could die from eating sacred food (Lloyd 1999, p. 16).

The legend of Perseus is loaded with mushroom allusions. Perseus beheads (or harvests) Medusa's head with a harpe, or small sickle.† Several scholars, including Shelley (1995, p. 94), identify this story of Per-

---

*See also (Ruck, Staples, and Heinrich 2001, pp. 59, 66, 68) for an extensive explanation of the Ixion legend and mushroom worship.

†Sacred heads and severed heads, like that of John the Baptist, play a significant role in cults of the dead. The veneration of sacred heads was especially popular in the medieval era in connection to legends of the Holy Grail. The Knights Templar may have continued the rites of the cult of the dead long after these rites were rejected by the Catholic church. The Templars practiced these rites until the group was suppressed in 1305. Yet we must ask: Why were heads venerated at all? It seems likely that once the cadaver was exhausted as a source for growing mushrooms it was natural for the head to be preserved and venerated. We can examine Keith Laidler's *The Head of God* for a history of head worship in Europe. In the Americas the Maya believed that the head of first father was hidden inside a ball and had great power. "This Holy-First-Father-Decapitated-Dead-Creating-Thing" is the singing ball of the Maya ball game (Gillette 1997, p. 79*ff*.).

seus and Medusa as explaining the rite used in harvesting the sacred mushroom. The serpents in Medusa's hair are emblems of evil and the disaster that can befall someone who plucks the mushroom incorrectly. According to the legend, anyone who looks at Medusa is turned to stone (mushrooms can cause a lethargy that is difficult to shake off), but Perseus is able to avoid this fate by using the mirrored surface of his shield to see her. Perseus harvests not only Medusa's head, but he also gathers the golden apples of the Hesperides, a reference to the golden-colored mushrooms that grow below the sacred tree and look like fallen red or yellow apples.*

The legend of Pandora's box is also tied to the sacred mushroom. In Greek mythology Pandora is created as a gift for Prometheus's brother, Epimetheus. This detail suggests a connection to the story of Prometheus, and her story is also similar to the biblical story of Eve in the book of Genesis. After Pandora is given to Epimetheus, a box is left in Pandora's care. When her curiosity gets the best of her, she opens it to see what's inside. A host of evils escapes from the box, and so Pandora (like Eve) is blamed for the diseases and misery that are visited upon all of humanity. Some scholars believe that the story of Pandora's box is based on the need to maintain the secrets of the mystery religions. The box contains the sacred instruments of the cult. The story is a warning to young initiates (especially young females) not to pry too closely into the mysteries that are in the care of their elders.† It seems likely that Pandora's box contains the secrets of the mushroom cult (or the mushrooms themselves), which should be hidden from the uninitiated. Similar boxes,

---

*We must note that Perseus is a descendant of Io, who was transformed into a cow and was guarded by Argos, the hundred-eyed Panoptes. Argos is called the many-eyed, which is code for the white-speckled cap of *Amanita muscaria* (Ruck, Staples, and Heinrich 2001, p. 51*ff.*). The mythology of the god Hermes is also loaded with such references, and it's Hermes who brings messages from the gods, probably in the form of visions.

†Other scholars, such as Lewis Paton in *Spiritism and the Cult of the Dead in Antiquity,* suggest that the story of Pandora has its origins in archaic religious rites. For Paton, Pandora is the earth goddess, and the cask that she opens is the *pithos,* or jar, in which the ancient Greeks were buried and from which the spirits of the dead emerge (2003, p. 77).

baskets, and other containers for sacred objects were common in Greek and Roman religions for centuries, and their images are easily found in many pieces of surviving artwork. Serpents were often represented as the guardians of these boxes.

When Pandora opens the box she releases a host of evils on humankind. In fact, Pandora's box is only one of many dangerous magical containers, such as the Ark of the Covenant.* Mushroom lore is filled with various magical containers, from the funeral box of Osiris to the two vases containing the blood of Medusa. Some of these containers (including baskets) were obviously used by the Greeks in religious rites to gather sacred mushrooms. Many illustrations depict the child god Dionysus carried in a basket, presumably after being gathered by the women of his cult (see, for example, Carpenter 1996, p. 240).†

Baskets play a significant role in several Greek legends. For example, in the story of Queen Creusa, two golden serpents are placed nearby to guard the wicker basket containing the queen's son, Ion. Unlike the hidden danger of Pandora's box, the threat is obvious to anyone who might want to look in the basket. Other details also suggest a connection to mushroom lore. For example, Queen Creusa places a cloth in the basket that bears a picture of Medusa (Ruck, Staples, and Heinrich 2001, p. 57). By using the image of a snake-haired deity, the punishment for looking inside is explicit.‡

There is one final aspect of the Prometheus legend that is vital to our understanding of the mushroom cult and the human sack. In one popular version of the Prometheus story Prometheus helps to prepare

---

*Simply touching the Ark could cause death. This idea is reflected in the film *Raiders of the Lost Ark* (1981) in which opening the Ark and the act of seeing the contents leads to a horrible death, a fact that Dr. Indiana Jones realizes just in the nick of time.

†Similar containers were used in Christianity, including the two cruets (small flat-bottomed vessels with narrow necks) that held the blood and sweat of Jesus. According to legend the cruets were brought to England by Joseph of Arimathea, the same man who loaned Jesus his tomb and took possession of Christ's body after the crucifixion (Matthew 27:57–60).

‡Obviously her child is divine, much like Moses, and he is born from the basket.

a feast for gods and men. A bull has been cooked, and it's to be served at the sacred feast. Prometheus decides to trick Zeus by wrapping some fat around some bones. He knows that Zeus will select this apparently tasty portion because he likes fat. At the same time the best parts of the meat are put in a second portion, which Prometheus intends for mortal men. As Prometheus plans, Zeus selects the fat and bones, while the better portions go to the mortals. Finding that he has been cheated, Zeus later condemns Prometheus to be chained to a mountain, and his liver is torn out again and again and eaten by an eagle.

This mythological event is mentioned frequently in Greek literature; probably the most remarkable example is the play *Prometheus Bound*. In this play the god Hephaestus is ordered to bind Prometheus to the mountain crag. In modern literature Prometheus is usually chained to the rocky stone face of the mountain, but in this play the chains are less important than the spike Hephaestus drives through his body.

HEPHAESTUS: Lo! this his arm is fixed inextricably.

KRATOS: Now rivet thou this other fast, that he
    May learn, though sharp, that he than Zeus is duller.

HEPHAESTUS: No one but he could justly blame my work.

KRATOS: Now drive the stern jaw of the adamant wedge
    Right through his chest with all the strength thou hast.

HEPHAESTUS: Ah me! Prometheus, for thy woes I groan.
    (lines 68–74)

The body of Prometheus is thus fastened with a spike, and he is left on the mountain to suffer in his captivity. (The spike driven through his heart also suggests many modern counterparts, including the Dracula story.)

This, however, is not the end of his punishment, for each day Zeus sends an eagle to attack the helpless Prometheus and tear out his liver. The eagle tears through his flesh, eats the liver, and flies away. Because

Prometheus is immortal, the liver grows back, and the same torment occurs again the next day and the day after. Aeschylus describes it:

HERMES: Thou shalt come back to light, and then his hound,
    The wingèd hound of Zeus, the ravening eagle,
    Shall greedily make banquet of thy flesh,
    Coming all day an uninvited guest,
    And glut himself upon thy liver dark.
    And of that anguish look not for the end,
    Before some God shall come to bear thy woes,
    And will to pass to Hades' sunless realm,
    And the dark cloudy depths of Tartaros. (lines 1113–22)

After the passage of many years the demigod Hercules eventually rescues Prometheus from the mountain.* Prometheus is released from his punishment and restored to freedom. The Prometheus story is a Greek passion story much like the story of Christ's suffering and crucifixion nailed to a cross. Further, the punishment of Prometheus is directly related to the idea of human sacrifice. Both of these gods are made to suffer for humankind—but what does this story really mean, and what is the origin of the rite on which the story is based?

There is one possibility that makes sense in the overall context of human sacrifice on Crete. The myth of Prometheus and his punishment on the mountain were perhaps contrived to explain how we might ritually dispose of the leftover skin of the human sacrifice after the mixture of liquefied flesh is drained from the leather sack.† The leftover skin

---

*Hercules was, like Christ, noted for having passed through the underworld.
†Today certain rituals are prescribed for disposing of the American flag once it's frayed and worn. The Minoans must also have been perplexed about how properly to dispose of the leather sack once it was no longer needed, because it was now the skin of a god. Early Minoan rituals probably included a ceremony in which a priest wore the skin of Prometheus and acted out his part. This probably included a procession to a nearby mountain peak sanctuary, where the skin was nailed to a crag with bronze spikes. *Prometheus Bound* is likely the late, fully developed and artistically enhanced version of the early Minoan rite.

and bones are the remaining flesh, and the bones and fat are the portion of Zeus. The sacrifice has, in a ritual sense, become Prometheus; the skin and bones are now holy. The skin of the sacrifice must be disposed of, but without profaning it. This poses a difficult problem.

How would an ancient culture dispose of the empty skin of a god? It seems likely that the Minoans used metal stakes to fix the sacred skin to a rocky mountainside where it could be seen and venerated from a distance. The skin, now containing only the leftover bones and flesh of the sacrifice, was treated as the portion of the gods. This idea explains the story in which Zeus is tricked into taking the portion of the feast composed of bones and fat. Once an empty sack was nailed to a cliff, the eagles (as carrion eaters) tore at the skin in order to eat the remaining flesh. Prometheus was one of the older gods called "Titans," and this word may be derived from the Greek verb τέμνω, meaning "to stretch" (Luschnig 2007, p. 182). Essentially Prometheus was a god whose skin was stretched out on the face of the mountain and fixed in place with nails. This practice was the source of the legend of Prometheus and his punishment by the eagle of Jove.

In his basic nature Prometheus is a savior god much like Osiris and the savior gods of other countries. Edward Carpenter explains in *The Origins of Pagan and Christian Beliefs*:

> . . . the Egyptian Osiris was called Savior, so was Horus; so was the Persian Mithras; so was the Greek Hercules who overcame death though his body was consumed in the burning garment of mortality, out of which he rose into heaven. So also was the Phrygian Attis called Savior, and the Syrian Tammuz or Adonis likewise—both of whom, as we have seen—were nailed or tied to a tree, and afterwards rose again from their biers or coffins. Prometheus, the greatest and earliest benefactor of the human race, was nailed by the hands and feet, and with arms extended, to the rocks of Mount Caucasus. Bacchus or Dionysus, born of the virgin Semele to be the Liberator of mankind (Dionysus Eleutherios as he was called), was torn to pieces,

not unlike Osiris. Even in far Mexico Quetzalcoatl, the Savior, was born of a virgin, was tempted, and fasted forty days, was done to death, and his second coming looked for. . . . (1996, p. 29)

These savior gods are similar in nature and function, reflecting through their common features the inherent need of human beings for divine direction and sacrifice.*

The Greek god Prometheus is clearly a savior god, much like Osiris and Jesus. Like the other savior gods, Prometheus's sacrifice is difficult to comprehend. Like the story of Pandora's box, the story of Prometheus suggests a punishment for a crime that we only vaguely understand. To most people the image of Prometheus chained to the mountain suggests the later image of Christ crucified. Further, just as Christ's blood had a profound magical power, the ichor that falls from Prometheus's wounded body is powerful (Russell 1998, p. 132). In this way Prometheus is like both Christ and Osiris; as the liquid efflux of his body has great supernatural power.†

---

*If, in fact, several of these passion stories developed out of the creation of a human sack and the later rituals used to dispose of the skin, then it seems likely that the story of the Roman soldiers casting lots for Christ's robe was derived from an old rite for choosing who would be responsible for disposing of the skin or perhaps being chosen for the sacrifice. The story of Simon from Cyrene may be related. Taking possession of the god's skin was, no doubt, an honor and a duty that had to be carried out by a person who was himself venerated and who might be chosen to be a sacrifice in the future.

†We can note that just as the eagle of Zeus is responsible for bringing divine food, ambrosia, down from the heavens, similarly in the Mythraic religion a bird carries divine food to earth (Shelley 1995, p. 95).

# 21

✠

# Adonis, Jason, and Jesus

## ADONIS

When Sir James Frazer wrote *Adonis, Attis, Osiris: Studies in the History of Oriental Religion* (part 4 of *The Golden Bough*) he presented a massive amount of evidence showing that these three gods were, if not the same god, then different manifestations of the same type of god: "So closely did the rites of Osiris resemble those of Adonis at Byblus that some of the people of Byblus themselves maintained that it was Osiris and not Adonis whose death was mourned by them. Such a view could certainly not have been held if the rituals of the two gods had not been so alike as to be almost indistinguishable" (1961, 2:127).

Adonis, Attis, and Osiris were fertility gods who died and were resurrected in sympathy with the death and rebirth of the natural world.*

Like many other gods, Adonis is associated with a miraculous plant.

---

*According to Martin A. Larson's *The Story of Christian Origins,* in the Semitic world "Osiris, displacing Tammuz, became Adonis" (1977, p. 29). In much the same way, Osiris became Dionysus among the Greeks.

According to Frazer, "the scarlet anemone is said to have sprung from the blood of Adonis, or to have been stained by it; and as the anemone blooms in Syria about Easter, this may be thought to show that the festival of Adonis, or at least one of his festivals, was held in the spring" (1:226). The creation of the anemone from the blood of Adonis suggests a connection to the other gods, including Osiris and Prometheus, in that sacred plants grow from their blood or body, or from the efflux of their bodies.

The proper name for Adonis was Tammuz, and it was under that name that he was worshipped among the people of Babylonia, Syria, and Palestine. As Frazer explains, "The appellation of Adonis is merely the Semitic Adon, 'lord' a title of honour by which his worshipers addressed him. In the Hebrew text of the Old Testament the name Adonai, originally perhaps Adoni, 'my lord' is often applied to Jehovah" (1:6).

The worship of Adonis/Tammuz was practiced very early in ancient Palestine. The prophet Ezekiel complains bitterly about the fact that Hebrew women worshipped him by "weeping for Tammuz" at the north gate of the Jerusalem Temple (Ezekiel 8:14). The ritual is similar to that of the Phoenicians: "In the great Phoenician sanctuary of Astarte at Byblus the death of Adonis was annually mourned, to the shrill wailing notes of the flute, with weeping, lamentation, and beating of the breast; but next day he was believed to come alive again and ascend up to heaven in the presence of his worshipers" (Frazer 1961, 1:225).

The sacrifices to Astarte and the weeping for Tammuz persisted in Judah and even in Jerusalem itself in spite of the complaints of Jeremiah (44:15–19) and Ezekiel. The association between Tammuz and Jesus is also suggested by the fact that Tammuz's followers often made a T-shaped mark with ashes on their foreheads, which they wore while weeping for Tammuz—a ritual that has continued in the Catholic churches on Ash Wednesday.

We can also note that the dove was sacred to Adonis. The symbolism of white doves plays no small role in various mushroom cults (Frazer 1961, 1:147). For example, "The Vedic fire god Agni also became a dove, and the lovers in the Song of Songs were also called doves. The Dove is clearly a metaphor for the visual appearance of the *Amanita muscaria* mushroom, which begins life as an egg shape and often ends as a bird shape, with wings extended" (Heinrich 1995, p. 101).

It seems likely that the whiteness of the dove's feathers brought to mind the whiteness of the fleshy gills on the underside of the mushroom cap.

We know that in Christian lore a supernatural dove descended on Jesus at the time of his baptism, and the dove continues as a symbol even today of the third leg of the Trinity, the Holy Spirit. Also interesting is the fact that the name Cephas, applied to Simon Peter, can be translated as "son of the dove" (Salibi 1998, p. 43).

## JASON AND JESUS

In *Persephone's Quest: Entheogens and the Origins of Religion,* R. Gordon Wasson gives a comprehensive overview of his long career in the new science of ethnobotany. In this book Wasson summarizes his previous work and compares the mushroom religions of several civilizations, including that of the Greeks and the native peoples of Central America. The similarities are many. For example, Wasson recognizes that many of these cultures viewed thunderbolts as the magical source of the sacred mushroom (Wasson 1986, p. 83*ff.*).

These cultures also have similar legends about one-legged men associated with the divine food of the gods.* Among the ancient Greeks they were called the shade foots (p. 167*ff.*). Among the Zapotec shamans of Mexico these creatures were the Kakulja Hurakan, the Lightning Bolt One-leg—a conflating of both ideas into one (Ruck, Staples, and Heinrich 2001, p. 93). The appearance of these ideas in both the Old World and the New World suggests that they were spontaneous—that is, the

---

*In Crete they used a symbol resembling an 8, which may have been a shield. Mackenzie describes a fully developed version of this symbol as a man with a single leg (1995, p. 161).

ideas were obvious symbols that occurred naturally to a people who worshipped the sacred mushroom with its single foot. These ancient peoples used similar images and stories as a kind of code to hide the true nature of their beliefs from the uninitiated and also to make their meaning clear to their followers.*

Modern scholars such as Robert Graves and Carl Ruck have found numerous mushroom-related images in Greek art, and many of the details of Greek stories are based on references to mushrooms. For example, Jason is described as "one footed" (he lost a sandal in the river while carrying Hera across the water), and he enters the city with a single muddy foot, also a mycological allusion (Ruck, Staples, and Heinrich 2001, p. 92*ff.*). Jason later sets out with the Argonauts on a quest to find the legendary Golden Fleece. This magical fleece is a mushroom allusion probably derived from using wooly sheep skins to filter the juice pressed from the red-gold mushrooms, a practice described in the ancient Vedic literature of India (Basham 1991, p. 14). The Golden Fleece was ruddy or golden because it was stained with mushroom juice and small bits of detritus from the yellow or red-tinted flesh of mushroom caps. When the fleece was hung over a tree branch to dry, the branch was also stained and thus became a "golden bough." All of these details from Greek mythology point to the mushroom cult and cult of the dead that began on Crete more than four thousand years ago and later spread to the Greek mainland.

There are also strong connections between the centaur Chiron and Prometheus. One version of the Prometheus story suggests that the immortal Chiron should be allowed to take the place of Prometheus staked out on the mountain. Chiron, who is wounded by a poisoned arrow, lives in great suffering because he is immortal. Allowing Chiron to enter Hades as a substitute for Prometheus would bring that suffering to an end. This may point to a time in Greek history

---

*For example, the Mayan god K'awil has a serpent leg that has the power of lightning and also is a source of visions (Gillette 1997, p. 66).

when horses (or in this case the horse/man Chiron) were offered in place of a human sacrifice.

The fact that Chiron was wounded in the knee and that several other Greek heroes are wounded in the extremities (including Achilles, whose heel is his only vulnerable point) suggests that this mythic detail originated in the sacrifice of humans (and later animals) to create a sack of liquefied flesh and mushrooms. The Greeks may have tapped the skin in order to test the liquid and make sure it was ready. It would make the most sense to do this in a foot or hand, where the incision could easily be tied off again. Just as Chiron was wounded in the knee and Achilles in the heel, then, a human sacrifice might have been tapped in the hands or feet to test whether the liquid was ready and had come to fullness. In all likelihood a particular sacred object was used to pierce the skin, and it would take on the supernatural power of the sacrifice. These cutting or piercing objects might include thorns, nails, needles, or even larger weapons such as spear heads or ritual knives. The many stories of heroes—including Hercules and the Fisher King, who receive deadly, poisonous wounds—may derive from this practice. Later on various fairy tales, including "Snow White" and "Sleeping Beauty," have similar details. The sacred wounds and weapons were destined to become important elements of religion and folklore.

As a great healer the centaur Chiron has many parallels in other cultures. For example, Drews further maintains that "now, as Epiphanius remarks in his *History of the Heretics,* Jesus bears in the Hebrew language the same meaning as curator, *therapeutes,* that is, physician and curer. But the Therapeutes and Essenes regarded themselves as physicians, and, above all, physicians of the soul" (1998, p. 58).

The Essenes were closely connected to the Nazarenes, along with other obscure Hebrew sects. In the Christian scriptures Jesus is identified as a Nazarene or Nazarite—which has caused some historians to think that he was from Nazareth. In fact, Jesus was probably a Naassene or Nazarene, a member of a religious sect of the time made up of healers. They believed that physical illness was a reflection of spiritual corruption. In addition, the high priest Ananias accused the apostle Paul of being both a troublemaker and a ringleader of the sect of the Nazarenes (Acts 24:5).

Drews also quotes an ancient document that says, "I exhort thee by Jesus the God of the Hebrews." The document appears to be Essene in origin and perhaps even pre-Christian, which may suggest that Jesus (or Jeshua/Joshua) was the name the Essenes used for their god (1998, p. 59). Furthermore, Hellenized Jews named their children Jason in place of Joshua/Yeshua, suggesting that the names Jason and Jesus have a common origin (Allegro 1970, p. 35). Both Jason and Jesus were associated with healing and perhaps with a god of healing known to both the Greeks and among the several ethnic groups of Palestine as Joshua/Yeshua/Jesus/Jason. The historical Jesus no doubt identified with his namesake and believed himself to be the embodiment of Joshua in his adopted role as the christened one (or Messiah) of the Nazarenes.

The knowledge of plants and their special properties was essential to healers in the ancient world. It's unlikely that the properties of hallucinogenic plants and mushrooms escaped their notice. Nor would they be unfamiliar with the practices of other cultures, including those of the Greeks and the Egyptians.

# 22

# From the Minotaur to Jesus

In 1900 when Sir Arthur Evans began his excavation of the palace of Knossos on Crete, he may not have really understood the full implications of this discovery. Evans unearthed a society that was largely dominated by the worship of a goddess (or goddesses). This fact alone makes the excavations on Crete one of the most significant for our understanding of Europe's prehistory. Since then many historians have asserted that Minoan society was primarily matriarchal, focused on the enjoyment of life and the search for ecstatic experiences and ignoring the more male pursuits of war and conquest.

More recently there have been books such as C. S. Barnes's *In Search of the Lost Feminine: Decoding the Myths That Radically Reshaped Civilization* that view ancient Crete as an example of what matriarchal society was like before it was overrun by the forces of patriarchy. Barnes suggests that there was a distinctly matriarchal mind-set or worldview and that this way of seeing the world collapsed only to be revived centuries later by the teachings of Jesus. Barnes also insists that Christ's teachings could easily have been influenced, at least indirectly, by Canaanite goddess worship (2006, p. 196), though we do not know and perhaps can never really know for certain if this is true. Yet we can see in the writings of the early Christians a total allegiance to the power of religious ecstasy. In its first centuries Christianity was devoted to discovering the secrets of how we could be a channel for the divine. We sometimes call this *theolepsy,* or "seized of God." The goal of the initiate is to possess and be possessed by God, who becomes an indwelling Holy Spirit—and this was accomplished by using sacred foods and oils.

It would be hard to find a society that was as single-minded in its approach to growing sacred mushrooms or one that had such a close and intimate relationship with the dead as the Minoans of Crete. The only parallel to the Minoan tholos tombs is the early Christian practice of communing with the dead in graveyards and catacombs. If we look, for example, at B. M. Billon's *Early Christian Art and Symbolism,* we find that the Christians of Rome frequently adorned their tombs with the symbols of the Eucharist, and they were particularly fond of the story of the loaves and fishes. Even the earliest symbol of Christ, the fish, is derived from the miracle of the loaves and fishes, as is the Eucharist itself (1976, p. 25*ff.*). All aspects of early Christian belief point to the sacred food: the inexhaustible body and blood of Christ.*

Why did these Christians invest so much in revering the miracle of the loaves and fishes? Perhaps the earliest Christians saw themselves as part of the body of Christ and that by painting the loaves and fishes on the walls of the catacombs they reminded themselves that like Jesus their bodies were anointed with sacred oils. Further, one day their corpses would be used to make holy oils or to produce the sacred food

---

*According to Mark Gaffney's *Gnostic Secrets of the Naassenes* the followers of the Nazarene way—that is, the earliest Christians of Jerusalem—were heavily invested in this symbolism (2004, p. 22*ff.*). Gaffney notes that the symbol of the fish may have derived from the worship of Oannes, an ancient Persian god associated with Osiris (p. 45). He further suggests that Christ understood his role as Son of Man to mean that he was the physical embodiment of divine wisdom, like Elisha, Osiris, Oannes, and other teacher/servant/ saviors. We might note too that in the winter months the Roman catacombs must have been chilly. The Christians also used the word *refrigeria* as a name for their sacred meals (Jensen 2008, p. 24).

of the Eucharist. In a sense the Corpus Christi, the body of Christ, would be multiplied through their own bodies in order that the multitudes could be fed. The words of the Gospel of John reflect this profound idea: "I am the vine, ye are the branches: He that abideth in me, and I in him, the same bringeth forth much fruit" (John 15:5 KJV).

This idea is suggested in numerous early Christian works. It's probably no accident that according to the account from the Acts of John, when the apostle John died, his corpse disappeared and was replaced with the holy manna. The word *manna* had early on been absorbed into the Christian mystery and become another euphemism for sacred food, as in John 6:58: "This is the bread which came down from heaven—not as your fathers ate the manna, and are dead. He who eats this bread will live forever" (KJV).

APPENDIX

# 1 John 2:20 and 2:27, Translations and Commentary

*When he was at the table with them, he took bread, blessed and broke it, and gave it to them. Then their eyes were opened, and they recognized him; and he vanished from their sight.*

LUKE 24:30–31

In *The Mystery of Manna: The Psychedelic Sacrament of the Bible,* Dan Merkur notes that the phrase "their eyes were opened"—used in Luke 24 to describe the effects of the new Eucharist—was borrowed from Genesis (3:4, 7) in which the phrase was used to describe the effects of eating the fruit of the Tree of Knowledge (Genesis 51). The power of this holy Eucharist is expressed, too, in the Gospel of John. Jesus says: "Truly, truly, I say to you, you seek Me, not because you saw signs, but because you ate of the loaves and were filled" (John 6:26).

Both the Hebrew scriptures and the Christian scriptures are filled with visions and wonders, and these visions are often accompanied by images of eating and drinking. We can't escape the fact that having visions of the divine often follow and almost certainly depend on eating sacred food. The visions of St. John described in Revelation, like those of Ezekiel a hundred years earlier, depended on eating the sacred hallucinogen.

Professor Luke Timothy Johnson's *Religious Experience in Earliest Christianity* describes the effects of what we have come to call the Holy Spirit but what was originally called the *pneuma:* "The pneuma comes to humans from another [power]. It indwells them, moves them, transforms and gives them life. It is poured out upon them and poured into them. It is drunk, and it fills humans. So pervasive is such language that the unsettling consequences of taking it literally rather than metaphorically seldom occur to the reader" (1998, pp. 8–9).

As a professor of Christian scriptures at Emory University, Professor Johnson can hardly be characterized as a radical in his reading of the Bible.* Yet he clearly sees a problem with the way people typically read the Christian scriptures, especially with the idea of taking specific words as metaphors when the context clearly suggests a literal understanding of the events.

I have suggested here that many of the religious experiences described in the Christian scriptures were based on the use of hallucinogens. In many cases the hallucinogens were used in a sacred unguent. According to Sir E. A. Wallis Budge in *Egyptian Magic,* the magical ointment was in common use: "To certain kinds of oil, magical properties have been attached from time immemorial in the East, and the important place that they occupied in the ceremonies and rituals of many nations proves that remarkable effects were expected to follow their use" (1971, p. 203).

Perhaps Christians too possessed just such a magic ointment or unguent.

This reading of the gospels may seem radical, but perhaps the Epistle 1 John is the smoking gun that proves this interpretation. 1 John describes an ointment or unguent that bestows a kind of supernatural

---

*His book was published by Augsburg Fortress, a publisher controlled by the Evangelical Lutheran Church in America. Johnson has gone on record in *The Real Jesus* attacking the liberal scholars of the Jesus Seminar. He is clearly not a liberal theologian.

knowledge or wisdom that teaches them everything that they need to know of Christ.*

Here are a variety of English translations of 1 John 2:20 and 2:27, ranging from the literal to the metaphorical. Over the centuries a metaphorical reading of the text has come occasionally to replace the literal one, but there is no good reason from the standpoint of translation to reject the literal meaning of the text.

### Wycliffe Bible, fourteenth century

2:20 But ye han anointyng of the Hooli Goost, and knowen alle thingis.

2:27 And that the anoyntyng which ye resseyueden of hym, dwelle in you. And ye han not nede, that ony man teche you, but as his anoyntyng techith you of alle thingis, and it is trewe, and it is not leesyng; and as he tauyte you, dwelle ye in hym.

### Tyndale, 1526

2:20 And ye have an ointment of the holy ghost, and ye know all things.

2:27 And the anointing which ye have received of him dwelleth in you. And ye need not that any man teach you: but as that anointing teacheth you all things, and is true, and is no lie: and as it taught you, even so bide therein.

### Tyndale, 1534

2:20 And ye have an oyntment of ye holy gost and ye knowe all thynges.

2:27 And ye anoyntynge which ye have receaved of him dwelleth in you. And ye nede not that eny man teache you: but as ye annoyntynge teaheth you all thynges and is true and is no lye: and as it taught you even so byde therin.

---

*The role of John in the formation of the early church is complex. We can read Elaine Pagels's *Beyond Belief* for a brief introduction. Certainly John believed that visions were an appropriate part of the Christian Church.

## Coverdale, 1535

2:20 But ye haue the anoyntinge of him yt is holy, & ye knowe all thiges.

2:27 And the anoyntinge which ye haue receaued of him, dwelleth in you: & ye nede not yt eny ma teach you, but as the anoyntinge teacheth you all thiges, euen so is it true, & is no lye. And as it hath taughte you, eue so abide ye therin.

## Geneva, 1557

2:20 But ye haue an ointment from that Holy one, and know all things.

2:27 But that anointing which ye receiued of him, dwelleth in you: and ye neede not that any man teach you: but as the same Anoynting teacheth you of all things, and it is true, and is not lying, and as it taught you, ye shall abide in him.

## Bishops Bible, 1568

2:20 Neuerthelesse, ye haue an oyntment of hym that is holy, and ye knowe all thynges.

2:27 And the annoyntyng whiche ye haue receaued of hym dwelleth in you: And ye nede not that any man teach you, but as the same annoynting teacheth you of all thynges, and it is true, and not lying: and as it taught you, ye shall abyde in it.

## King James Version, 1611

2:20 But ye have an unction from the Holy One, and ye know all things.

2:27 But the anointing which ye have received of him abideth in you, and ye need not that any man teach you: but as the same anointing teacheth you of all things, and is truth, and is no lie, and even as it hath taught you, ye shall abide in him [in him: or, in it].

## Webster Translation, 1833

2:20 But ye have an unction from the Holy One, and ye know all things.

2:27 But the anointing which ye have received from him abideth in you, and ye need not that any man should teach you: but as the same anointing teacheth you concerning all things, and is truth, and is no lie, and even as it hath taught you, ye shall abide in him.

## Darby Translation, 1890

2:20 And ye have the unction from the holy one, and ye know all things.

2:27 And yourselves, the unction which ye have received from him abides in you, and ye have not need that any one should teach you; but as the same unction teaches you as to all things, and is true and is not a lie, and even as it has taught you, ye shall abide in him.

## Young's Literal Translation, 1898

2:20 And ye have an anointing from the Holy One, and have known all things.

2:27 And you, the anointing that ye did receive from him, in you it doth remain, and ye have no need that any one may teach you, but as the same anointing doth teach you concerning all, and is true, and is not a lie, and even as was taught you, ye shall remain in him.

## American Standard Version, 1901

2:20 And ye have an anointing from the Holy One, and ye know all the things.

2:27 And as for you, the anointing which ye received of him abideth in you, and ye need not that any one teach you; but as his anointing teacheth you; concerning all things, and is true, and is no lie, and even as it taught you, ye abide in him.

## Weymouth New Testament, 1903

2:20 As for you, you have an anointing from the holy One and have perfect knowledge.

2:27 And as for you, the anointing which you received from Him remains within you, and there is no need for any one to teach you. But since His anointing gives you instruction in all things—and is true and is no falsehood you are continuing in union with Him even as it has taught you to do.

## Bible in Basic English, 1965

2:20 And you have the Spirit from the Holy One and you all have knowledge.

2:27 As for you, the Spirit which he gave you is still in you, and you have no need of any teacher; but as his Spirit gives you teaching about all things, and is true and not false, so keep your hearts in him, through the teaching which he has given you.

## The New American Bible (Roman Catholic), 1970

2:20 But you have the anointing that comes from the holy one, and you all have knowledge.

2:27 As for you, the anointing that you received from him remains in you, so that you do not need anyone to teach you. But his anointing teaches you about everything and is true and not false; just as it taught you, remain in him.

## Good News Bible, 1994

2:20 But you have had the Holy Spirit poured out on you by Christ, and so all of you know the truth.

2:27 But as for you, Christ has poured out his Spirit on you. As long as his Spirit remains in you, you do not need anyone to teach you. For his Spirit teaches you about everything, and what he teaches is true, not false. Obey the Spirit's teaching, then, and remain in union with Christ.

## Word English Bible, 1997

2:20 You have an anointing from the Holy One, and you all have knowledge.

2:27 As for you, the anointing which you received from him remains in you, and you don't need for anyone to teach you. But as his anointing teaches you concerning all things, and is true, and is no lie, and even as it taught you, you will remain in him.

## Holy Bible, English Standard Version (Crossway), 2001

2:20 But you have been anointed by the Holy One, and you all have knowledge.

2:27 But the anointing that you received from him abides in you, and you have no need that anyone should teach you. But as his anointing teaches you about everything—and is true and is no lie, just as it has taught you—abide in him.

## Douay-Rheims Bible, 2003

2:20 But you have *the unction from the Holy One,* and *know all things.*

2:27 And as for you, let the unction, which you have received from him, abide in you. And *you have no need* that any man teach you; but as his unction teacheth you of all things, and is truth, and is no lie. And as it hath taught you, abide in him.

In *The Epistles of John,* one of the volumes in the prestigious Anchor Bible series, Raymond E. Brown examines the letters of John and looks specifically at the word *chrisma* and the idea of anointing. Brown notes that the early English translations favored *ointment,* and most recent translations favor *anointing.* Of course, it's obvious that modern translators would favor a word capable of a metaphorical interpretation, given the emphasis placed on spirit over matter in modern theology. The idea that a literal ointment is needed in order to receive the Holy Spirit does not sit well with modern Christians. Even Catholics seem to feel a little uncomfortable with the idea that a specific type of ointment is needed, even though in the early years of the Christian Church the investiture of bishops was sometimes delayed for lack of a specific type of ointment or oil.

According to Brown, the *ma* ending of *chrisma* suggests a noun form in Greek, rather than an action. This reading is consistent with Josephus, who mentions the mixing of oils and perfumes into a sweet-smelling chrisma. In fact, a great deal of evidence points to a literal ointment in a literal anointing, rather than a figurative spirit anointing.

Perhaps Professor Brown's greatest point is that John "never tells his own adherents that they are the only ones who have been anointed" (1982, p. 344). It seems likely too that anointing in other cults also had the power to grant supernatural knowledge, or gnosis. The nature of these visions probably varies widely, based on the ingredients used in chrisma. All of these other cults and sects had their own anointing, and John was well aware that other groups had similar rites. He specifically warns his own followers against these competing cults (1 John 2:18–19). A similar competition between the Hebrew and other cults also is reflected in Deuteronomy 32:31–32.

We know that there were controversies in the early church regarding the Eucharist. Different groups claimed to have the only true Eucharist. Interestingly, however, none of them claimed to have the only Eucharist. In addition, several competing groups had their own anointing, but neither John nor the other religions tried to claim to have the only anointing. Yet if this anointing was purely spiritual, John could and no doubt would have claimed to have the only real, true supernatural anointing. We can only gather that John had a real, literal, and material anointing that he shared with his followers.

Over time, the church abandoned this special anointing described by John. Once the church was well established, it made sense politically to drop the use of hallucinogens, but some Christians refused to abandon the old ways. For example, the Naassenes continued to use the anointing, and they traced its use back to the time of King David. Two centuries after John wrote his first epistle, the Naassenes claimed to have a true literal anointing, saying: "Out of all we are the only true Christians who complete the mystery at the third gate [of regeneration] and there are anointed with an unutterable chrisma from a horn as was David" (Hippolytus 1868, 5.9.22).

The Naassenes claimed to use a true anointing, and it was a very real and literal anointing, like that of King David (Isaiah 61:1–3).

As the Church of Rome came to dominate the rest of the churches, the Romans began to destroy all records of the true anointing and the true Eucharist. As Dan Russell explains: "All the original Hebrew and Aramaic writings of the real Israelite apostles, the Nazarenes, were destroyed as heretical by the Roman Church in the second and third century" (1998, p. 215).

All that was left within the Church of Rome were the empty rituals, the invisible spiritual anointing, and the symbolic Eucharist embodied in plain wine and white bread. In many Protestant Christian churches today, all that is left of the original Eucharist is grape juice and bleached crackers. Instead of the work of the Holy Spirit, we have nothing left but the cartoon magic of the Keebler elves.

In his book *This Tree Grows out of Hell*, Ptolemy Tompkins describes how a similar fate overtook the ancient Maya: "As the secrets of the living earth were forgotten or atrophied into sterile doctrines passed on only by priestly elites, the disembodied soul, the dream body experienced concretely by the shaman, became more and more a topic for debate and less a living reality" (1990, p. 57).

With the exception of a few heretical Christians—long since exterminated—the ecstatic movement begun by Jesus, James, John, and Paul has withered on the vine. All that is left now are priests and cathedrals, televangelists, Internet websites, and megachurches, along with their endless spawn of Christian singles groups, AA meetings, Christian t-shirts, bumper stickers, Christian rock, Christian rap, Christian heavy metal, and endless other social manifestations of our endless "belief in things not seen" (Hebrews 11:1).

The rest is now history.

# Bibliography

Unless otherwise indicated all scriptural quotations are from the New American Standard Bible (*The Holy Bible: Updated New American Standard Bible Containing the Old Testament and the New Testament.* Grand Rapids, Mich.: Zondervan, 1995).

Aeschylus. *Prometheus Bound.* Girard, Kans.: Haldeman-Julius Co., 1922.

Akers, Brian P. "Introduction." *The Sacred Mushrooms of Mexico: Assorted Texts.* Lanham, Md.: University Press of America, Inc., 2007.

Alcorn, J. B. "The Scope and Aims of Ethnobotany in a Developing World." In Richard Evans Schultes and Siri von Reis, eds. *Ethnobotany: Evolution of a Discipline.* Portland: Ore.: Timber Press, 2005.

Alexiou, Stylianos. *Minoan Civilization.* Heraklion: Spyros Alexiou Sons, 1969.

Allegro, John. *The Sacred Mushroom and the Cross.* New York: Doubleday, 1970.

Allen, J. Romilly. *Early Christian Symbols in Great Britian and Ireland.* Kila, Mont.: Kessinger Publishers, 2004.

St. Ambrose. "Concerning the Mysteries." *Nicene and Post-Nicene Fathers,* series 2, vol. 10. Edinburgh: T & T Clark, 1882. www.bible.ca/history/fathers/NPNF2-10 (accessed March 12, 2012).

Andrews, Carol. *Amulets of Ancient Egypt.* Austin: University of Texas Press, 1998.

*Apostolic Constitutions. Ante-Nicene Christian Library* vol. 17. Translated by Rev. Marcus Dods; text edited by Rev. Alexander Roberts and James Donaldson. Edinburgh: T&T Clark, 1870.

Armstrong, David E. *Alcohol and Altered States in Ancestor Veneration Rituals of Zhou Dynasty China and Iron Age Palestine.* Lewiston, N.Y.: Edwin Mellen, 1998.

Arthur, James. *Mushrooms and Mankind.* Escondido, Calif.: Book Tree, 2000.

Baigent, Michael. *The Jesus Papers.* New York: HarperSanFrancisco, 2006.

Baigent, Michael, Richard Leigh, and Henry Lincoln. *Holy Blood, Holy Grail.* New York: Delacorte, 1982.

Balter, Michael. *The Goddess and the Bull.* New York: Free Press, 2005.

Barnes, C. S. *In Search of the Lost Feminine: Decoding the Myths That Radically Reshaped Civilization.* Golden, Colo.: Fulcrum Publishing, 2006.

Barnstone, Willis. *The Restored New Testament.* New York: W. W. Norton, 2009.

Basham, Arthur Llewellyn. Edited and completed by Kenneth G. Zysk. *The Origins and Development of Classical Hinduism.* Oxford: Oxford University Press, 1991.

Benitez, Fernando. "The Hallucinogenic Mushrooms." In Brian P. Akers, ed., *The Sacred Mushrooms of Mexico: Assorted Texts.* Lanham, Md.: University Press of America, Inc., 2007.

Billon, B. M. *Early Christian Art and Symbolism.* Devon, England: Stockwell, 1976.

Blinkenberg, Christopher. *The Thunderweapon in Religion and Folklore: A Study in Comparative Archeaology.* New Rochelle, N.Y.: Caratzas, 1987.

Bloch-Smith, Elizabeth. "The Cult of the Dead in Judah: Interpreting the Material Remains." *Journal of Biblical Literature* 2, no. 111 (1992): 213–24.

Bottalini, Cesare. *Quaresimale.* In Piero Camporesi, *The Incorruptible Flesh: Bodily Mutation and Mortification in Religion and Folklore.* Cambridge: Cambridge University Press, 1988.

Bradshaw, Paul F. *Eucharistic Origins.* London: Oxford, 2004.

Branigan, Keith. "Cemeteries and Social and Political Landscapes." In Keith Branigan, ed. *Cemetery and Society in the Aegean Bronze Age.* Sheffield, U.K.: Sheffield Academic, 1998.

———. *Hellas: The Civilizations of Ancient Greece.* New York: McGraw-Hill, 1980.

Brown, Raymond Edward. *The Epistles of John.* Anchor Bible Series. Garden City, N.Y.: Doubleday, 1982.

Budge, E. A. Wallis. *The Divine Origin of the Craft of the Herbalist.* Kila, Mont.: Kessinger Publishing, 1997.

———. *Egyptian Magic.* New York: Dover, 1971.

———. *From Fetish to God in Ancient Egypt.* New York: Dover, 1988.

———. *The Gods of the Egyptians.* New York: Dover, 1969a.

———. *The Liturgy of Funerary Offerings.* New York: Dover, 1994.

———. *Osiris and the Egyptian Resurrection.* New York: Dover, 1969b, 1973.

Butz, Jeffrey J. *The Secret Legacy of Jesus: The Judaic Teachings that Passed from James the Just to the Founding Fathers.* Rochester, Vt.: Inner Traditions, 2010.

Camporesi, Piero. *The Incorruptible Flesh: Bodily Mutation and Mortification in Religion and Folklore.* Cambridge: Cambridge University Press, 1988.

Carpenter, Edward. *The Origins of Pagan and Christian Beliefs.* London: Senate, 1996.

Castleden, Rodney. *Minoans: Life in Bronze Age Crete.* London: Routledge, 1990.

Cavanagh, William. "Innovation, Conservatism and Variation in Mycenaean Funerary Ritual." In Keith Branigan, ed. *Cemetery and Society in the Aegean Bronze Age.* Sheffield, U.K.: Sheffield Academic, 1998.

Cole, Susan Guettel. "Voices from beyond the Grave: Dionysus and the Dead." In Thomas H. Carpenter and Christopher A. Faraone, eds., *Masks of Dionysus.* Ithaca, N.Y.: Cornell University Press, 1993.

Craffert, Pieter F. *The Life of a Galilean Shaman: Jesus of Nazareth in Anthropological-Historical Perspective.* Eugene, Ore.: Cascade Books, 2008.

Cyprian. *To Januarius. Ante-Nicene Christian Library,* vol. 8. Translated by Rev. Marcus Dods; text edited by Rev. Alexander Roberts and James Donaldson. Edinburgh: T&T Clark, 1868.

Dalrymple, Theodore. *Not with a Bang but a Whimper: The Politics and Culture of Decline.* Chicago: Ivan R. Dee, 2008.

Davies, Jon. *Death, Burial and Rebirth in the Religions of Antiquity.* London: Routledge, 1999.

DeKorne, James B. *Psychedelic Shamanism: the Cultivation, Preparation and*

*Shamanic Use of Psychotropic Plants*. Port Townsend, Wash.: Loompanics Unlimited, 1994.

Denzinger, Heinrich. *The Sources of Catholic Dogma*. Fitzwilliam, N.H.: Loreto, 2002.

Didache, or *The Teaching of the Twelve Apostles*. Translated by Tim Saunders. www.voting.ukscientists.com/didache.html.

*Didascalia Apostolorum. Ante-Nicene Christian Library,* vol. 17. Translated by Rev. Marcus Dods; text edited by Rev. Alexander Roberts and James Donaldson. Edinburgh: T&T Clark, 1870.

Dietrich, Bernard C. "Death and Afterlife in Minoan Religion." *Kernos.* http://kernos.revues.org/643 (accessed April 12, 2011).

Dothan, Trude, and Moshe Dothan. *People of the Sea: The Search for the Philistines*. New York: Scribner, 1992.

Diodorus Siculus. *Library of History*. Cambridge: Harvard University Press, 1998–2001.

Drews, Arthur. *The Christ Myth*. Amherst, N.Y.: Prometheus, 1998.

Du Chaillu, Paul B. *The Viking Age*. New York: Scribners, 1889.

Eliade, Mircea. *Shamanism: Archaic Techniques of Ecstasy*. Princeton University Press, 1972.

Ellis, Hilda Roderick. *The Road to Hel: A Study of the Conception of the Dead in Old Norse Literature*. New York: Greenwood, 1968.

Elwin, Verrier. *Myths of Middle India*. Delhi: Oxford University Press, 1991.

Elworthy, Frederick Thompson. *The Evil Eye*. New York: Julian Press, 1986.

Escalante, Robert, and Antonio Lopez. "Sacred mushrooms of the Matlatzinca." In Brian P. Akers, ed., *The Sacred Mushrooms of Mexico: Assorted Texts*. Lanham, Md.: University Press of America, Inc., 2007.

Euripides. *Hercules Furens*. London: Cornish, 1884.

Eusebius. *History of the Church*. New York: Barnes & Noble, 1995.

Evans, Arthur. "The Tomb of the Double Axes and Associated Group; And, Pillar Rooms and Ritual Vessels of the 'Little Palace' at Knossos." *Archaeologia* 65, nos. 1–94 (1914).

*Exploring the Da Vinci Code: Henry Lincoln's Guide to Rennes-le-Chateau*. New York: Disinfo, 2005.

Firmicus Maternus, Julius. *The Error of the Pagan Religions*. New York: Newman Press, 1970.

Frazer, Sir James George. *Adonis, Attis, Osiris: Studies in the History of Oriental Religion* (part 4 of *The Golden Bough*). New York: University Books, 1961.

Freke, Timothy, and Pete Gandy. *The Jesus Mysteries: Was the "Original Jesus" a Pagan God?* New York: Three Rivers, 2001.

Fuller, John Grant. *The Day of St. Anthony's Fire.* New York: The Macmillan Company, 1968.

Gaffney, Mark H. *Gnostic Secrets of the Naassenes.* Rochester, Vt.: Inner Traditions, 2004.

Gartz, Jochen. *Magic Mushrooms Around the World: A Scientific Journey across Cultures and Time.* Los Angeles: LIS Publications, 1996.

Gaster, Theodor H. *Thespis: Ritual, Myth, and Drama in the Ancient Near East.* Garden City, N.Y.: Anchor, 1961.

Gershenson, Daniel E. *Apollo the Wolf-god.* Washington D.C.: Institute for the Study of Man, 1991.

Gibson, Shimon. *The Cave of John the Baptist: The Stunning Archaeological Discovery that has Redefined Christian History.* New York: Doubleday, 2004.

Gillette, Douglas. The *Shaman's Secret: The Lost Resurrection Teachings of the Ancient Maya.* New York: Bantam, 1997.

Gimbutas, Marija. *The Goddesses and Gods of Old Europe, 6500–3500: Myths and Cult Images.* Berkeley: University of California Press, 1982.

Ginzburg, Carlo. *Ecstasies: Deciphering the Witches' Sabbath.* New York: Pantheon, 1991.

Glazov, Gregory Yuri. *The Bridling of the Tongue and the Opening of the Mouth in Biblical Prophecy.* Sheffield, U.K.: Sheffield Academic, 2001.

Godbey, Allen H. "Incense and Poison Ordeals in the Ancient Orient." *The American Journal of Semitic Languages and Literatures* 46, no. 4 (July 1930): 217–38.

*GOD'S WORD Translation.* Iowa Falls, Iowa: World Bible Publishers, 1995.

"Gospel of Philip" in Robinson, James M. ed. *The Nag Hammadi Library in English*, third edition. San Francisco: Harper & Row, 1988.

"Gospel of Thomas" in Robinson, James M. ed., *The Nag Hammadi Library in English*, third edition. San Francisco: Harper & Row, 1988.

Graves, Robert. *Food for Centaurs*. Garden City, N.Y.: Doubleday, 1960.

———. *The Greek Myths*. New York: George Braziller, 1957.

Graves, Robert, and Raphael Patai. *Hebrew Myths: The Book of Genesis*. New York: Greenwich, 1983.

———. *The White Goddess*. New York: Vintage, 1948.

Green, Miranda J. *Dictionary of Celtic Myth and Legend*. London: Thames and Hudson, 1997.

Hall, Manley. *The Secret Teachings of All Ages*. Los Angeles: Philosophical Research Society, 1928.

Hallote, Rachel S. *Death, Burial, and Afterlife in the Biblical World*. Chicago: Ivan Dee, 2001.

Hamilkis, Yannis. "Eating the Dead: Mortuary Feasting and the Politics of Memory in the Aegean Bronze Age Societies." In Keith Branigan, ed. *Cemetery and Society in the Aegean Bronze Age*. Sheffield, U.K.: Sheffield Academic, 1998.

Hartland, E. Sidney. "Sin-Eating." In James Hastings, ed. *Encyclopedia of Religion and Ethics*. New York: Charles Scribner's Sons, 1908–1927.

Hawkes, Jacquetta. *Dawn of the Gods: Minoan and Mycenaean Origins of Greece*. New York: Random House, 1968.

Heinrich, Clark. *Strange Fruit: Alchemy, Religion and Magical Foods, A Speculative History*. London: Bloomsbury, 1995. (Also available as *Magic Mushrooms in Religion and Alchemy*. Rochester, Vt.: Park Street Press, 2002.)

Herrero de Jáuregui, Miguel. *Orphism and Christianity in Late Antiquity*. New York: De Gruyter, 2010.

Hillman, D. C. A. *The Chemical Muse: Drug Use and the Roots of Western Civilization*. New York: St. Martins, 2008.

Hippolytus. *Ante-Nicene Christian Library*, vol. 6. Translated by Rev. Marcus Dods; text edited by Rev. Alexander Roberts and James Donaldson. Edinburgh: T&T Clark, 1868.

Hislop, Rev. Alexander. *The Two Babylons, or The Papal Worship*. New York: Loizeaux Bros., 1945.

Homer. *Iliad*. Cambridge, Mass.: Harvard University Press, 1954, 7.

———. *Odyssey*. Cambridge, Mass.: Harvard University Press, 1960, 6.

Hood, M. S. F. "Tholos Tombs of the Aegean." *Antiquity* 34, no. 135 (1960): 66–176.

Hornug, Erik. *The Secret Lore of Egypt: Its Impact on the West*. Ithaca, N.Y.: Cornell University Press, 2001.

Howey, M. Oldfield. *The Encircled Serpent: A Study of Serpent Symbolism in All Countries and Ages*. Kila, Mont: Kessinger Publishing, 2005.

Hughes, Dennis D. *Human Sacrifice in Ancient Greece*. London: Routledge, 1991.

Iamblichus. *Iamblichus on the Mysteries of the Egyptians, Chaldeans, and Assyrians*. Chiswick: Whittingham, 1821.

Ignatius. *Ante-Nicene Christian Library* vol. 1. Translated by Rev. Marcus Dods; text edited by Rev. Alexander Roberts and James Donaldson. Edinburgh: T&T Clark, 1867.

Ignatius. "Epistle to the Philadelphians." In J. B. Lightfoot, trans. *Apostolic Fathers*. London: Macmillan, 1891.

Irenaeus. "Against Heresies." *Ante-Nicene Christian Library*, vol. 9. Translated by Rev. Marcus Dods; text edited by Rev. Alexander Roberts and James Donaldson. Edinburgh: T&T Clark, 1883.

Jensen, Robin M. "Dining with the Dead." In Laurie Brink and Deborah Green, eds. *Commemorating the Dead: Texts and Artifacts in Context*. New York: De Gruyter, 2008.

Johnson, Luke Timothy. *Religious Experience in Earliest Christianity: A Missing Dimension in New Testament Study*. Minneapolis: Augsburg Fortress, 1998.

Joinville, Jean, sire de. *Memoirs of the Crusades*. London and New York: J. M. Dent, E. Dutton, 1933.

Keating, John Fitzstephen. *The Agape and the Eucharist in the Early Church: Studies in the History of the Christian Love-feasts*. LaVergne, Tenn.: BiblioLife, 2009.

Kennedy, H. A. A. *St. Paul and the Mystery Religions*. London: Hodder and Stoughton, 1913.

Kerenyi, Carl. *Dionysos: Archetypal Image of Indestructible Nature*. Princeton, N.J.: Princeton University Press, 1996.

———. *Eleusis: Archetypal Image of Mother and Daughter*. Princeton, N.J.: Princeton University Press, 1991.

King, Philip J. "The Marzeah Amos Denounces." *Biblical Archeological Review* 14 (July/Aug 1988): 34–45.

Knab, Timothy J. *A War of Witches: A Journey into the Underworld of the Contemporary Aztecs*. New York: HarperCollins, 1995.

Koester, Helmut comments on cover of MacMullen, Ramsay. *The Second Church: Popular Christianity A.D. 200–400.* Atlanta: Society of Biblical Literature, 2009.

Komarnitsky, Kris D. *Doubting Jesus' Resurrection: What Happened in the Black Box?* Drapper, Utah: Stone Arrow Books, 2009.

Laidler, Keith. *The Head of God.* London: Weidenfeld and Nicholson, 1998.

Lambert, Michael. "Ancient Greek and Zulu Sacrificial Ritual: A Comparative Analysis." *Numen* 40, no. 3 (September 1993): 293–318.

Lang, Andrew. *Myth, Ritual and Religion,* 2 vols. London: Senate, 1996.

Larson, Martin A. *The Story of Christian Origins.* Tahlequah, Okla.: Village Press, 1977.

Leclercq, H. (1907). "Agape." *The Catholic Encyclopedia.* New York: Robert Appleton Company. Retrieved November 28, 2011, from New Advent: www.newadvent.org/cathen/01200b.htm.

Lee, Earl. *Among the Cannibal Christians.* Tucson, Ariz.: See Sharp Press, 2000.

Lincoln, Henry. *The Holy Place: Saunière and the Decoding of the Mystery of Rennes-le-Château.* New York: Arcade, 2004.

Lloyd, John T. *God-Eating: A Study in Christianity & Cannibalism.* Tucson, Ariz.: See Sharp Press, 1999.

Logan, A. H. B. *The Gnostics: Identifying an Early Christian Cult.* London: T and T Clark, 2006.

Luschnig, C. A. E. *An Introduction to Ancient Greek.* Indianapolis: Hackett, 2007.

Mackenzie, Donald A. *Crete & Pre-Hellenic Myths and Legends.* London: Senate, 1995. (Reprint of *Myths of Crete and Pre-Hellenic Europe.* London: Gresham Publishing Co., n.d.)

MacMullen, Ramsay. *The Second Church: Popular Christianity A.D. 200–400.* Atlanta: Society of Biblical Literature, 2009.

McCane, Byron. *Roll Back the Stone: Death and Burial in the World of Jesus.* Harrisburg: Trinity Press International, 2003.

McKenna, Terence. *Food of the Gods: The Search for the Original Tree of Knowledge.* New York: Bantam, 1992.

Merkur, Dan. The *Mystery of Manna: The Psychedelic Sacrament of the Bible.* Rochester, Vt.: Park Street Press, 2000.

Minucius Felix, Marcus. *Ante-Nicene Christian Library,* vol. 13. Translated by Rev. Marcus Dods; text edited by Rev. Alexander Roberts and James Donaldson. Edinburgh: T&T Clark, 1869.

Morgan, Adrian. *Toads and Toadstools.* Berkeley, Calif.: Celestial Arts, 1995.

Morris, Christine, and Alan Peatfield. "Feeling through the Body: Gesture in Cretan Bronze Age Religion." In Y. Hamilikis et al., eds. *Thinking through the Body: Archaeologies of Corporeality.* New York: Kluwer, 2002.

Nilsson, Martin. *Minoan-Mycenaen Religion and Its Survival in Greek Religion.* Second rev. ed. New York: Biblo and Tannen, 1970.

Olivier, Guilhem. *Mockeries and Metamorphoses of an Aztec God: Tezcatlipoca, Lord of the Smoking Mirror.* Boulder: University Press of Colorado, 2003.

O'Kane, James. *Notes on the Rubrics of the Roman Ritual.* New York: P. Oshea, 1883.

Ott, Jonathan. *Hallucinogenic Plants of North America.* Berkeley, Calif.: Wingbow Press, 1976.

Pagels, Elaine. *Beyond Belief.* New York: Random House, 2003.

Palmer, Leonard R. *Mycenaeans and Minoans: Aegean Prehistory in the Light of the Linear B Tablets.* New York: Knopf, 1962.

Paton, Lewis Bayles. *Spiritism and the Cult of the Dead in Antiquity.* Kila, Mont.: Kessinger, 2003.

Picknett, Lynn, and Clive Prince. *The Sion Revelation: The Truth about the Guardians of Christ's Sacred Bloodline.* New York: Simon and Schuster, 2006.

Piggott, Stuart. "The Tholos Tomb in Iberia." *Antiquity,* no. 107 (1953): 137–43.

Plutarch. *Plutarch's Lives: The Translation Called Dryden's.* Boston: Little, Brown, & Co., 1868.

Pope, Marvin H. "The Cult of the Dead at Ugarit." In G. D. Young, ed. *Ugarit in Retrospect.* Winona Lake, Ind.: Eisenbrauns, 1981.

———. "A Divine Banquet at Ugarit." In James M. Efrid, ed. *The Use of the Old Testament in the New.* Durham, N.C.: Duke University Press, 1972.

"Prometheus." In Smith, William. *A New Classical Dictionary of Greek and Roman Biography, Mythology and Geography.* New York: Harper, 1851.

Radding, Charles, and Frances Newton. *Theology, Rhetoric, and Politics in the Eucharistic Controversy,* 1078–79. New York: Columbia University Press, 2003.

Rahn, Otto. *Crusade Against the Grail: The Struggle between the Cathars, the Templars, and the Church of Rome.* Rochester, Vt.: Inner Traditions, 2006.

Rahner, Hugo. *Greek Myths and Christian Mystery.* New York: Biblo and Tannen, 1971.

Ravicz, Robert. "The Mixtec in a Comparative Study of the Hallucinogenic Mushroom." In Brian P. Akers, ed., *The Sacred Mushrooms of Mexico: Assorted Texts.* Lanham, Md.: University Press of America, Inc., 2007.

Roberts, Alison. *Golden Shrine, Goddess Queen: Egypt's Anointing Mysteries.* Rottingdean, East Sussex: NorthGate, 2008.

Robertson, John M. *Pagan Christs: Studies in Comparative Hierology,* second ed. London: Watts, 1911.

Robinson, James M. ed., *The Nag Hammadi Library in English,* third edition. San Francisco: Harper & Row, 1988.

Rordorf, Willy. "The Didache." In *The Eucharist of the Early Christians.* New York: Pueblo Publishing, 1978.

Ross, Anne. *Druids.* Charleston, S.C.: Tempus, 1999.

Ruck, Carl A. P., Blaise Daniel Staples, and Clark Heinrich. *The Apples of Apollo: Pagan and Christian Mysteries of the Eucharist.* Durham, N.C.: Carolina Academic Press, 2001.

Ruskin, John. *The Works of John Ruskin,* vol. 10. London: G. Allen, 1903–1912.

Russell, Dan. *Shamanism and the Drug Propaganda: the Birth of Patriarchy and the Drug War.* Camden, N.Y.: Kalyx, 1998.

Salibi, Kamal. *Who Was Jesus? A Conspiracy in Jerusalem.* New York: I. B. Tauris, 1998.

Schultes, Richard. *Plants of the Gods: Their Sacred, Healing, and Hallucinogenic Powers.* Rochester, Vt.: Healing Arts Arts Press, 2001.

Shelley, William Scott. *The Elixir: An Alchemical Study of the Ergot Mushrooms.* Notre Dame, Ind.: Cross Cultural Publishers, 1995.

Sidky, H. *Witchcraft, Lycanthropy, Drugs and Diseases: an Anthropological Study of the European Witch-Hunts.* New York: Peter Lang, 1997.

Smith, W. Robertson. *The Religion of the Semites.* New York: Meridian, 1956.

Sophocles, *The Three Theban Plays: Antigone, Oedipus the King, Oedipus at Colonus*. Translated by Robert Fagles. Edited by Bernard Knox. New York: Penguin Books, 1982.

Sordi, Marta. *The Christians and the Roman Empire*. Norman: University of Oklahoma Press, 1994.

Spess, David L. Soma: *The Divine Hallucinogen*. Rochester, Vt.: Park Street Press, 2000.

Stamets, Paul. *The Mushroom Cultivator*. Olympia, Wash.: Agarikon Press, 1983.

Stetkevych, Jaroslav. *Muhammad and the Golden Bough: Reconstructing Arabian Myth*. Bloomington: Indiana University Press, 1996.

Temple, Robert, and Olivia Temple. *The Sphinx Mystery: the Forgotten Origins of the Sanctuary of Annubis*. Rochester, Vt.: Inner Traditions, 2009.

Tertullian. *Ante-Nicene Christian Library*, vols. 11 and 15. Translated by Rev. Marcus Dods; text edited by Rev. Alexander Roberts and James Donaldson. Edinburgh: T&T Clark, 1882, 1870.

———. "The Resurrection of the Dead." *Ante-Nicene Christian Library*, vol. 15. Translated by Rev. Marcus Dods; text edited by Rev. Alexander Roberts and James Donaldson. Edinburgh: T&T Clark, 1882, 1870.

Theophilus of Antioch. "To Autolycus" *Ante-Nicene Christian Library*, vol. 3. Translated by Rev. Marcus Dods; text edited by Rev. Alexander Roberts and James Donaldson. Edinburgh: T&T Clark, 1867.

Tierney, Patrick. *The Highest Altar: The Story of Human Sacrifice*. London: Bloomsbury, 1989.

Tompkins, Ptolemy. *This Tree Grows out of Hell: Mesoamerica and the Search for the Magical Body*. New York: HarperSanFrancisco, 1990.

Tubb, Jonathan N. *Canaanites: Peoples of the Past*. Norman: University of Oklahoma Press, 1998.

Twain, Mark. *Innocents Abroad*. Hartford, Conn.: American Pub. Co., 1869.

Urrutia, Benjamin. "Psalm 51 and the 'Opening of the Mouth' Ceremony." *Scripta Hierosolymitana: Publications of the Hebrew University of Jerusalem* 28 (1982): 222–23.

Valerius Flaccus. *Argonautica*. Translated by Mozley, J. H. Loeb Classical Library Volume 286. Cambridge, Mass.: Harvard University Press, 1928.

Vincent, Marvin Richardson. *Word Studies in the New Testament*. Peabody, Mass.: Hendrickson, 1984.

Vulliamy, C. E. *Immortality: Funerary Rites and Customs*. London: Senate, 1997.

Waite, Arthur Edward. *The Holy Grail: The Galahad Quest in Arthurian Literature*. Kila, Mont.: Kessinger Publishers, 1993.

Wasson, R. Gordon. *The Wondrous Mushroom: Mycolatry in Mesoamerica*. New York: McGraw-Hill, 1980.

———. *The Road to Eleusis: Unveiling the Secret of the Mysteries*. New York: Harcourt, Brace Jovanovich, 1978.

Wasson, R. Gordon, et al. *Persephone's Quest: Entheogens and the Origins of Religion*. New Haven: Yale University Press, 1986.

Wasson, R. Gordon, and Valentina Wasson. *Mushrooms, Russia and History*. New York: Pantheon Books, 1957.

Wilken, Robert L. *The Christians as the Romans Saw Them*. New Haven, Conn.: Yale University Press, 1984.

Wilkinson, J. Gardner. *The Manners and Customs of the Ancient Egyptians*. London: John Murray, 1878.

Zevit, Ziony. *The Religions of Ancient Israel: A Synthesis of Parallactic Approaches*. New York: Continuum, 2001.

# Index

# BOOKS OF RELATED INTEREST

**Plants of the Gods**
Their Sacred, Healing, and Hallucinogenic Powers
*by Richard Evans Schultes, Albert Hofmann, and Christian Rätsch*

**Entheogens and the Future of Religion**
*Edited by Robert Forte*

**Spiritual Growth with Entheogens**
Psychoactive Sacramentals and Human Transformation
*Edited by Thomas B. Roberts, Ph.D.*

**Barbarian Rites**
The Spiritual World of the Vikings and the Germanic Tribes
*by Hans-Peter Hasenfratz, Ph.D.*

**The Encyclopedia of Psychoactive Plants**
Ethnopharmacology and Its Applications
*by Christian Rätsch*

**Pagan Christmas**
The Plants, Spirits, and Rituals at the Origins of Yuletide
*by Christian Rätsch and Claudia Müller-Ebeling*

**Magic Mushrooms in Religion and Alchemy**
*by Clark Heinrich*

**High Society**
The Central Role of Mind-Altering Drugs in History,
Science, and Culture
*by Mike Jay*

INNER TRADITIONS • BEAR & COMPANY
P.O. Box 388
Rochester, VT 05767
1-800-246-8648
www.InnerTraditions.com

Or contact your local bookseller